S0-AGO-681

IN DEFENSE OF THE SHENANDOAH VALLEY,
JACKSON ADVANCED PAST THIS SAWMILL TO ENGAGE
WITH UNION TROOPS AT KERNSTOWN.

(U.S. Army Military History Institute,
Carlisle Barracks, PA)

ON THE FRONT LINES

The sharpshooters of the enemy then made their appearance, and a body of them took possession of the brick house and outbuildings about three or four hundred yards in our front, and opened fire on us at once. . . . At this moment a shot wounded me in the knee.

It did not hurt much. I had been struck a few minutes before on the shoulder by a spent ball, which hit hard enough to raise a knot, but did not break the skin.

As the ball fell, I stooped down, took it up and put it into my pocket, thinking no more of it until I received this second shot which I thought was of the same character; but in a few minutes I became so sick that I was compelled to lie down.

One of my comrades ran to me and asked if I was shot. I replied, "I don't think I am; it was a spent ball." By this time I was so sick that I thought my time to die had come, and as I looked at my knee, I saw blood running freely down my pants. . . .

Thomas J. "Stonewall" Jackson

ONE OF JACKSON'S FOOT CAVALRY

★★★

BY

John H. Worsham

An Old F., Richmond, Va.

Introduction by Robert K. Krick
General Series Editor, Paul Andrew Hutton

BANTAM BOOKS
New York • Toronto • London • Sydney • Auckland

ONE OF JACKSON'S FOOT CAVALRY
A Bantam Domain Book

PRINTING HISTORY
The Neale Publishing Company edition published 1912
Bantam edition/May 1992

General Series Editor, Paul Andrew Hutton

ISBN 0-553-29382-6

Published simultaneously in the United States and Canada

PRINTED IN THE UNITED STATES OF AMERICA

OPM   0   9   8   7   6   5   4   3   2   1

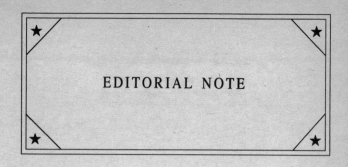

EDITORIAL NOTE

This book is a reprint of the first edition of John H. Worsham, ONE OF JACKSON'S FOOT CAVALRY: HIS EXPERIENCE AND WHAT HE SAW DURING THE WAR 1861–1865, published by The Neale Publishing Company, New York, in 1912. The complete text of the original is reprinted.

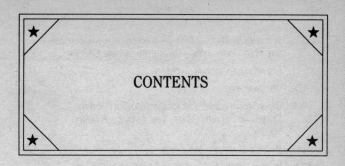

CONTENTS

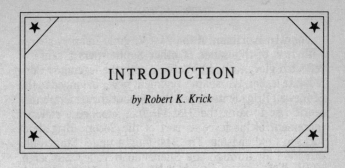

INTRODUCTION

by Robert K. Krick

THOMAS JONATHAN "STONEWALL" JACKSON loomed larger than life over the war-torn American land during one dramatic year beginning in May 1862. A remarkable string of victories in the face of daunting circumstances catapulted the Virginian to prominence, and more than a few eccentricities contributed to his aura. Young men who marched and battled and died for the Confederacy came to feel deep pride in their association with the famous man. A surgeon who visited the army in the spring of 1863, for instance, wrote to his wife in astonishment about the "boisterous exclamations ... the eccentric Stonewall Jackson elicits wherever he goes." John Esten Cooke never fought under Jackson but he skillfully captured a prevalent feeling when he wrote after the war:

> And men shall tell their children,
> Tho' all other memories fade,
> That they fought with *Stonewall Jackson*
> In the old "Stonewall Brigade"!

John H. Worsham of the 21st Virginia Infantry shared with tens of thousands of other Southerners a sense of reflected glory earned by serving with the legendary Confederate leader. Worsham's regiment never belonged to the Stonewall Brigade itself, but throughout the general's meteoric rise to fame the 21st Virginia supplied a stalwart increment of his force as part of the Second Brigade of Jackson's old division. The 21st fought under Stonewall's direction all through the Shenandoah Valley campaign, which first made the general's reputation. It served at his instance around Richmond, suffered brutal losses protecting his center at Cedar Mountain, followed him to Second Manassas, Sharpsburg, and Fredericksburg, and stood close behind the point where the general fell mortally wounded at Chancellorsville. John Worsham, a twenty-one-year-old Richmond youth when the war broke out, sturdily followed Jackson almost every step of the way.

In the spring of 1861, Thomas Jonathan Jackson could claim no wider circle of influence than a few dozen citizens of Virginia's Shenandoah Valley and a few hundred men who had been his students at Lexington's Virginia Military Institute. A substantial proportion of this handful considered the military-school professor an eccentric failure. Stories of his inflexible personal style and his unimaginative teaching performance seemed to be the only reason to talk about Thomas Jackson. Two years later the awkward misfit had become the most famous man in North America and perhaps in the world. In war, the peacetime failure had found his natural element.

Young T. J. Jackson had in fact accomplished a great deal on a personal level before the American Civil War provided him with a vast arena in which to create military legends. He was born in Clarksburg, Virginia (it became part of the new state of West Virginia a few weeks after Jackson's death), in 1824. Both of Tom Jackson's parents died while he was very young and the boy had to adjust to life in the homes of various relatives. When he had the good fortune to win an appointment to the United States

Military Academy at West Point, the teenage Jackson faced an enormous challenge because his preparatory education had been haphazard. By dint of stern application to duty the cadet met the academy's rigorous scholastic demands with enough success to forge steadily upward in class standing. Jackson ranked a lowly fifty-first at the end of his first year, but had improved to seventeenth among fifty-nine graduates when he graduated in 1846 (George E. Pickett stood dead last in the class). A classmate declared, revealingly if not entirely accurately, that if the course at West Point had been a bit longer, Tom Jackson would have reached the head of his class.

As a newly minted officer in the summer of 1846, Lieutenant Jackson joined most of his military generation in heading for the scenes of the Mexican War. He won real distinction as an artillerist there, including brevet promotions for gallantry. The deadly ennui of peacetime regular-army life after Mexico rapidly drove Jackson into conflict with a superior officer and then to resignation in order to accept a post on the faculty of Virginia Military Institute. For a decade the quiet and deeply religious officer did his level best to teach young men things they did not wish to learn; his best often was barely enough to get by. VMI cadets knew something of the Mexican exploits of their wooden professor and respected that image. They also had the evidence of their senses that he was a clumsy professor. One of them actually attempted to kill the stern Jackson after having been mistreated in striking fashion; in ultimate irony, the murderous cadet later commanded Jackson's famous Stonewall Brigade late in the war.

T. J. Jackson led the institute cadets to Richmond at the outbreak of war in 1861, then went to Harpers Ferry to command that critical frontier outpost. On July 21, 1861, he stood solid as a rock with his brigade of Virginians near the crest of Henry House Hill during the battle of Manassas or Bull Run and earned his immortal nom de guerre "Stonewall." It is intriguing to speculate how much less rapidly the general's reputation might have grown, and

how it might survive today, had it not been nurtured and
abetted by that enchanting military nickname. What
Thomas Jackson did in 1862 and 1863 stands clear on the
record for students to examine, and he certainly deserves
all of the military fame that has gathered around his eccentric head. A component of his popular image, though,
hangs upon the catchy label that lends itself to such media
as country songs, high-school team mascots, and billboard
advertisements. More Europeans have heard of Stonewall
than could possibly have heard of plain Thomas J. Jackson,
no matter what his historic performance might have been.

After standing like a stone wall at Manassas, Jackson had
little opportunity for distinction for many months as the
war settled into quiet stalemate. Late in 1861 Jackson went
back to the Shenandoah Valley whence he had marched to
war, bearing a commission as major general and charged
with defending the lower valley. An inauspicious winter
campaign west from Winchester yielded far more head-
aches than kudos for Jackson. By March 1862 he was
mightily frustrated and so was his country. The fledgling
Confederate States of America stood on the brink of extinc-
tion that month. After a brave beginning and a few initial
successes, the cause of the seceded Southern states had
foundered on a series of reverses. Combined land and naval
forces carried the Union flag into Tennessee early in 1862
and won major victories at Fort Henry and Fort Donelson.
A vast invading army under General George B. McClellan
inched ponderously up Virginia's peninsula toward Richmond to besiege the capital city of both the state and the
Confederacy.

Time and events had tarnished the bright prospects of
most of the South's early heroes. Dispirited civilians
looked frantically for hopeful signs. Victories and leaders
were badly needed, and soon. Stonewall Jackson and his
fewer than four thousand troops perched precariously in
the lower Shenandoah Valley hardly seemed candidates for
a hero's mantle, but in fact Jackson's hour had arrived. The
ungainly professor turned the war on its ear during a

period of eleven weeks in the spring of 1862 and made history with a campaign that will always be studied as a military classic. After an unpromising beginning at Kernstown in March (which accomplished the general's strategic imperative, tawdry tactical appearances notwithstanding), Jackson patiently knitted together an army drawn from several sources and awaited his opening. It came in May, when he struck at widely separated points to win three battles, expending his soldiers' sweat in copious volume. He marched them hard enough to be called the "Foot Cavalry" of Worsham's title, but spilled in consequence relatively little of their blood.

Jackson left the Shenandoah Valley—with which his name always will be associated—in June 1862 and moved toward Richmond, where R. E. Lee and his army hoped to break the federal stranglehold on the capital. Although Jackson performed there far below his usual standard, perhaps because of a sort of stress fatigue that sapped his vital forces, the Seven Days battles saved Richmond and inaugurated a series of spectacular successes that Lee won with Jackson's collaboration. General Jackson returned to independent campaigning in July, suppressing General John Pope in operations in central Virginia that reached a climax at the Battle of Cedar Mountain on August 9. John Worsham's regiment suffered about its worst day of the war at Cedar Mountain. Worsham's description of that disaster is among his most important battle narratives.

Stonewall Jackson's brilliant marching and daring initiatives led to further success for Lee's army at Second Manassas (or Bull Run) at the end of August 1862. The next month he led the maneuver element of the army in wide-ranging operations north of the Potomac and west of Washington that ended in a bloody stalemate at Sharpsburg (or Antietam). The Confederates won a sweeping but easy victory at Fredericksburg in December 1862 without drawing on Jackson's daring offensive style, thus ending active operations in a year that had carried Stonewall from relative obscurity to dazzling prominence.

Four days after Jackson took the field for spring campaigning in 1863, he met a fatal bullet. On April 29 the federal army opposite Fredericksburg pushed across the river near town in a feint designed to screen their main movement far upstream. Lee and Jackson moved toward the main threat on May 1 and determined to fight near Chancellorsville, despite being outnumbered by more than two-to-one odds. The next morning Jackson led nearly thirty thousand veterans on a thirteen-mile march in a startling gamble designed to cross the front of the enemy army in search of its exposed right flank and rear. Lee and Jackson won their amazing gamble and in the process crafted what must be considered Lee's greatest victory—but at a cost far too high, because at the end of his mighty flank attack Stonewall Jackson fell mortally wounded by the mistaken fire of North Carolinians in his own command. Lee lost, as he put it, his right arm. The Confederacy lost, it is easy to postulate, one of its most important implements if independence was to be won on the field of battle.

From the beginning of the 1862 valley campaign the 21st Virginia and John Worsham served Jackson well as among the stoutest of his steady "Foot Cavalry." The general's troops included many valley men and a preponderance of hardy farm boys. Worsham and his company stood in sharp contrast to that stereotype. John was a city boy from Richmond and so were his comrades in the 21st Virginia's Company F. Born in Richmond on July 8, 1839, Worsham was the son of a tailor who lived and worked in the midst of the city. After a private-school education, young Worsham worked as a clerk for a downtown merchant. War fever early in 1861 prompted him to enlist in the elite local military company known as "F Company" (long before it became Company F of the 21st Virginia). One observer called the members of the company "the pride, the boast and the love of Richmond!" When John joined the organization, he looked like a soldier, being a strapping six-footer with hazel eyes and light hair and complexion.

F Company went to war gaily caparisoned in fancy uniforms that Worsham described in loving detail in *One of Jackson's Foot Cavalry*. The outfit included calfskin knapsacks and white gloves, the whole festooned with yards of gold braid. Worsham's amused description of the unit's naive beginnings serves as a striking point of departure for a classic story that deals most often with weary and sweating foot soldiers.

Worsham and his mates answered frantic early war alarms around Richmond and then on the Potomac River east of Fredericksburg. Their first real campaign took them west from Staunton in mid-July into rainy mountain country, where they faced months of confusion and frustration. Late in December 1861, Worsham's regiment joined Stonewall Jackson in Winchester, thus forming an affiliation that lasted until the general's death. John saw Jackson during the march through town and wrote of "a pair of dark flashing eyes" beneath the low brim of a "faded gray cap." At Winchester the regiment formed another lasting association when it joined a brigade that included the 42nd and 48th Virginia Infantry regiments and the First Virginia Infantry Battalion.

The savage winter campaign at the beginning of 1862 seemed to Worsham to be "the most terrible experience during the war." Roads consisting of a "sheet of ice" forced the men to move "in the side ditches and in the woods." "Guns were constantly being fired by the men falling" and "each day was colder than the day before." Worsham noted with horror that "many men were frozen to death" and many more were barefoot, "having burned their shoes while trying to warm their feet at the fires."

Worsham saw his first real fighting at Kernstown in March 1862, where the 21st Virginia participated in "a regular stand-up fight" to open Jackson's valley campaign. Jackson's foot cavalry earned its title in the valley after

Kernstown in what Private Worsham called with unmistakable pride "the most brilliant [campaign] of modern times." John marched hard toward McDowell, but did not fight in the May 8 battle there. At Front Royal on May 23 he witnessed an affecting scene when one of his comrades met a brother among the mass of federal soldiers taken prisoner. During the final stages of the campaign Worsham and the 21st drew guard duty over the prisoners, "a job little relished by the men, since we had only about two hundred and fifty men to guard about three thousand prisoners!" In summarizing Jackson's success and its impact on his weary marching columns, Worsham clearly stated the credo of the foot cavalry: "to accomplish so much with so little loss, we would march six months!"

When Stonewall Jackson led his victorious veterans to Richmond in June 1862 to help General Lee lift the siege of the Confederate capital, Worsham met Lee and President Jefferson Davis as he approached the battlefield at Gaines' Mill. That evening John toured the strong position from which the Northerners had just been driven and reported seeing a machine gun emplaced there, "with its handle to turn out a bullet at every revolution."

Worsham and his regiment followed Jackson north from Richmond in late July and fought in the front line at Cedar Mountain on August 9, 1862. Worsham's narrative supplies important details of the general's narrow escape there and then describes a maelstrom of hand-to-hand combat "such . . . as was not witnessed during the war," employing "guns, bayonets, swords, pistols, fence rails, [and] rocks."

The terrible losses in the 21st Virginia made Cedar Mountain the regiment's toughest battle. Not many days later the regiment's fate had changed dramatically as Jackson's foot cavalry marched far and fast around the enemy and wound up in the midst of the federal supply trains. The ensuing bacchanalia at Manassas Junction lingered fondly in the memory of every participant through the lean years to come. Worsham remembered the joys of "potted ham, lobster, tongue, candy, cakes, nuts, oranges, lemons, pick-les, catsup, mustard, etc." For more than a few of the hard-marching Confederates, "etc." included captured spirits. In the Battle of Second Manassas that followed, Worsham participated in an exciting advance reconnais-sance, survived the death of four men standing next to him hit by a single cannonball, and witnessed the famous episode in which Confederates fought with rocks when their ammunition supply ran out. At the end of the battle John Worsham was one of three men present for duty in his company.

At Antietam in September, Worsham and the company's surviving fragment fought in the face of dominant federal artillery. "It seemed that the air was alive with shells!" Worsham recalled. By happy contrast, the 21st Virginia occupied a quiet zone in the next battle, at Fredericksburg in December. The winter that followed featured the usual camp diversions and a broad, deep religious revival that swept through Lee's army. John Worsham's memoir is renowned for its battle descriptions, but it deserves equal attention for the rich flavor of Confederate winter encamp-ments and soldierly diversions that it provides. Worsham describes the revival, the role of slaves, sharpshooting practice, discipline and executions, camp routine, and other aspects of military society in rear areas.

Recruiting duty took John Worsham to Richmond dur-ing the Chancellorsville campaign in May 1863, while the 21st fought another hard battle and Stonewall Jackson fell mortally wounded by the mistaken fire of his own troops. Worsham did not quite catch up with the army in time to reach Gettysburg. That circumstance serves history well because Sergeant Worsham (he had been promoted in April) found himself in the midst of a hot fight at Williamsport, Maryland, on July 6, 1863; his account is a key source on that battle.

At Payne's Farm on the Mine Run battlefield in Novem-ber 1863 Worsham witnessed an episode in an adjacent regiment of his brigade that nicely typifies the style of *One of Jackson's Foot Cavalry,* blending drama, dark comedy, and battle detail. A "large and stout" captain in the 50th Virginia, dismayed by his men's inadequate performance, chided them and "walked out to the brow of the hill, lay down on its top, broadside to the enemy," and told his troops "if they were afraid, they could use him as a breastwork." Worsham reported that the pragmatic soldiers called the captain's bluff: "Several of them very promptly accepted his challenge, lying down behind him, resting their guns on him, firing steadily . . . until the fight was over."

Worsham's eye for the unusual came upon another bizarre scene during the May 1864 Battle of the Wilderness. The 21st Virginia fought from the edge of Saunders Field on the Orange Turnpike on May 5–6, 1864. A Yankee and a Rebel seeking shelter from the sheets of lead flying overhead found themselves in the same midfield ravine and got into "a regular fist and skull fight" that spilled out of the draw and into the field. Worsham described the pugilists with glee and insisted that soldiers of both sides ceased firing to watch and cheer. One week later the 21st Virginia barely missed the bloodbath at Spotsylvania's "Bloody Angle." The regiment had spent the night far out in front of the lines on picket duty and on the morning of May 12 eventually managed to find a looping route away from the crisis and back to friendly lines.

In the early summer of 1864 John Worsham and the 21st left Lee's army and followed General Jubal A. Early back to the scenes of the triumphal 1862 Shenandoah Valley campaign. Early pushed the federals north out of the valley and boldly followed them to the outskirts of Washington. Worsham provides an irresistible portrait of General John B. Gordon at the Battle of Monocacy on July 9. A desperate race for a critical rail fence, under Gordon's direction, seemed to John to be "the most exciting time I witnessed during the war. The men were perfectly wild." The rest of the march toward Washington was not so exciting; Worsham was barefoot by then and tore his feet so badly that the scars remained visible to his death.

John Worsham's Civil War ended soon after the return from the Washington suburbs. He was hit hard in the left knee at the Third Battle of Winchester late on September 19, 1864, and remained incapacitated for duty for the rest of the war. *One of Jackson's Foot Cavalry* endeavors to report on the experiences of the 21st Virginia during the war's closing months, but the narrative of course lacks the immediacy of Worsham's lively eyewitness accounts. More interesting is his testimony on the occupation of Richmond in April 1865, written from firsthand observation as a convalescent in the city.

Soon after the war John Worsham emigrated from the burned and shattered capital city and went into business at Scottsville, on the James River. There he engaged in milling and operated a line of barges on the river and its adjacent canal. In the 1880s Worsham, by now married and the father of four children, returned by Richmond, where he worked as an insurance auditor then as a bookkeeper for a printing establishment.

Throughout his postwar years the proud veteran kept up his ties with his Confederate comrades. He was one of more than three dozen veterans of Company F who rallied for the dedication of the Lee Monument in Richmond in 1890. Late in the century articles from Worsham's pen began to appear in local newspapers. The *Southern Historical Society Papers* published several of them. These articles obviously prompted Worsham to work on a connected memoir of his war experiences. His book as published included the substance of the earlier articles, often altered only in mild editorial fashion: en route to Cedar Mountain, for instance, he described the "sizzling" of passing musket balls in an 1899 article and changed the word to "ting" in the book version of the same sentence.

In both his articles and the book, John Worsham displayed pride in his Confederate service, but avoided almost entirely any of the jingoistic Southern sentiment toward Northerners that had been prevalent during the war. By the turn of the century rapprochement had taken a firm hold on the nation. That Worsham actually remained less than thoroughly reconstructed seems obvious from a letter he wrote in 1904 with no intention that it be published—and in fact it never has been. Writing to a Confederate staff officer, Worsham described "a very pleasant memory" of Harpers Ferry. The staff officer rode up to Colonel Andrew Jackson Grigsby of the Stonewall Brigade "and informed him" in Worsham's presence "that the white flag had been raised and that Capt Poague's guns were loaded and that he wanted to know what to do about it. The old Colonel's reply has always stuck to me," Worsham noted with fond amusement. "Tell him to fire them off the way they are pointed, he wont kill more of the D— yankees than he ought to."

One of Jackson's Foot Cavalry appeared as part of a fine array of Southern memoirs published by Walter Neale and the Neale Company of New York. Some of the best Confederate books, and some that remain among the most sought after, came from Neale's press during the period 1904–1915. Worsham must have been delighted by the critical acclaim that reviewers accorded his volume. A review copied widely by Southern newspapers praised the book extravagantly: "If Dickens had followed Stonewall Jackson, he would have written just such a book as this. . . . [Worsham's] humor, his pathos, his fancy, his descriptive power, made him just the man to write this spirited account of the great campaigns in which he took part. . . . Worsham has made realistic the humorous, the dramatic, and the weirdly picturesque."

The Northern press was hardly less laudatory. Papers in Chicago, Pittsburgh, and Boston called Worsham's work an "interesting narrative" and "well told"; said that it was written in "thrilling and fascinating style," such that "the reader can imagine himself right up front with 'Stonewall' Jackson"; and pronounced it "highly entertaining" and "thoroughly interesting and instructive."

The publisher offered *One of Jackson's Foot Cavalry* for sale for $2.15, including postage. Although the first edition is regarded today among collectors as a classic Confederate rarity, it is not really so scarce as a number of other famous Neale titles. Accordingly, the book must have sold well during its first two years on the market. Early in 1915, however, as Walter Neale was sliding toward insolvency, he put his entire stock on sale at half price. The cut-rate advertisements, which are enough to make a Confederate bibliophile sigh wistfully and long for the advent of time travel, quote the rave review about Worsham's Dickensian qualities. At its demise the Neale Company had published nearly five hundred titles, but few if any have more claim to fame than does John Worsham's story of service under Stonewall Jackson.

The last years of Worsham's long life must surely have been brightened by the recognition earned by his book. The end came for the elderly veteran on September 19, 1920—ironically on the fifty-sixth anniversary of the day that his war ended near Winchester in 1864. Worsham was buried in Richmond's Hollywood Cemetery, that great city of the Confederate dead.

Nearly a half century after the author's death, *One of Jackson's Foot Cavalry* came back on the market as one of the spate of reprints done during the Civil War Centennial. That 1964 version was reset in type with rather extensive rearrangement of Worsham's language. Another reprint appeared during the 1980s. This current Bantam edition reproduces Worsham's words exactly as he wrote them.

The American Civil War continues to grip the nation's imagination in the 1990s, as a flurry of releases in various media on both popular and scholarly fronts visibly attest. Stonewall Jackson retains his power to fascinate, and he probably always will. The experiences of Confederate enlisted men offer us the riveting perspective of men defending their homes, still—fortunately—an experience unique for Americans in any large-scale war. Among the large number of soldier narratives that compete for attention,

John H. Worsham's book demands recognition. The reviewers writing early in 1913 about Worsham were right. *One of Jackson's Foot Cavalry* is indeed, to repeat their descriptive words, spirited, humorous, dramatic, weirdly picturesque, well told, thrilling and fascinating, highly entertaining, and thoroughly interesting.

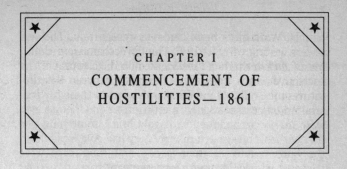

CHAPTER I

COMMENCEMENT OF HOSTILITIES—1861

SOON AFTER THE INVESTMENT of Fort Sumpter, S.C., December 20th, 1860, a military spirit prevailed all over Virginia. All the old volunteer companies were filled at once, and new ones were organized, and when the State seceded, a large portion of the men had joined some of the military organizations. I joined an old volunteer company. It was known as "F Company" of Richmond; one of the crack companies of that day. In its ranks were some of the best men of the city. It numbered about eighty men. New members were added so rapidly that it soon numbered about one hundred and fifty.

This company had a fine cadet gray uniform, consisting of a frock coat, which had a row of Virginia fire-gilt buttons on its front; around the cuff of the sleeve, a band of gold braid and two small fire-gilt buttons; on the collar the same gold braid so arranged that it looked very much like the mark of rank for a first lieutenant, which was afterwards adopted by the Confederacy. The pants had a black stripe about one and a quarter inches wide along the outer seams. The cap was made of the same cadet gray cloth,

1

trimmed with black braid, and two small fire-gilt buttons, and on its front the letter F. The non-commissioned officers had their mark of rank worked on the sleeves of their coats with black braid. The difference between the uniforms of the officers and the privates was in these particulars: the officers' coats were a little longer and their sleeves were highly ornamented with gold braid, something like that of the Confederate uniform; they had gold braid down the outer seams of their pants, and their caps were trimmed with gold braid. Each sergeant carried, besides his gun, a sword attached to his belt. When on duty every man was required to wear white gloves. He carried in his knapsack a jacket made of cadet gray cloth. We had black cloth overcoats, the skirt reaching a little below the knee, the capes a little below the elbow, and the buttons were Virginia fire-gilt.

Our knapsacks were a specialty; they were imported from Paris, made of calfskin tanned with hair on, the color being red and white, the skin was fitted around a box frame. Inside they were divided into partitions; and outside, there were openings into some of these so that one could handle articles inside of them without opening the whole knapsack, and there were straps on the outside for blanket, overcoat, oilcloth and shoes, and other straps and some hooks handy for attaching any article we wished to carry. We also imported our canteens.

For a week or two before the State seceded, the companies in Richmond were drilling men nearly all the time; a squad of green men at one hour, another squad at the next, so on throughout the entire day; and at night a company drill. Each man was required to report at company headquarters once during the day. The tolling of the fire bells was the signal to meet at the companies' armories, prepared to go wherever ordered.

I was quietly walking home from church, after the morning service on Sunday, April 21, 1861, when the bells commenced to toll. I broke into a run at once, going home as fast as I could. I put on my uniform, etc., and was soon at our armory. Here it was rumored that the gunboat *Pawnee* was coming up James River, with the intention of capturing or bombarding the city. As soon as all the men reported, the company was formed and marched to Wilton on James River, about ten miles below the city. Passing Rocketts, the port of Richmond, we found the citizens assembled there by thousands; old men, boys, women, girls, women with babies in their arms, in fact nearly the whole population. The fields in Rocketts, as well as the wharves, were literally alive with human beings, commingled with horses and vehicles, as some had ridden down in buggies and carriages. Some had shotguns, some had rifles, some pistols, some swords, some canes, and some had made large piles of stones on the wharves, to use against the enemy. They were all determined that the ship should never get to the wharf. It makes me laugh now, after my experience of war, to think what the citizens were then doing!

We arrived at Wilton about sunset, where we were joined by the Richmond Howitzers. A picket from F Company was established along the river. The Howitzers' guns were placed in position. Orders were given to fire on the *Pawnee* as soon as she came within shooting distance. The men of F Company, not on duty, stacked arms, and were ordered to remain near them during the night. We had nothing to eat, and did not know when or where we would get anything. One of our officers, however, had remained behind, and about eight or nine o'clock that night came up with a wagon loaded with cooked ham, bread, etc., and we had a jolly time over our supper, the first of the war. After eating, the men gathered about in squads talking; finally lying down on the grassy ground and going to sleep; the first experience of the war, and that without either blanket or oilcloth. The night passed without incident; the expected *Pawnee* did not come. The next day we returned to Richmond on two barges, that were sent down the river for us. We won a great deal of glory in this campaign, as everyone thought we had done wonders. In marching from

Rocketts up Main Street to our quarters, which were between Eighth and Ninth Streets, we had an ovation nearly all the way. Thus closed the "Pawnee War."

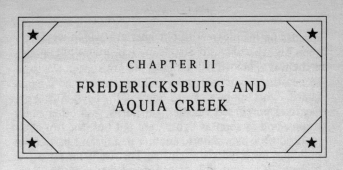

Virginia was thoroughly aroused. Soldiers were coming into Richmond from all directions, the streets were filled with marching men, and the sound of the drum was heard every hour of the day and night. It will show the enthusiasm of the people of the State when it is said that four weeks after Virginia seceded, eighty thousand organized soldiers had offered their services in defense of the cause!

On the morning of Wednesday, April 24, 1861, several telegrams were received in Richmond announcing that the enemy were landing at Aquia Creek, the terminus of the Richmond, Fredericksburg & Potomac R. R. Our company and the Richmond Light Infantry Blues were ordered at once to that place. We marched to the R. F. & P. R. R. depot, then on Broad Street, corner of Eighth Street, where we embarked on cars for the seat of war, Aquia Creek. On reaching Fredericksburg, we were informed that the Yankees had made a demonstration to Aquia Creek, but did not land; and we received orders to stop there. F Company debarked, and marched to the courthouse and

5

camped for the night. A load of straw was sent us, which we spread on the floor and benches, making a very good bed; and citizens invited us to their homes to supper. We went to bed that night in regular military order, had a camp guard, lights out by taps, etc. Some of the boys, during the day, had purchased whistles, tin horns, and other noisy things, and as soon as lights were put out, the fun commenced: One blew a horn, another in a distant part of the building answered on a whistle. This went on for a few minutes. When the officers commanded silence, no attention was paid to them. When the officers said to the sergeant, "Arrest those men," the sergeant would strike a light, and go where he thought the noise originated; but each man looked so innocent that he could not tell who it was. By this time, another would blow. Soon there were four sergeant, running here and there, trying to catch the delinquents. This was kept up until the perpetrators became tired, not one being detected.

In the morning we were supplied with breakfast by the citizens. We remained in the town, living in this manner several days. Then we marched to the Fair Grounds, where we found that the Blues had preceded us. Here we went regularly into camp, which was called Camp Mercer. Our company was assigned to the sheds of the horse department, the floors were covered with straw, and three men were assigned to a stall.

Camp duty began at once, guard mounting, policing, drills, etc., and dress parade every fair evening, most of the young ladies of the town coming out to witness it; and they seemed to enjoy it as much as we did their presence. The men formed messes, each consisting of about ten men, each employing a negro man as cook, and we got on nicely, as we thought. The regular rations were issued to us, but in order to become accustomed by degrees to eating them, we sent the cook or some member of the mess into town, to get such articles as the market afforded.

The following are the names of the members of F Company, who went to Fredericksburg:

Captain, R. Milton Cary.
First Lieut.—(Did not go.)
Second Lieut., Richard H.
Cunningham.
Jr. Second Lieut., Phillip A.
Welford.
First Sergeant, Edward Mayo.
Second Sergeant, Henry T.
Miller.
Third Sergeant, John A. Pizzini.
Fourth Sergeant, Edward G.
Rawlings.
First Corporal, John Tyler.
Second Corporal, Thomas
Ellett.
Third Corporal—(Did not go.)
Fourth Corporal—Shirley King.

PRIVATES

Anderson, Archer.
Anderson, Junius H.
Anderson, Henry V.
Archer, William S.
Ayers, Edward W.
Barker, William C.
Baughman, Charles C.
Baughman, George C.
Baughman, Greer H.
Beers, Henry H.
Binford, James M.
Binford, Robert E.
Blunt, Ira W.
Bridges, Jr., David B.
Bridges, Richard M.
Broch, R. Alonzo.
Bullington, Henry N.
Cabell, J. Caskie.
Child, Jesse.
Chamberlain, J. Hampden.
Chapman, Isaac W.
Clarke, Maxwell T.
Clopton, Dr. John.
Cocke, Lorenzo G.
Cole, Addison C.
Cowardin, John L.
Craig, John A.
Danforth, Henry D.
Dill, Jr., Adolph.
Doggett, Francis W.
Ellerson, Jock H.
Ellett, Robert.

Etting, Samuel M.
Exall, Charles H.
Exall, William.
Field, William G.
Fontaine, R. Morris.
Gentry, John W.
Gibson, William T.
Gilliam, Robert H.
Gray, W. Granville.
Gray, Somerville.
Green, John W.
Green, Thomas R.
Harrison, Thomas R.
Harvie, William O.
Haynes, George A.
Henry, Dr. Patrick.
Hobson, Deane.
Hudgins, Malcolm L.
Hull, Irving.
Jenkins, William S.
Jones, David B.
Jones, Jr., Phillip B.
Jordan, Reuben J.
Kellogg, Timothy H.
Lindsay, Roswell S.
Lorentz,—.
Macmurdo, Richard C.
Maddox, R. G.
Mayo, Joseph E.
McEvoy, Charles A.
Meade, Everard B.
Mebane, J. A.

Meredith, J. French.
Mitchell, Samuel D.
Mittledorfer, Charles.
Morris, Walter H. P.
Mountcastle, John R.
Norwood, Jr., William.
Nunnally, Joseph N.
Pace, George R.
Pace, Theodore A.
Page, Mann.
Pardigon, C. F.
Payne, James B.
Peaster, Henry.
Pegram, William A.
Pegram, William R. J.
Peterkin, George W.
Picot, Henry V.
Piet, William A.
Pollard, William G.
Powell, John G.
Powell, John W.
Price, Channing R.
Randolph, J. Tucker.
Randolph, M. Lewis.
Redd, Clarence M.
Reeve, David I. B.
Reeve, John J.
Rennie, G. Hutcheson.
Rison, John W.
Robertson, William S.
Robinson, Christopher A.
Robinson, Richard F.
Singleton, A. Jackson.
Sizer, Milton D.
Skinker, Charles R.
Smith, Edward H.
Sublett, Peter A.
Tabb, Robert M.
Talley, Daniel D.
Tatum, A. Randolph.
Tatum, Vivian H.
Taylor, Charles E.
Taylor, Clarence E.
Taylor, Edward B.
Taylor, Robert T.
Tompkins, Edmond G.
Tyler, James E.
Tyler, R. Emmett.
Van Buren, Benjamin B.
Waldrop, Richard W.
Watkins, A. Salle.
Watkins, Harrison H.
White, Robert C.
Willis, Joseph N.
Worsham, John H.
Worsham, Thomas R.
Wren, J. Porter.
Wright, Phillip B.
Zimmer, Lewis.
Surgeon, Frank B. Cunningham.
Assistant Surgeon, Peter Lyon.

A few of these men joined us after we went to Fredericksburg, and some left us to join other commands, after staying with us two or three weeks. Samuel F. Pilcher was left in Richmond to drill men for a second company, and on account of sickness never came to the command.

While in Camp Mercer we were joined by a company of infantry, one of cavalry, and the Purcell Battery of Artillery from Richmond. W. R. J. Pegram of F Company (Specks, as he was called) helped Captain Lindsay Walker to drill this battery, and was soon made a lieutenant; this is the same

W. R. J. Pegram of the artillery, who was soon known in the army of Northern Virginia as the fighting captain, major, lieutenant colonel, and colonel, and was killed at Five Forks in 1865.

I saw the first man of the war punished for disobedience of orders, while we were in this camp; he was a member of Walker's battery, and was strapped on one of the wheels of a cannon in such a manner as to keep him from moving. This punishment is known as "strapping to the wheel." We were treated most hospitably by the citizens of Fredericksburg, some of us visiting the city each day; and were always welcomed and invited to meals, and we left with sad hearts. This was the most comfortable camp we had during the war, but at that time we thought it was execrable.

We stayed at Fredericksburg about three weeks, and were ordered to Aquia Creek. We camped in a house at Game Point, situated on a high hill to the left of the Richmond, Fredericksburg & Potomac R. R., and about three-quarters of a mile from Aquia Creek. The R. L. I. Blues also went to Aquia Creek and camped lower down the river, about one and a half miles from us.

The cook of my mess would not leave Fredericksburg, and at Game Point we determined to cook for ourselves. I will never forget the first meal. We made a fire under the shade of a tree, made up our bread of meal (the government commenced to give it to us thus early), sliced our fat meat, and commenced to cook, and in about two minutes both meat and bread were burned black on one side! We took them off the fire, cooled them, and tried again, and succeeded very well in burning the other side. We finally cooked everything we had and sat down on the ground to eat. The bread had no salt in it, no one had thought of that; the meat was so salt we could not eat it. We were disgusted, but the next day we had better success, and in a few days we got along all right.

We had a camp guard and two picket posts or rather lookout posts, as the duties at each was to watch the river for the enemy. While I was on guard at our quarters, one night General Ruggles, the commanding officer of this department, paid us a visit. I presented arms as soon as I saw him, and turned out the guard, thinking to do him all the honor we could. I was horrified when a non-commissioned officer slipped up to me and told me such honor was not done after dark.

PRAYER IN CAMP

The following letter was written while we were in this camp and explains itself:

George W. Peterkin, Esq,:
    Dear Sir—We, the undersigned comrades in arms with yourself, have been struck with the propriety of evening prayer, and desire, if agreeable to you, that you, from this time, and so long as we may remain together, conduct that service.
                                        Respectfully,

J. M. Binford,
R. E. Binford,
John W. Powell,
J. P. Wren,
R. T. Taylor,
C. R. Skinker,
Jesse Child,
William Exall,
J. A. Mebane,
D. D. Talley,
R. M. Bridges,
John Tyler,
D. J. Burr Reeve,
John J. Reeve,
R. E. Tyler.
Joseph N. Nunnally,
C. M. Redd,
H. D. Danforth,
W. Granville Gray,

George A. Haynes,
G. R. Pace,
John R. Macmurdo,
S. D. Mitchell,
John H. Chamberlayne,
Robert Ellett,
R. C. White.
Shirley King,
A. C. Cole,
H. H. Watkins,
Dean Hobson,
R. S. Lindsay,
W. S. Archer,
Thomas Ellett,
J. H. Ellerson,
J. W. Chapman,
William A. Piet,
C. H. Exall,
A. R. Tatum,

S. M. Etting,	P. A. Wellford,
John A. Pizzini,	H. N. Bullington,
Edward Mayo,	E. H. Smith,
E. G. Tompkins,	William C. Barker,
Louis Zimmer,	M. H. Clarke,
D. B. Jones,	E. G. Rawlings,
H. H. Beers,	E. W. Ayres,
R. Milton Cary,	and others.

This gallant young soldier and truly good man conducted the service each night, and by his Christian example won the respect and affection of every member of the company; and when he left us in 1862, to take a staff appointment, it was like breaking up a household.

This is the same George W. Peterkin who has for a number of years been the honored and respected Bishop of West Virginia.

On May 29th, 1861, we had our first experience of war. One of the enemy's gunboats stopped off Aquia Creek, fired a few shots and left. On June 7, three gunboats made their appearance and commenced to bombard the earthworks near the wharf. Capt. Walker put some of his small three-inch rifle cannon into the works, and replied, the enemy throwing six, eight, and ten inch shots at Walker. This firing lasted several hours, when the enemy withdrew about two or three miles down the river, staying all night, and renewing the attack the next morning with five gunboats; keeping the fire up until about 5 P.M., when they withdrew. The R. L. I. Blues and F Company were stationed, during the firing, behind some hills in the rear of the works, and nearly all the shots of the enemy passed over us. The family living inside the earthworks had a chicken coop knocked to pieces. The old cock confined in it came out of the ruins, mounted the débris, flapped his wings and crowed. That was the only casualty on our side. Capt. Walker's shots struck the vessels several times, and as they were wooden boats, he must have damaged them some. We afterwards heard that one of them was the notable *Pawnee*.

We had several alarms at night, when the entire company would turn out, and march to the river to the place designated. On one of these occasions, we marched in rain which poured down in torrents. The darkness was illumined by most vivid flashes of lightning, and great peals of thunder intensified the storm. We stayed out all night, putting a picket along the river, two men on a post. We crossed Aquia Creek twice during alarms, one time staying all night on the point.

We were joined by a regiment from Arkansas, and one from Tennessee and several companies from Virginia. The hills around Aquia were fortified by earthworks, and large naval guns were placed in them. Our company turned out one night and pulled one of those large guns up one of the steepest hills to its position, after a failure on the part of a large team of horses and oxen! It was demonstrated very forcibly that men are the best and quickest force for handling large and heavy guns like those.

We drilled every good day and took our first lessons in skirmish drill, and the bayonet exercise, or the Zouave drill; and before we left, we became very well drilled in each. We enjoyed ourselves very much notwithstanding the duties, fishing on the wharf, bathing in the river, taking rambles through the woods, having on one of the hills in the neighborhood a fine and extensive view of the Potomac.

On June the 14th, F Company was ordered to Richmond to join a regiment that was being formed there. The men were told it was to be a crack regiment; our own and a Maryland company commanded by Capt. J. Lyle Clarke, then in Camp Lee, were to be the nucleus, the other companies to be of the same standing. No time was designated for the formation of the regiment, and when formed it would be an independent one. With those inducements the men readily consented to the arrangement, and therefore the order to go to Richmond.

The following changes took place in officers and non-commissioned officers, while we were at Fredericksburg and Aquia Creek.

First Lieut. James R. Crenshaw and Corporal Edward T. Robinson did not accompany us, and soon after we got to Fredericksburg Capt. Cary was made a Colonel; those vacancies were filled by promotions as follows:

Captain, Richard H. Cunningham.

First Lieut., Edward Mayo.

Second Lieut., Phillip A. Welford.

Jr. Second Lieut., Henry T. Miller.

First Sergeant, John A. Pizzini.

Second Sergeant, Edward G. Rawlings.

Third Sergeant, John Tyler.

Fourth Sergeant, Thomas Ellett.

First Corporal, M. Louis Randolph.

Second Corporal, Jesse Child.

Third Corporal, J. Tucker Randolph.

Fourth Corporal, Shirley King.

First Corporal, M. Louis Randolph resigned June 4, 1861.

Jesse Child was made First Corporal June 5.

J. Tucker Randolph was made Second Corporal June 5.

Shirley King was made Third Corporal June 5.

George R. Pace was made Fourth Corporal June 5.

F Company gave up Capt. Cary with much reluctance. He was the organizer of F Company, a fine soldier, strict disciplinarian, and splendid drill master. They tell this on him to show his promptness: At the time of the John Brown raid, Gov. Wise one night sent for him, told him he wanted his company to go to Harper's Ferry at once, and asked him, "How many men can you carry, and how soon can you meet me at the R. F. & P. R. R. depot?" Capt. Cary replied, "Sixty men in sixty minutes." The old governor, much pleased with the answer, told him to report within two hours.

When F Company left Richmond for Fredericksburg,

each man carried his equipment of gun, etc., a knapsack, canteen, tin cup, and haversack; most of them wore linen gaiters and havelocks, the latter being a head covering, a protection from the sun. Many wore around their waists, next to their skin, a flannel belt or worsted string, to prevent bowel complaint (?). In our knapsacks we carried a fatigue jacket, several pairs of white gloves, several pairs of drawers, several white shirts, undershirts, linen collars, neckties, white vest, socks, etc., filling our knapsack to overflowing. Strapped on the outside were one or two blankets, an oilcloth, and extra shoes. Most of the knapsacks weighed between thirty and forty pounds, but some were so full that they weighed fifty pounds!

The best article carried by the soldiers was a needle case, as it was called, containing needles of various sizes, thread, buttons, etc. It soon became the most valuable of our possessions, and when we went into camp we would see the men occupied in sewing or patching their clothing, and towards the last of the war, it was in almost constant use. Notwithstanding this, it was hard to keep the ragged clothing from showing a portion of the skin of its wearer.

Every man carried a Bible, given with her blessing by mother or sweetheart, and I suppose every man in the Confederate army carried one. This Bible was read as a book never was before. I read mine through the first year. They were a blessing to many, and life savers, too, as I heard of and saw many lives saved by bullets striking the Bible, carried in the breast pocket.

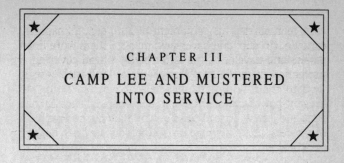

On our arrival at Camp Lee, we were given tents, which we put up in regular military style near the center of the grounds, and commenced a regular camp life; drilling, guard mounting each morning, policing, inspections, and evening dress parade. The latter was witnessed daily by quite a number of our lady friends from Richmond.

We were mustered into service for one year on June 28, 1861 (to date from April 21), on the Capitol Square by Inspector General J. B. Baldwin. Each boy under 21, and there were many, brought a written permit from parent or guardian, and this was approved by the Governor of Virginia before he was mustered in.

I cannot give a copy of that muster roll, as it cannot be found, but give that of the 30th, only two days later, which is practically the same.

"Muster Roll of Captain Richard H. Cunningham, Jr.'s Company F of Light Infantry from the City of Richmond, known as 'F Company,' constituting part of the Force of Virginia Volunteers, called into the Service of the State by the Governor, under an Ordinance of the State Convention

	Names Present and Absent.			Joined for Service and Enrolled at General Rendezvous			Mustered into Service.		
No.	Privates in Alphabetical Order.	Rank	Age	When	Where	By Whom	When	Where	By Whom
1	Richard H. Cunningham, Jr.	Capt.	27	Apr. 21	Richmond	R. Milton Cary	June 28	Richmond	Gen. Baldwin
1	Edward Mayo	1st Lt.	30	Apr. 21	Richmond	R. Milton Cary	June 28	Richmond	Gen. Baldwin
2	Philip A. Wellford	2nd Lt.	27	Apr. 21	Richmond	R. Milton Cary	June 28	Richmond	Gen. Baldwin
1	Henry T. Miller	2nd Lt.	26	Apr. 21	Richmond	R. Milton Cary	June 28	Richmond	Gen. Baldwin
1	John A. Pizzini	1st Sgt.	27	Apr. 21.	Richmond	R. Milton Cary	June 28	Richmond	Gen. Baldwin
3	Edward G. Rawlings-	1st Sgt.	36	Apr. 21	Richmond	R. Milton Cary	June 28	Richmond	Gen. Baldwin
3	John Tyler	1st Sgt.	25	Apr. 21	Richmond	R. Milton Cary	June 28	Richmond	Gen. Baldwin
4	Thomas Ellett	1st Sgt.	28	Apr. 21	Richmond	R. Milton Cary	June 28	Richmond	Gen. Baldwin
1	Jesse Child	Corpl.	30	Apr. 21	Richmond	R. Milton Cary	June 28	Richmond	Gen. Baldwin
2	J. Tucker Randolph	Corpl.	18	Apr. 21	Richmond	R. Milton Cary	June 28	Richmond	Gen. Baldwin
3	Shirley King	Corpl.	19	Apr. 21	Richmond	R. Milton Cary	June 28	Richmond	Gen. Baldwin
4	George R. Pace	Corpl.	25	Apr. 21	Richmond	R. Milton Cary	June 28	Richmond	Gen. Baldwin
1	Anderson, Henry V.	Private	21	Apr. 21	Richmond	R. Milton Cary	June 28	Richmond	Gen. Baldwin
2	Anderson, Junius H.	Private	26	Apr. 21	Richmond	R. Milton Cary	June 28	Richmond	Gen. Baldwin
3	Anderson, Archer	Private	23	Apr. 21	Richmond	R. Milton Cary	June 28	Richmond	Gen. Baldwin
4	Archer, William S., Jr.	Private	17	Apr. 21	Richmond	R. Milton Cary	June 28	Richmond	Gen. Baldwin
5	Baughman, Greer H.	Private	19	Apr. 21	Richmond	R. Milton Cary	June 28	Richmond	Gen. Baldwin
6	Baughman, Charles C.	Private	21	Apr. 21	Richmond	R. Milton Cary	June 28	Richmond	Gen. Baldwin
7	Barker, William C.	Private	28	Apr. 21	Richmond	R. Milton Cary	June 28	Richmond	Gen. Baldwin
8	Bridges, Richard M.	Private	17	Apr. 21	Richmond	R. Milton Cary	June 28	Richmond	Gen. Baldwin
9	Bridges, David Jr.	Private	19	Apr. 21	Richmond	R. Milton Cary	June 28	Richmond	Gen. Baldwin
10	Bullington, Henry N.	Private	20	Apr. 21	Richmond	R. Milton Cary	June 28	Richmond	Gen. Baldwin
11	Beers, Henry H.	Private	20	Apr. 21	Richmond	R. Milton Cary	June 28	Richmond	Gen. Baldwin
12	Brock, Robert A.	Private	22	Apr. 21	Richmond	R. Milton Cary	June 28	Richmond	Gen. Baldwin
13	Binford, James M.	Private		Apr. 21	Richmond	R. Milton Cary	June 28	Richmond	Gen. Baldwin
14	Binford, Robert E.	Private		Apr. 21	Richmond	R. Milton Cary	June 28	Richmond	Gen. Baldwin
15	Blunt, Ira W.	Private	29	Apr. 21	Richmond	R. Milton Cary	June 28	Richmond	Gen. Baldwin
16	Cocke, Lorenzo G.	Private	25	Apr. 21	Richmond	R. Milton Cary	June 28	Richmond	Gen. Baldwin
17	Clarke, Maxwell T.	Private	31	Apr. 21	Richmond	R. Milton Cary	June 28	Richmond	Gen. Baldwin

No.	Name	Rank	Age	Date	Place	Officer	Date	Place	Officer
18	Craig, John A.	Private	21	Apr. 21	Richmond	R. Milton Cary	June 28	Richmond	Gen. Baldwin
19	Chapman, Isaac W.	Private	21	Apr. 21	Richmond	R. Milton Cary	June 28	Richmond	Gen. Baldwin
20	Cole, Addison C.	Private	30	Apr. 21	Richmond	R. Milton Cary	June 28	Richmond	Gen. Baldwin
21	Doggett, Francis W.	Private	27	Apr. 21	Richmond	R. Milton Cary	June 28	Richmond	Gen. Baldwin
22	Danforth, Henry D.	Private	20	Apr. 21.	Richmond	R. Milton Cary	June 28	Richmond	Gen. Baldwin
23	Dill, Adolph, Jr.	Private	20	Apr. 21	Richmond	R. Milton Cary	June 28	Richmond	Gen. Baldwin
24	Ellett, Robert	Private	18	Apr. 21	Richmond	R. Milton Cary	June 28	Richmond	Gen. Baldwin
25	Exall, Charles H.	Private	20	Apr. 21	Richmond	R. Milton Cary	June 28	Richmond	Gen. Baldwin
26	Exall, William	Private	22	Apr. 21	Richmond	R. Milton Cary	June 28	Richmond	Gen. Baldwin
27	Fontaine, Richard M.	Private	19	Apr. 21	Richmond	R. Milton Cary	June 28	Richmond	Gen. Baldwin
28	Gray, William G.	Private	25	Apr. 21	Richmond	R. Milton Cary	June 28	Richmond	Gen. Baldwin
29	Gray, Somerville	Private	20	Apr. 21	Richmond	R. Milton Cary	June 28	Richmond	Gen. Baldwin
30	Green, John W.	Private	23	Apr. 21	Richmond	R. Milton Cary	June 28	Richmond	Gen. Baldwin
31	Gibson, William T.	Private	29	Apr. 21	Richmond	R. Milton Cary	June 28	Richmond	Gen. Baldwin
32	Gentry, John W.	Private	20	Apr. 21	Richmond	R. Milton Cary	June 28	Richmond	Gen. Baldwin
33	Gilliam, Robert H.	Private	22	Apr. 21	Richmond	R. Milton Cary	June 28	Richmond	Gen. Baldwin
34	Green, Thomas R.	Private	24	Apr. 21	Richmond	R. Milton Cary	June 28	Richmond	Gen. Baldwin
35	Haynes, George A.	Private	20	Apr. 21	Richmond	R. Milton Cary	June 28	Richmond	Gen. Baldwin
36	Henry, Patrick	Private	24	May 16	Game Point	R. H. Cunningham, Jr.	June 28	Richmond	Gen. Baldwin
37	Hudgins, Malcolm L.	Private	17	May 16	Game Point	R. H. Cunningham, Jr.	June 28	Richmond	Gen. Baldwin
38	Jinkins, William S.	Private	27	Apr. 21	Richmond	R. Milton Cary	June 28	Richmond	Gen. Baldwin
39	Jones, Philip B. Jr.	Private		Apr. 21	Richmond	R. Milton Cary	June 28	Richmond	Gen. Baldwin
40	Jones, David B.	Private	25	Apr. 21	Richmond	R. Milton Cary	June 28	Richmond	Gen. Baldwin
41	Jordan, Reuben J.	Private	20	Apr. 21	Richmond	R. Milton Cary	June 28	Richmond	Gen. Baldwin
42	Kellogg, Timothy H.	Private	30	Apr. 21	Richmond	R. Milton Cary	June 28	Richmond	Gen. Baldwin
43	Lindsay, Roswell S.	Private	21	Apr. 21	Richmond	R. Milton Cary	June 28	Richmond	Gen. Baldwin
44	Mebane, James A.	Private	19	Apr. 21	Richmond	R. Milton Cary	June 28	Richmond	Gen. Baldwin
45	Mittledorfer, Charles	Private	22	Apr. 21	Richmond	R. Milton Cary	June 28	Richmond	Gen. Baldwin
46	Morris, Walter H. P.	Private	21	Apr. 21	Richmond	R. Milton Cary	June 28	Richmond	Gen. Baldwin
47	Meade, Everard B.	Private	22	Apr. 21	Richmond	R. Milton Cary	June 28	Richmond	Gen. Baldwin
48	Mountcastle, John R.	Private	20	Apr. 21	Richmond	R. Milton Cary	June 28	Richmond	Gen. Baldwin
49	Mitchell, Samuel D.	Private	19	Apr. 21	Richmond	R. Milton Cary	June 28	Richmond	Gen. Baldwin
50	Mayo, Joseph E.	Private	21	May 10	Fredericksburg	R. Milton Cary	June 28	Richmond	Gen. Baldwin
51	Macmurdo, Richard C.	Private	26	May 18	Game Point	R. H. Cunningham, Jr.	June 28	Richmond	Gen. Baldwin

	Names Present and Absent. Privates in Alphabetical Order.	Rank	Age	Joined for Service and Enrolled at General Rendezvous When	Where	By Whom	Mustered into Service. When	Where	By Whom
No.									
52	Norwood, William, Jr.	Private		Apr. 21	Richmond	R. Milton Cary	June 28	Richmond	Gen. Baldwin
53	Nunnally, Joseph N.	Private	20	Apr. 21	Richmond	R. Milton Cary	June 28	Richmond	Gen. Baldwin
54	Powell, John G.	Private	26	May 10	Fredericksburg	R. Milton Cary	June 28	Richmond	Gen. Baldwin
55	Payne, James B.	Private	24	Apr. 21	Richmond	R. Milton Cary	June 28	Richmond	Gen. Baldwin
56	Picot, Henry V.	Private	24	Apr. 21	Richmond	R. Milton Cary	June 28	Richmond	Gen. Baldwin
58	Page, Mann	Private	26	Apr. 21	Richmond	R. Milton Cary	June 28	Richmond	Gen. Baldwin
59	Pegram, William A.	Private	18	Apr. 21	Richmond	R. Milton Cary	June 28	Richmond	Gen. Baldwin
60	Peterkin, George W.	Private	20	Apr. 21	Richmond	R. Milton Cary	June 28	Richmond	Gen. Baldwin
61	Peaster, Henry	Private	25	Apr. 21	Richmond	R. Milton Cary	June 28	Richmond	Gen. Baldwin
62	Pollard, William G.	Private	24	Apr. 21	Richmond	R. Milton Cary	June 28	Richmond	Gen. Baldwin
63	Pace, Theodore A.	Private	16	May 6	Fredericksburg	R. Milton Cary	June 28	Richmond	Gen. Baldwin
64	Reeve, David I. B.	Private	23	Apr. 21	Richmond	R. Milton Cary	June 28	Richmond	Gen. Baldwin
65	Reeve, John J.	Private	20	May 10	Fredericksburg	R. Milton Cary	June 28	Richmond	Gen. Baldwin
66	Robinson, Christopher A.	Private	22	Apr. 21	Richmond	R. Milton Cary	June 28	Richmond	Gen. Baldwin
67	Robinson, Richard F.	Private	18	Apr. 21	Richmond	R. Milton Cary	June 28	Richmond	Gen. Baldwin
68	Robertson, William S.	Private	20	May 18	Game Point	R. H. Cunningham, Jr.	June 28	Richmond	Gen. Baldwin
69	Rennie, George H.	Private	21	May 18	Game Point	R. H. Cunningham, Jr.	June 28	Richmond	Gen. Baldwin
70	Redd, Clarence M.	Private	22	Apr. 21	Richmond	R. Milton Cary	June 28	Richmond	Gen. Baldwin
71	Smith, Edwin H.	Private	29	Apr. 21	Richmond	R. Milton Cary	June 28	Richmond	Gen. Baldwin
72	Sublett, Peter A.	Private	21	Apr. 21	Richmond	R. Milton Cary	June 28	Richmond	Gen. Baldwin
73	Skinker, Charles R.	Private	22	Apr. 21	Richmond	R. Milton Cary	June 28	Richmond	Gen. Baldwin
74	Singleton, Andrew J.	Private	19	Apr. 21	Richmond	R. Milton Cary	June 28	Richmond	Gen. Baldwin
75	Sizer, Milton D.	Private	25	Apr. 21	Richmond	R. Milton Cary	June 28	Richmond	Gen. Baldwin
76	Tompkins, Edmond G.	Private	24	Apr. 21	Richmond	R. Milton Cary	June 28	Richmond	Gen. Baldwin
77	Taylor, Robert T.	Private	29	Apr. 21	Richmond	R. Milton Cary	June 28	Richmond	Gen. Baldwin
78	Taylor, Edward B.	Private	18	Apr. 21	Richmond	R. Milton Cary	June 28	Richmond	Gen. Baldwin
79	Taylor, Charles E.	Private	17	Apr. 21	Richmond	R. Milton Cary	June 28	Richmond	Gen. Baldwin
80	Taylor, Clarence E.	Private	20	Apr. 21	Richmond	R. Milton Cary	June 28	Richmond	Gen. Baldwin
81	Tyler, James E.	Private		Apr. 21	Richmond	R. Milton Cary	June 28	Richmond	Gen. Baldwin

No.	Name	Rank		Date	Place	Officer	Date	Place	General
82	Tyler, Robert E.	Private	24	Apr. 21	Richmond	R. Milton Cary	June 28	Richmond	Gen. Baldwin
83	Tatum, Augustus R.	Private	20	Apr. 21	Richmond	R. Milton Cary	June 28	Richmond	Gen. Baldwin
84	Tatum, Vivian H.	Private	23	Apr. 21	Richmond	R. Milton Cary	June 28	Richmond	Gen. Baldwin
85	Talley, Daniel D.	Private	20	Apr. 21	Richmond	R. Milton Cary	June 28	Richmond	Gen. Baldwin
86	Tabb, Robert M.	Private	30	Apr. 21	Richmond	R. Milton Cary	June 28	Richmond	Gen. Baldwin
87	Van Buren, Benjamin B.	Private	24	Apr. 21	Richmond	R. Milton Cary	June 28	Richmond	Gen. Baldwin
88	Willis, Joseph N.	Private	21	Apr. 21	Richmond	R. Milton Cary	June 28	Richmond	Gen. Baldwin
89	Watkins, Henry H.	Private	20	Apr. 21	Richmond	R. Milton Cary	June 28	Richmond	Gen. Baldwin
90	Watkins, Aurelius S.	Private	21	Apr. 21	Richmond	R. Milton Cary	June 28	Richmond	Gen. Baldwin
91	Wren, Joseph P.	Private	30	Apr. 21	Richmond	R. Milton Cary	June 28	Richmond	Gen. Baldwin
92	White, Robert C.	Private	21	Apr. 21	Richmond	R. Milton Cary	June 28	Richmond	Gen. Baldwin
93	Worsham, John H.	Private	21	Apr. 21	Richmond	R. Milton Cary	June 28	Richmond	Gen. Baldwin
94	Waldrop, Richard W.	Private		Apr. 21	Richmond	R. Milton Cary	June 28	Richmond	Gen. Baldwin
95	Worsham, Thomas R.	Private		Apr. 21	Richmond	R. Milton Cary	June 28	Richmond	Gen. Baldwin

The following members enrolled on 21st April, 1861, served for the time specified:

No.	Name	Rank	Date	Place	Officer	Remarks
1	Baughman, George Jr.	P'vt	Apr. 21	Richmond	R. Milton Cary	Resigned June 27, 1861.
2	Chamberlayne, John H.	Pvt	Apr. 21	Richmond	R. Milton Cary	Resigned May 27, 1861. Appointed Lt. in Provisional Army of Virginia.
3	Etting, Samuel M.	Pvt	Apr. 21	Richmond	R. Milton Cary	Resigned June 27, 1861.
4	Hobson, Deane	Pvt	Apr. 21	Richmond	R. Milton Cary	Resigned May 20, 1861. Since joined Richmond Howitzers.
5	Harrison, Thomas R.	Pvt	Apr. 21	Richmond	R. Milton Cary	Resigned May 27, 1861.
6	McEvoy, Charles A.	Pvt	Apr. 21	Richmond	R. Milton Cary	Resigned June 27, 1861, per order of Gov. Letcher.
7	Meredith, John F.	Pvt	Apr. 21	Richmond	R. Milton Cary	Resigned June 6, 1861.
8	Randolph, Mereweather L.	Pvt	Apr. 21	Richmond	R. Milton Cary	Resigned June 4, 1861. Appointed Lt. in Provisional Army of Virginia.
9	Ellerson, John H.	Pvt	Apr. 21	Richmond	R. Milton Cary	Resigned June 27, 1861.
10	Clopton, John	Pvt	Apr. 21	Richmond	R. Milton Cary	Resigned June 6, 1861.

adopted April 17, 1861. Enrolled for Active Service at Richmond, on the 21st of April, 1861; Mustered into Service at Richmond on the 28th day of June, 1861, for one year from the 21st day of April, 1861, unless sooner discharged."

	Recapitulation.	Capt.	1st. Lieut.	2nd Lieut.	Sergeants	Corporals	Privates	Total	Aggregate
Present	For duty	1	1	2	4	4	86	94	98
	Sick						5	5	5
Absent	With leave						4	4	4
	Strength, Present and Absent	1	1	2	4	4	95	103	107

I certify on honor, that this "Muster Roll" exhibits the true state of the company therein described, for the period mentioned; that the "Remarks" set opposite the name of each officer and soldier are accurate and just.

(Signed) R. H. CUNNINGHAM, JR.,
Commanding the Company.

I certify on honor, that I have at the Camp of Instruction on this 30th day of June, 1861, carefully examined this Roll and that I have mustered the company.

(Signed) WILLIAM GILHAM,
Col. and Mustering Officer.
Date, June 30, 1861.
Location, Camp of Instruction.

While in Camp Lee, some of the company visited the city daily, some with passes, others "ran the blockade" on their uniform. As before stated, our uniforms gave the impression of a first lieutenant, and when we wanted to go to the city and could not get a pass, we would march boldly by a sentinel on duty at some of the many openings around the grounds, give him the salute, and he would present arms as we passed out. So many of our company went to the city in this way, that orders were finally issued that every one leaving the grounds should go out of the gate; and as some officer was always stationed there, we were afraid to try it too often.

I cannot help telling of a good thing I heard from an officer. One night I was particularly anxious to go to the city, and no one was allowed to go out at night, unless he had the countersign. This was only given to those on duty, and in consequence none of us could go out at night. As night approached, I walked to the guard quarters at the gate, and took a seat among some of my company who were on duty, hoping something would turn up, and let me into the secret. I was there some time, but no one would talk about it, and as it was getting dark, I had about made up my mind to leave, and try to dodge the sentinel by walking out, hoping he would think me one of the guards. The captain of the guard now made his appearance, and called by name the non-commissioned officer who was on duty, and said, "The countersign to-night is 'Richmond,' and the password, 'Chickahominy.' " I was so overjoyed that I came near letting the officer know that I was not one of the guard. As soon as he walked away I quietly left, went to our quarters, told many of the company, and they left for the city. About half of the company did the same.

Our company was called on suddenly about sunset, on Monday, July 1, to "fall in," and we marched, at a double quick, through rain and mud to the Penitentiary. Here we found the weaving department on fire, and much excitement; our company was put on guard duty. After remaining several hours, the fire having been put out and quiet restored, we were again ordered to "fall in," and marched to the corner of Fifth and Franklin Streets in the city and were dismissed, being allowed to go to our homes for the remainder of the night. We were given orders to assemble at the same point next morning at 10 o'clock, when we marched back to Camp Lee.

Quite a stir was created in camp one day by the announcement that a flag would be presented to Company B. This was a very handsome silk flag, was made by the ladies

of Baltimore and "ran the blockade" into Richmond, and
was presented to the company by President Davis. He made
one of his brilliant speeches in the presence of the regiment, and a large number of visitors from Richmond, most
of whom were ladies. The occasion passed off with great
enthusiasm.

About two weeks after reaching Camp Lee, the 21st
Regiment of Virginia Infantry was formed, including the
Maryland company, two or three others, and F Company.
The following officers were appointed:

William Gilham, Colonel, from the Va. Military
Institute.

John M. Patton, Lt. Colonel, from Richmond.

Scott Shipp, Major, from the Va. Military Institute.

William H. Morgan, Adjutant, from the Va. Military
Institute.

Dr. Robert L. Coleman, Surgeon, from Richmond.

Dr. R. Lewis, Assistant Surgeon, from Richmond.

H. E. C. Baskerville, Commissary, from Richmond.

Virginus Dabney, Sergeant Major.

Timothy H. Kellogg, Commissary Sergeant, from
Richmond.

In a few days an order was sent to these officers to
complete the regiment at once from such companies as
were then in camp, and be ready to move as soon as possible; as troops were very much needed in the field. This
order was complied with, and the regiment was completed.
The following is a list of companies and their captains, in
alphabetical order, as I am unable to give them in the order
of their rank:

Company "B" of Baltimore, Maryland, Captain J.
Lyle Clarke.

Brunswick Grays, Brunswick Co., Captain Robertson.

Buckingham Leitches, Buckingham Co., Captain James
Leitch.

Chalk Level Grays, Pittsylvania Co., Captain —
Mustain.

Cumberland Grays, Cumberland Co., Captain Francis
    D. Irving.
"F" Company, Richmond, Captain Richard H. Cunning-
    ham, Jr.
Meherrin Grays, Mecklenberg Co., Captain William
    R. Berkeley.
Oliver Grays, Buckingham Co., Captain John Oliver.
Red House Volunteers, Charlotte Co., Captain John
    B. Moseley.
Turkey Cock Grays, Pittsylvania Co., Captain William
    A. Witcher.

The regiment numbered about eight hundred and fifty,
rank and file. We were soon ready, and reported to the
authorities. Our company now equipped itself with everything that could be gotten to make us comfortable. As we
had been in the field several weeks and knew the necessi-
ties, had marched, slept without protection, done picket
duty, been in one engagement; we thought ourselves veterans, and as such, were going to take along with us everything the authorities would allow. Each mess purchased a
nice chest. As our own was a fair specimen, I will try to
describe it and its contents. The chest was made of oak, and
was about three feet long, eighteen inches deep and wide.
In it were several trays; it was strapped securely with iron,
at each end were iron handles, and its top was secured by
substantial iron hinges and a strong lock. We had in it a
dozen knives and forks, two or three butcher knives, a
dozen teacups and saucers, a dozen plates, several dishes
and bowls, a sugar dish and cream pitcher, salt and pepper
boxes, a tin box, containing a dozen assorted boxes of
spices, a dozen glasses, a sifter, rolling pin, coffee tin, etc.;
besides these, we carried outside a frying pan, coffee pot,
camp kettle, teapot, bread oven that afterwards played such
a prominent part in the army as the "spider," two water
buckets, ax, etc.

The regiment got orders to be ready to take the cars at
the Central Depot on the 18th of July, 1861, for Staunton.

Promptly on that morning we marched out of Camp Lee into Broad Street, where we wheeled into platoons, F Company in front, and marched to the depot. Our friends turned out by thousands and the march was made amidst the inspiring cheers of the multitude that bade us good-by. The day was terribly hot, and many of the men fell out of rank during the march, overcome by the heat.

In addition to the usual arms of an infantryman, each man carried a long bowie knife, and a pistol at his belt.

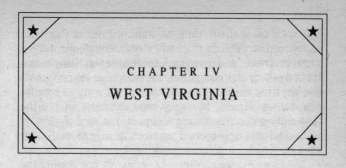

CHAPTER IV
WEST VIRGINIA

We left Richmond about 11 A.M. on the 18th of July, 1861, for Staunton, which place we reached in slow time on the next morning about 7 o'clock. We were marched to the Fair Grounds, and camped in a wood on a large hill overlooking the depot and city. During the day we made additional purchase of articles that we thought would be of use and comfort to us, and hired teams to carry our company baggage. The next morning we left Staunton, marching to Buffalo Gap; the regiment having a wagon train of thirty-five wagons, most of which were four-horse mountain wagons. Our company had five, having hired four of that number to carry our baggage, knapsacks, chests, etc., the one furnished by the government carrying our tents and cooking utensils. When we reached Buffalo Gap, flour was issued to us as rations, and we were promised beef as soon as some of the regiment would kill some cattle that were in a pen in sight. Some of the F boys volunteered to do the killing, if others would do the dressing, etc. The force was soon made up, the F boys quietly loading their guns, and shooting the required number of beeves, the others dressing them, and in a short time we had our regular supper. This is the commencement of our rations of beef and flour, a ration that was issued to us many years. While the beef was being dressed, camp was laid off, tents pitched, fires made. Some of the men took a delightful bath, others climbed the steep mountain and viewed the surrounding country. Guard was placed around the camp, and as bedtime approached we went quietly to rest, after our first regular march as a regiment.

Next morning we continued our march, and during the day we heard firing of artillery so plainly in our front, that our officers sent someone ahead to find out what it meant. After waiting some time one of them rode forward, and when he returned after several hours' absence, he could give no account of it, saying that as far as he went it seemed just ahead, and no one he saw could give any information in regard to it. We went into camp at Ryan's, and while we were eating supper a dispatch was received by a courier, saying a great battle had been fought and won by the Confederates at Manassas. We must have been one hundred miles in an air line from Manassas. The firing was as distinct that day as any I heard afterwards that was five to six miles off.

The company's first misfortune overtook us at Ryan's; the government took one of our company's wagons, and the driver of another refused to go any farther. Some of the mess chests were left, and some of the men had to carry their knapsacks. The next day we reached McDowell in a drizzling rain, and met the men of Garnett's command, who had been defeated a few days before at Carrick's Ford. They were a forlorn looking set, and told awful tales of having nothing to eat except berries and roasting ears! None of us believed what they said. It was not many months before we were made to realize that it was the truth. We now lost another of our company's wagons and more mess chests were left behind. The next day we marched to Monterey. We were living high, buying as many chickens as we wanted, nearly grown, for six pence—

8^{1}/$_{3}$ cents—each, butter and eggs at corresponding prices per pound and dozen, and when we could stop for a meal, the price was nine pence—12^{1}/$_{2}$ cents.

Continuing our march, we reached Napp's Creek Valley on the 25th, and forded that creek seventeen times during the day's march, the road crossing from one side to the other every few hundred yards. Gen. Loring, the officer in command of this expedition, passed us to-day while we were on the march. His attention being called to the regiment, he remarked that they were a fine looking body of men, but no soldiers. Until they are able to sleep in winter amidst the snow and ice without tents, they are not soldiers! This was repeated to our company, and the men were very indignant, and put him down at once as an officer who knew nothing; and each man in the company wanted to call him to account for the insinuation, and would have told him they never expected to sleep in snow or surrounded by ice. Alas, for our judgment! It was not many months before we were of the same opinion as Gen. Loring, and we then knew that we had at this time learned nothing about the duties of soldiers in the field. On the evening of the 26th, we reached Huntersville, the county seat of Pocahontas.

We stayed there several days, concentrating a force large enough to cope with the enemy in our front. We were joined by several regiments of infantry, several companies of cavalry, and several batteries of artillery. During our stay there a great many of the men became sick with measles and typhoid fever, and when we left on the evening of the 3d of August, at least one-third of the 21st Va. Regt. was sick in the hospitals. The courthouse and only church had been converted into hospitals, and some of the private houses were full of the sick, and tents had to be erected for others. Our company's baggage was reduced so much that we only had one wagon when we left. The march continued until we reached Valley Mountain on the 6th, where our regiment pitched tents on the side of this mountain, and we went into camp.

Gen. R. E. Lee, having been assigned to the command of this department, joined us here, and pitched his headquarter's tents about one or two hundred yards from our company. He soon won the affection of all by his politeness and notice of the soldiers. He very often had something to say to the men, and it soon became known that when some of the people in the neighborhood sent him something good to eat, as soon as the messenger got out of sight, the articles were sent to some sick soldier. This affection increased as the years rolled on, and I suppose no body of men under his command had more love and respect for our great leader than these men who first served under him!

Here is an incident showing Gen. Lee's kindness of heart. He was well aware of the arduous duties we had to do at that time. On a rainy night a private of Company E of our regiment was on guard duty. Soon after getting to his post he took a seat on a log, thinking he could protect himself and his gun from the rain better in this position. While in this position he was approached by the corporal of the guard, who accused the man of being asleep on his post. This the man denied and stated that the ground being so soft from rain, he did not hear him approach. The corporal arrested him, and took him to the guard house, turning him over to the officer of the guard. At that time it was thought a capital offense for a man to be caught asleep on post, and punishable by death. In the morning the captain of the guard consulted with the officers of the regiment as to what should be done. All of them thought he ought to be shot. Things began to look blue for the man, when as by inspiration the captain said, "Well, Gen. Lee is here, and he knows, and I'll carry you to him." As they approached Gen. Lee's tent, they saw he was alone, and at a table writing. On getting to the tent the general bade them good-morning and invited them in. When they entered, the general said, "What can I do for you, captain?" The captain stated the case, and said the officers of the regiment did not know what to do, so he came to consult him. Gen. Lee at once replied, "Captain, you know the arduous duties these men have to do daily. Suppose the man who was found on his post asleep had been you, or me, what do you think should be done to him?" The captain replied that he had not thought of it in that way. Then Gen. Lee turned to the man and said, "My man, go back to your quarters, and never let it be said you were found asleep on your post."

The sick became so numerous here, and the regiments were so diminished at one time, that I suppose there were not more than one-fourth of the men available for duty. I know that in my own regiment we had to picket to the front and when one picket was relieved and the men returned to camp in the evening, most of them were detailed immediately, and ordered to get ready with rations, etc., to go on duty again in the morning. We worked a great deal on the roads. Some of the men while at work one day under the direction of a corporal, were observed by Gen. Loring in his rounds. He dismounted, gave some directions as to work, and then took a seat on a log near him. The corporal joined him, and seating himself near the general, made some remarks about the work, and said to Gen. Loring, "General, we officers have a good time up here, don't we?" General Loring looked at him, and then asked his rank. He replied: "Corporal!" The general, who was a profane man, let some "cuss words" loose at him, and told him to take a spade; and it is said the corporal made the dirt fly as long as Gen. Loring was in sight.

Gen. Lee ordered a forward movement on Sept. 9th. The men were given thirty rounds of ammunition each, which in a short time thereafter were increased to forty rounds, which number was always carried by each man to the end of the war, unless on some special occasion we were required to carry eighty.

We met the enemy at Conrad's Mill on the 11th, when some skirmishing and artillery firing took place. As we advanced up the road, we passed our first dead Yankee. He made a lasting impression, as he lay on the side of the road, his face upturned and a fresh pool of blood at his side, showing that his life had just passed away.

The enemy retired during the night. The next day a picket from the 21st Va. Regt. was sent to the front, remaining there until the 15th, when we fell back to Valley Mountain, reaching there on the 17th.

The failure here was owing more to mud than anything else. In all my experience of the war I never saw as much mud. It seemed to rain every day and it got to be a saying in our company that you must not halloo loud, for if you should, we would immediately have a hard shower, and when some of the men on their return from picket had to shoot their guns off to get the load out, it brought on a regular flood. Granville Gray always said it rained thirty-*two* days in August. I was told by wagoners that it was hard for them to haul from Milboro, a distance of sixty miles, any more than it took to feed their teams back and forth. I saw dead mules lying in the road, with nothing but their ears showing above the mud.

We remained at Valley mountain until the 24th, when Gen. Lee left us and joined Gen. Floyd on Sewell's Mountain, taking all the troops with him but our regiment, the Irish Battalion, a battery of artillery and a company of cavalry. These troops were left in command of Col. Gilham of the 21st Va. Regt. He fell back to Middle Mountain, about two miles from Valley Mountain, which position could be more easily defended. We marched to the place of our encampment on Middle Mountain, stacked arms, and returned to Valley Mountain for our camp equipage. Having no wagon, we had to carry everything needed on our backs, and had to make several trips to do it. What was left at Valley Mountain was gathered together and burned. What a fall for F Company! You will remember that we left Staunton with five wagons loaded with baggage belonging to the company. We are now moving the camp of our regiment without a single wagon.

We left Middle Mountain on the 28th, after a heavy rain. All the creeks had become small rivers, and as we forded

them the water came up to our waists. We had now one
two-horse and one three-horse wagon to move everything
belonging to the command, and began to think, as Gen.
Loring did, that we were men, but not soldiers. After a
short march each day we reached Elk Mountain about dark
on Oct. 1. A detail of a lieutenant and six men and a non-
commissioned officer was made from F Company, and sent
back eight miles on the road to picket. We reached our
destination about midnight. Two sentinels were posted at
once, one in the road, the other in a path that led over the
mountain, headquarters of the camp being at a spring on
the road near a house, but on the opposite side of the road.
The next morning, not long after day, the inmates of the
house, a woman and her children, commenced to stir, and
soon made their appearance. About sunrise the woman
came to the yard fence, and commenced to abuse us in the
most violent language I ever heard from a woman. It was
some time before we could tell why she was abusing us.
She had quite a large number of beehives, and the troops
marching by her house the day before molested none of
them. When she arose in the morning, and knew that one
of her best hives was gone, and a squad of men were at her
spring, it was quite natural that she should think we took
it. Our lieutenant, Edward Mayo, tried to impress on her
that we did not; but she knew better, as she had gone to bed
with everything all right, and when she awoke, we were
there and the hive was gone. This was convincing proof to
her. We were ordered not to go on her side of the road, nor
have any talk with the inmates of the house, as Lieutenant
Mayo would show her that we were gentlemen at any rate.
We had no rations, as we moved in the night, before we
could get any. It is true that some of the men had a little
sugar and coffee, and some a little raw meat and a few
biscuit. After the old lady had cooled off, as we supposed,
our lieutenant went over to the house and tried to borrow
or hire a coffee pot, but the old lady said she would see him
and us in a hot place sooner. On his return we built a small
fire, boiled the meat, and divided the bread amongst us.

The woman now, to add to our misery, commenced to bring out her milk and carry it to the hog pen, pouring gallon after gallon to the hogs. We did not say a word to any of the household during the day. A little before night our lieutenant went over again to see what he could do, and with the offer of a little coffee, an article he found the old lady was very fond of and had been without for some time, he got the use of a teakettle to make some coffee in, and she baked us an oven of corn bread. He carried the articles back, and stayed in the porch, had quite a long chat, and returning, told us she promised to let us have the kettle and some more bread in the morning. In the morning we got them, with the promise of a dinner for the party. About dinner time we were relieved, and ordered to report back to camp. We waited for our dinner, and the old lady certainly did try herself. She gave us as nice a dinner as we ever had, including dessert, which made amends for the way in which she first treated us. She also apologized, and we left truly friends, and all kissed the baby.

We left Elk Mountain on the 9th, for Edray, marching amidst the most beautiful scenery I ever saw, the trees having taken on their brilliant colors of fall. We remained in Edray and had a picket on Elk Mountain until the 14th, when we moved to Greenbrier river. Soon after leaving our camp and getting into the road, we passed two men who were sitting on the ground, facing a rail fence. Their hands and feet were put through the rails, and tied together on the opposite side of the fence, in such a position that they could not move. A little further on, we passed two who were lying on top of the fence, their hands and feet tied to some of the rails underneath, so as to keep them from moving. These men had been guilty of disobeying some order, and were punished in that manner.

We went regularly into camp, on the banks of the beautiful Greenbrier, on a piece of low ground that was almost level, affording plenty of room for camp and drill. It was a magnificent camp. The weather was fine, and the time of year such as to make it bracing; the men soon improved so much, and fattened too, that they became better looking than when they left home. We had a picket on the other side of Edray, about twelve miles from camp. About fifteen men and an officer went and stayed three days. It was my fortune to go there with the first detail, and I went again afterwards, and I thought it the most delightful duty of the war.

While we were in this camp we were informed that in a few days there would be an election for President and Vice-President of the Confederate States of America. This had been talked about with much interest for some time, but without the usual excitement of an election, as there was only one ticket in the field. All the South looked to Mr. Davis as their leader, and no other person was even thought of. Much interest was taken by the soldiers, as it would be the first election held in camp. They discussed as to who were entitled to vote, and where the voting place would be located. On a cloudy morning in November it was announced that the eventful day had arrived, and the precinct was open. Some of the regiment had been appointed judges. The voting precinct was in a tent in our camp, across the entrance of which a pole had been placed, to mark the line between the voters and judges. It had been decided that all enlisted soldiers, regardless of age, that were of good standing, could vote. The following ticket was eagerly voted:

VIRGINIA ELECTORAL TICKET
Election November 6th, 1861.

For President
Jefferson Davis,
of Mississippi.

For Vice-President
Alex. H. Stevens,
of Georgia.

ELECTORS
For the State at Large
John R. Edmunds, Halifax.
A. T. Caperton, Monroe.

For the District
1st. Joseph Christian, Middlesex.
2nd. Cincinnatus W. Newton, Norfolk City.
3rd. R. T. Daniel, Richmond City.
4th. W. F. Thompson, Dinwiddie.
5th. Wood Bouldin, Charlotte.
6th. W. L. Goggin, Bedford.
7th. B. F. Randolph, Albemarle.
8th. James W. Walker, Madison.
9th. Asa Rogers, Loudoun.
10th. Samuel C. Williams, Shenandoah.
11th. Samuel M. D. Reid, Rockbridge.
12th. H. A. Edmundson, Roanoke.
13th. J. W. Sheffey, Smyth.
14th. H. J. Fisher, Mason.
15th. Joseph Johnson, Harrison.
16th. E. H. Fitzhugh, Ohio.

The election passed off with much enthusiasm, and at the close of day, when it was announced that the entire regiment had voted for Jefferson Davis and Alex. H. Stevens, there were loud and repeated cheers for them and the Confederacy.

One morning while we were in the camp, the guard near the river reported a deer swimming the river, and making for the middle of our camp. All was in commotion in a minute. The deer came over and ran down the middle street of our encampment, and took to the hills in the rear. Many men took their guns and went in pursuit, I amongst the rest; and, hoping to head the deer off and get a shot, I ran in an oblique direction to the top of the hill, but did not see the deer, as it had been turned the other way by some of the men. The exertion made me breathe rapidly, and I took my time back to camp. One of the guard quietly approached, told me I was arrested, and marched me to the guard house, which was the shade of a tree on the river side. During my absence, an order had been issued to the guard to arrest every man found with a gun in his hand; my comrades, being near enough, heard the order given, dropped their guns, quietly walked into camp, and afterwards went back for them. I was the only man arrested. Another deer ran through our camp before we left. We made excursions in the neighborhood, sometimes fording the river, sometimes mounting a log and riding over on that, often getting a ducking by the logs turning.

We left Greenbrier river on November 11th, and reached the Warm Springs the night of the 13th, marching twenty-two miles that day, the last five (on Peter Sublett's dead level) all the way up hill! The hotel was open at that time, and the officers of F Company treated the company to supper. I cannot tell you of that supper. I only know none was ever enjoyed more. After supper we took a bath in the warm pool, and as the atmosphere was cool, we thought the water hot, but we enjoyed it. Next morning the men of F Company took breakfast at the hotel, and we marched to the Bath Alum Springs, pitched tents, and went regularly into camp. We had a good snow here. Our camp was on the edge of a piece of land that had been recently cleared of its wood, the wood being cut into logs about eight feet long, and piled ready for burning. Every day we toted enough of these logs to our tents to make a great fire that would last about twenty-four hours. At night we gathered around these fires, and had a big time telling tales, singing, etc. I think the company enjoyed this camp very much. Here a comrade, J. E. Mayo, and I took our muskets and went out of camp to see if we could get a deer; we cut our bullets into slugs and loaded with them. We had not gone more than three hundred yards when two deer sprang up, but we thought they were too far for our slugs. A little farther on we came to a branch that seemed to run around a hill. It was agreed that he should go over the hill, and I would follow the branch; and when he got in sight of the branch, he should halloo. I waited for the signal, and hearing it, started up the bottom, went a short distance, jumped a doe, called out to him to look out, and soon heard a shot which killed the deer. We carried it at once to camp, and had a big time over our deer. We stayed at Bath Alum Springs until the 30th, when we marched to Milboro, staying there until December 4th, and then took the cars for Staunton.

We left Milboro late in the evening on flat cars, and did not reach the camping place on the side of the railroad near Staunton until late in the night. That was a fearful ride at that season of the year; it was cold, and our riding on a flat car made it more so. The water tank at Panther Gap was literally one mass of ice; some of the men got a small quantity of wood and built fires in the spiders and ovens that afforded a little warmth for a few. It was only a few minutes after leaving the cars before we had trees cut down and rousing fires going. Did it ever occur to the reader how quickly soldiers could make fires? It made no difference whether it was raining, snowing, or blowing a great gale, in five minutes after getting into camp, a regiment would have fifty fires burning. Wet wood and green wood made no difference.

While we were in this camp, we elected officers to fill the vacancy occasioned by the resignation of First Lieutenant Edward Mayo. P. A. Wellford was made first lieutenant, H. T. Miller second, and W. Granville Gray, Junior, second.

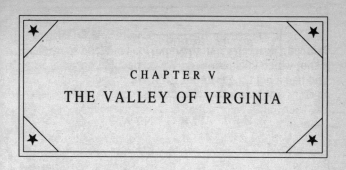

WE WERE ENCAMPED in Augusta County, about one and a half miles north of Staunton. In the valley, that great place for wheat, flour, and hogs, and democrats, the latter could always be heard from in counting the votes after an election.

We remained here until the 10th of December, when we took up our march to join Jackson at Winchester. We marched along quietly each day, until we reached Mt. Jackson on the 20th. It was the custom, during the war, to march with the right of the regiment in front one day, and the left next day. On the 20th the left was marching in front. That threw our company in the rear, as we were the right company. During the day the left led off several times in quick time, which gave our company hard marching. Few know how much easier it is to march in front of a regiment than in the rear. That night our company decided that we would get even next day with the left, and if the officers did not interfere, we would give it to them. Soon after getting into the road the next morning, our captain told Sergeant Rawlings, who was leading the company, to

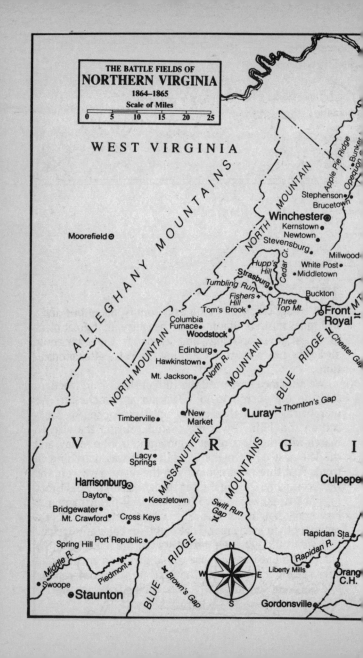

THE BATTLE FIELDS OF
NORTHERN VIRGINIA
1864–1865
Scale of Miles
0   5   10   15   20   25

WEST VIRGINIA

ALLEGHANY MOUNTAINS

NORTH MOUNTAIN

NORTH MOUNTAIN

Moorefield

Apple Pie Ridge

Bunker

Opequon

Stephenson
Brucetown

Winchester
Kernstown
Newtown
Stevensburg
Millwood
White Post
Middletown

Cedar Cr.

Hupp's
Hill
Strasburg
Tumbling Run
Fishers
Hill
Tom's Brook
Columbia
Furnace
Woodstock
Edinburg
Hawkinstown
Mt. Jackson

Buckton

Three
Top Mt.
**Front
Royal**

Chester Gap

North R.

MASSANUTTEN MOUNTAINS

BLUE RIDGE MT.

New
Market
Timberville

Luray   Thornton's Gap

V   I   R   G   I

Lacy
Springs

Harrisonburg
Dayton
Keezletown

Bridgewater
Mt. Crawford   Cross Keys

Spring Hill   Port Republic

Middle R.

Piedmont

Swoope   **Staunton**

MOUNTAINS

Swift Run
Gap

Culpepe

Rapidan Sta.

Rapidan R.

Liberty Mills

**Orang
C.H.**

BLUE RIDGE

Brown's Gap

N
W   E
S

Gordonsville

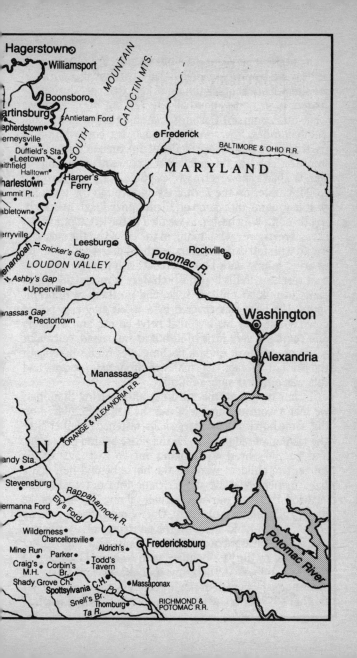

step out. Now Sergeant Rawlings was just the man to do it, as he was a powerful man physically, with great endurance. He stepped out at quick time, and kept that pace during the march. In six hours and a half after leaving Mt. Jackson, we went into camp at Strasburg, marching twenty-three and one-half miles. It was said by some of the boys who timed us, that we marched three miles at one time in thirty-three minutes. This was the quickest march we made during the war. We had a snow storm while at Strasburg, and marched to Winchester on the 25th, passing through the town the next day, going into camp on the Romney Road. In marching through Winchester, as we filed to the left at one of the cross streets, we saw standing in the crowd on the sidewalk a man with full dark whiskers and hair, dressed in uniform, wearing a long dark blue overcoat with a large cape, his coat reaching to his boots, which were worn outside of his pants in regular military style, and on them were bright spurs. His head was covered by a faded gray cap, pulled down so far over his face that between cap and whiskers one could see very little of it; but as we passed we caught a glimpse of a pair of dark flashing eyes from underneath the brim of his cap. That man was Stonewall Jackson, and this was our first sight of him.

In our march on the third day after leaving Staunton, we met a woman riding a horse; she had five children on this same horse. She had large bags, fastened together after the fashion of saddle bags, on the horse behind the saddle, and a child's head was looking out on each side of the horse, two children were on the horse behind her, and a baby in her arms. When she came into our midst, and realized that the war was actually going on, she broke down and commenced to cry. One of our officers rode up to her, hat in hand and with the politeness of a Virginian, said some pleasant word to her. This, and the respect shown her by the passing men, soon restored her. She said her husband was in the army, and she, fearing to stay at their home by herself in the lower valley, was going to her mother's higher up, where she hoped to be out of reach of

Stonewall Jackson

the enemy, in case the lower valley should be abandoned by our army. She would have to travel about fifty miles. The children seemed to be in splendid spirits and to enjoy our passing. Although this was a sight none of us ever saw before, every one treated her with the respect due the first lady of the land. Here is war, real war. Such scenes as families leaving home with nothing but what they could carry on their person, was witnessed many times by the writer.

In going down the valley, we had a feast all the way; the people had just finished killing hogs, and every house had sausage, spare ribs, chine, liver, etc., to give us. We passed Lacy's Spring or Big Spring for the first time, situated on the side of the pike. The volume of water from this spring is large enough to run a large mill, and it looked more like a small river than a spring branch.

At that time everything in the valley had a thrifty look, the horses and cattle were fat and sleek, the large barns overflowing with the gathered crops, the houses which were small in comparison with the barns, looked comfortable, the fences, post and rail or stone, were in splendid order; in fact everything looked well, and showed a thriving population. It was truly a land of milk and honey.

While in camp at Winchester, the Irish Battalion and the 48th, 42d, and 21st Va. Regiments were formed into a brigade, and were known as the second brigade of Jackson's division. Col. Wm. Gilham, being the ranking officer, took command. The marching we had now done made all of us discard everything but necessaries, and we began to think that Ritchie Green did a very smart thing, when we left Richmond, to carry nothing in his knapsack but one paper collar and a plug of tobacco!

We elected a lieutenant here, to fill the vacancy occasioned by the resignation of Second Lieutenant Henry T. Miller. W. Granville Gray was made second lieutenant, and James B. Payne, Junior, second lieutenant.

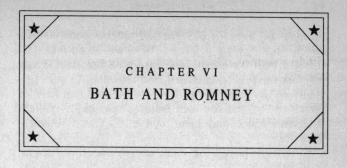

CHAPTER VI
BATH AND ROMNEY

G EN. JACKSON having decided on a winter campaign, marched his army from the neighborhood of Winchester January 1, 1862, a beautiful day, the sun shining brightly and the atmosphere bracing. The second brigade camped near Pughtown that night, the 21st Va. Regt. in a large wood, where gathering the fresh fallen leaves into large piles, placing our oilcloths on them and laying down, covering with our blankets, we enjoyed the bed as much as any we ever slept on.

We marched the next morning at early dawn, and at night camped at Unger's X Roads. The next day, the 3d, we met the enemy about five miles from Bath, Morgan County. The 21st Va. Regt. was marching near the rear of the column. Gen. Jackson sent an order for F Company to report to the front, and we marched by our troops, who had halted in the road. When we reached the front, we halted and were ordered to load, which was done under fire, as the enemy were a short distance in front, on a hill behind a fence. As soon as we had loaded, we were deployed as skirmishers, and ordered forward through a wood, halting on its edge behind a fence. There we became heavily engaged with the enemy, and kept up a fire until it was too dark to see. Firing ceased, and returning to our regiment, we went into camp. This was the first real fight of the company, and the men behaved splendidly. William Exall was killed and Lieut. James B. Payne seriously wounded.

It snowed during the night and the weather became very cold.

The enemy were at Bath in force. In the morning Gen. Jackson advanced on their position in three columns, the second brigade moving along the road with F Company as advance guard. We moved slowly, in order to let a column on our left get into position on the mountain ridge. We came in sight of the enemy, who were in line of battle on that ridge, about one and a half miles from Bath. Our column had marched along the road until it got almost on the flank of their line, before they moved. It was too far for musket firing, but the men of each side engaged in much abuse of each other. As soon as our skirmish line on the ridge came within shooting distance, firing commenced, and the enemy began to retreat. Gen. Jackson now arrived at the front and took the lead on horseback, a few couriers following him; as he passed our company, he ordered us to double quick, and we soon ran. This was a grand sight. The second brigade marching by the flank and running down the road, the Yankees in sight on the ridge to our left, running too, our column on the ridge following them as fast as they could run! In this way our column entered Bath, going through the village, doubling back on the road which wound up the ridge. When we reached the top of the ridge, we could see the Yankees disappearing at the far end of a field, going toward the Potomac river. We followed, but the road ran through a defile, and we could not go as fast as the enemy, because we had to look out for their rear guard, who occasionally came in sight and fired. The enemy went over the river during the night. We captured some stores and a few prisoners.

I saw Col. Turner Ashby to-day for the first time; he impressed me as being a dashing man. He passed us with a company of cavalry, taking a road to our left. One of our columns following on another road, had a spirited combat with the enemy. On the next day, the 5th, Gen. Jackson moved his force towards Hancock, a village on the Maryland side of the Potomac. He sent for F Company to come to the front and lead the column across the river; a high honor to come from him. We marched out of camp singing, and kept it up until we arrived at the front. While we were singing the "Pirate's Glee," and were well in the chorus, every man having joined in with a zest, and had taken up the inspiring words, "We'll nail the black flag to the mast," we came suddenly on Gen. Jackson. He pulled off his cap, and his eyes twinkled with evident delight as we passed.

We marched to a certain point and halted, and stayed there several hours, the Yankees throwing a shell at us occasionally from a battery in Hancock. The ground was covered with snow, and it was cold, and we were not allowed to make fires. As night approached, we marched back and with our regiment, camped for the night. It was snowing and hailing, which continued all night, and was intensely cold. The ground the next morning was covered several inches with snow and ice. Gen. Jackson gave up the advance on this road, owing to the ice in the Potomac river, and on the 8th we returned to Unger's X Roads. The march was a terrible one; the road had become one sheet of ice from frequent marching over it, and the men would march in the side ditches and in the woods, where it was practicable; guns were constantly being fired by the men falling, and many accidents were occasioned thereby. In some instances the horses had to be taken from the cannon and wagons, and men with chains and ropes pulled them, the horses being sent forward through the woods; and at many hills, the pioneers had to cut small trenches across the road, in order that the men might have a footing. It was late in the night when we stopped to camp. Although the men underwent great exertion in this march, the cold was so intense that their suffering was great. I saw Gen. Jackson marching along the road on foot with the men several times.

Col. Gilham and Major Shipp of the 21st Va. Regt. received an order to report to the Va. Military Institute for duty, and they left on the 9th. The men had become very much attached to both, and were sorry to give them up. As a token of their respect, F Company purchased a fine horse and presented it to Col. Gilham, attaching to the bridle one of our F's. The next day we had hail again; the second brigade marched only about four miles, marching as they did the day before, men to help cannon and wagons. The next day my regiment marched about five hundred yards, and the head of the brigade marched about four miles. Owing to the terrible weather, our line was scattered over ten miles of road. My mess was so near the camping place of last night, that we went back to it, put the chunks together, and in a short time were comfortable and asleep for the night, rejoining the company in the morning in time for roll call. The only way we could get along at all was to have heavy details of men with each wagon and cannon to help, and at times to pull them. Each day was colder than the day before, and we crossed most of the streams, cannon, wagons, and men, on the ice.

On the 14th it snowed and hailed again. In our march we passed for several miles along the road a growth of flat cedar or arbor vitae. We continued our march in the same way, until we reached the neighborhood of Romney on the 17th. There the head of the column had quite a spirited combat with the enemy, capturing their camp and some stores. The second brigade went into camp in a wood near the town, and picketed the road we had marched over. Here the sun came out and shone on us, the first time for nineteen days.

Our mess lost its "spider" on this march, and I thought one might be purchased in the neighborhood to replace it. One day I took a stroll into the country to get one, and went to several houses without success. Finally I came to a very comfortable looking house, and found an old lady who was very talkative. She made many inquiries where we were from, how long we were going to stay, etc.; she seemed particularly pleased on learning I was from Richmond, and we had a long chat about the city. I finally told her what I wanted. She called a servant girl and held a consultation, and finally decided that she would let me have a certain oven that was too large for her family. It was brought from one of the outhouses and a bargain was made, after much discussion. She wished to know if it suited me. It was an unusually large one, and had a broken lid. It did not suit me, but was the only one I had been able to get, and I told her that it did. As to the price, she did not know what to say. She finally said, "That is a good oven. I bought it in Winchester sixteen years ago, and gave two dollars and fifty cents for it. It's a good oven, even if the lid is cracked (a piece was broken out of it), it's done me good service. Well, as you want it, under the circumstances, you may have it for two dollars and seventy-five cents." That took all the wind out of me; I am sure you could have knocked me down with a feather, but I paid her the money, and the service that oven rendered us proved it was a bargain.

The first night or two after the ground became covered with snow. We cleaned the snow off, so as to have the ground to lie on, but the thawing of the ground underneath us made it muddy, and our oilcloths would be badly soiled when we got up in the morning; we then tried the snow, and found it made a better bed and was equally as warm. After that, we never removed the snow on going into camp. Some nights we would spread our tent on the snow, put our oilcloths on that, and a blanket on that, then the party would lie down, a comrade cover them up with the remaining blankets, and then throw the sides of the tent over that, leaving nothing but the head out; he would then crawl from the bottom into his place. In this way I managed to sleep very comfortably several nights on this expedition.

On the 24th, the 21st Va. Regt. marched into the town of Romney, taking up its quarters in the houses that had been deserted. F Company had the bank building. We lived well there; my mess employed an old darky, about two squares off, to cook our rations, she adding to them any good thing she could get. There was a hotel that had buckwheat cakes in splendid style, fine butter and syrup for breakfast, and only charged twenty-five cents for meals. It took only three days for us to eat it out.

Gen. Jackson left us here, going to Winchester and taking a part of his force with him, leaving Gen. Loring in command at Romney. We staid until the evening of February 3d, when Romney was given up, and Gen. Loring's force was marched towards Winchester. We marched late in the night, and it snowed again. Our wagons had gone ahead, and when I arrived at their camping place, I sat down on a bucket at one of the wagoner's fire to warm, fell asleep, and stayed on my bucket until morning! We reached Winchester on the 6th, and went into camp, after being away a little over a month, undergoing the most terrible experience during the war. Many men were frozen to death, others frozen so badly they never recovered, and the rheumatism contracted by many was never gotten rid of. Many of the men were incapacitated for service, large numbers were barefooted, having burned their shoes while trying to warm their feet at the fires.

Do any of my readers recollect Randall Evans at Winchester? He is the old colored man who could get up such famous dinners. After a long time in camp, or on a march with the usual army fare, to go to Randall Evans, and get a meal such as he could serve, would make one forget all about bread and beef, both without salt! I never saw a soldier leave *his* place who was not perfectly satisfied

with the army and everything else, and it was brought
about by being full of food, as Randall did not keep anything to drink. What Tom Griffin was to Richmond, so was
Randall Evans to Winchester. After the Romney campaign,
we came very near eating Randall out.

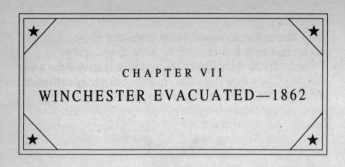

GEN. JACKSON sent several regiments of his army to Gen. Johnston at Manassas. We remained in our camp on the Romney road until the 27th of February, when my brigade marched through Winchester and camped on the Berryville road, staying there until March 7th; at which time we marched through Winchester, and camped on the Staunton pike, where we stayed until the 11th. Then everything was packed, and we were ready for a general move. These movements were occasioned by the enemy having crossed the Potomac, and it being reported that they would advance on Winchester. We marched through Winchester again, this time to the Martinsburg road, as we heard that the enemy were advancing on this road, and were not far off. They were commanded by Gen. Banks, afterwards known as Jackson's commissary, who later supplied our army so bountifully. Gen. Jackson made disposition to meet them. A line of battle was formed across the pike, a battery placed on Fort Hill and the 21st Va. Regt. ordered to support it. We took our position along with the battery and lay down awaiting the enemy. We heard occasional

50

guns in our front. When night came the enemy had not made their appearance.

Gen. Jackson considered the enemy too strong for him, and withdrew during the night, marching through Winchester a short distance, and resting until morning. Then we continued our march slowly up the valley, until we reached Mt. Jackson on the 18th. The second brigade went into camp about one mile below Mt. Jackson, and the balance of the army marched to Rude's Hill, about two miles above that village, where they camped. We sent a picket down the Valley pike and on the 20th marched to Rude's Hill and joined the balance of our little army. The enemy had followed us slowly, but at Mt. Jackson stopped, and retired down the valley.

Gen. Jackson was a great man for saving everything captured from the enemy. His way was to save everything already on hand and never destroy if there was a chance to save. It was a saying in the command that he would carry off a wheelbarrow load, rather than let it fall into the hands of the enemy. While we were camped around Winchester, he was diligently at work getting everything out of reach of the enemy, in case he should be compelled to leave; even the locomotives and cars, that were captured at Martinsburg, were sent to the rear. Because the valley pike was such an excellent road, he could do this. He sent parties of men along the pike, who cut down trees, and used the timber in bracing the bridges to enable them to endure great weight. When everything was ready, large teams of horses and mules were hitched to the locomotives and cars at Martinsburg, and they were hauled to Strasburg, a distance of about fifty miles, where they were put on the Manassas Gap railroad for the use of the Confederacy. In this way many locomotives and cars were saved. During this movement, I saw at one time five cars on their way to Strasburg.

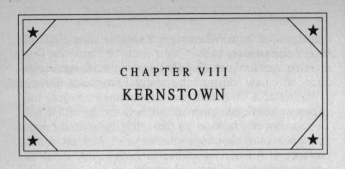

CHAPTER VIII
KERNSTOWN

GEN. JACKSON'S ARMY was now at Rude's Hill. The enemy had retired from our front to obtain, as we supposed, a better camping place. On the evening of March 21st, we received orders to cook three days' rations, and be ready to move at early dawn the next morning. When the line was formed in the morning, and we marched to the road, instead of turning up the valley pike, as we supposed our course would be, we took a quick march in the direction of the enemy, and soon passed through Mt. Jackson.

The day was raw and blustering. We marched twenty-seven miles, stopped near Fisher's Hill and bivouacked for the night. Early the next morning we marched, and kept it up, until we reached Barton's Mill, about noon, having marched about sixteen miles. Our brigade stopped to rest until most of the troops came up. We had heard cannon firing in our front and knew our advance under Ashby had overtaken the enemy. It was a surprise to the men that we had come so far without encountering them. But it was known to Gen. Jackson that they had fallen back to the neighborhood of Winchester, and were sending some of their number away to join their army at Manassas. Our march was to find out what they were doing. It was ascertained that they had made a stand at Kernstown.

The 21st Va. Regiment was now ordered forward, and after going down the pike a short distance, turned to the left, and marched across an open field towards the hills that were covered with woods. When we were about half way across the field, we came in sight of the Yankee line of battle near Kernstown, and a battery posted on a hill a little in their rear. The battery opened on us at once. We were ordered to double quick, soon began to run, and reached the hills without an accident. F Company were thrown forward as skirmishers and advance, the regiment following in line of battle a short distance, when the company was ordered to join them, and we marched by the flank. A gun or two of the Rockbridge battery now joined us, we marched under a hill, and they to the right on top of the ridge. These guns were occasionally in their march exposed to the view of the enemy's battery, and they fired at them, the shells passing over our regiment. One of them struck one of the drivers of the guns, tearing his leg to pieces, and going through the horse. Both fell; the shell descended and passed through our ranks and struck a stump not far off, spinning around like a top, and before it stopped one of the company ran and jumped on it, taking it up and carrying it along as a trophy. This is the first man of the war I saw struck by a shell; it was witnessed by the majority of the regiment.

Gen. Jackson now made his appearance, and had a talk with our commander, Lt.-Col. Patton. We were thrown forward into line of battle again, and marched a short distance to the top of a hill, and in full sight of the enemy's line of battle. They were advancing, too, at this point. I saw five flags; we opened fire at once, and they scattered. In a few minutes I saw only two flags, and soon after only one, which marched in a field on our right to a pile of rocks on which it was planted; the regiment gathered around it. Our

regiment and the guns of the Rockbridge battery have been
fighting this force. Our line was lengthened by the arrival
of the third brigade on our left. A part of our regiment
moved to a fence on the right, and facing the enemy in the
field, fired at them. Some of F Company were kneeling
down, firing from behind the fence, some were standing
straight up; soon all were standing, and taking deadly aim
as they fired. As the excitement increased, they mounted
the fence, and many sat on it, loading and firing until every
cartridge was shot away. A regiment was sent to the support of the Yankees, but they never got any nearer than the
party around the flag, and they soon became intermingled
with them. All our ammunition being gone, we gradually
retired, passing through the 5th Va. Regt. that had formed
in our rear. Our artillery had taken position and were firing
on the enemy, but when we retreated they were compelled
to do so. In going through a gap in a stone wall, one of
their guns became entangled and disabled and was left.
One of our company in going to the rear was encountered
by Gen. Jackson who inquired where he was going. He
answered, that he had shot all his ammunition away, and
did not know where to get more. Old Stonewall rose in his
stirrups, and gave the command, "Then go back and give
them the bayonet," and rode off to the front.

The remainder of the little army had been heavily engaged, and although confronted by large odds, held its
own, and only retired after shooting all its ammunition
away. It seems to me that the 21st Va. Regt. would have
held its line indefinitely, if it had been supplied with ammunition. It was a regular stand-up fight with us, and as
stated the men along the fence left its protection and
fought as I never saw any fighting during the war. After
this, they were glad to take advantage of anything.

We were whipped after desperate fighting, and I think
only for want of ammunition. Night found our little army
in retreat towards the valley pike, where the stragglers
were gathered up, and the men lay down on the ground for
a few hours' rest. The next morning we took up a slow and

sullen march up the valley, the enemy following. Arriving at Middletown, I learned that Tucker Randolph, one of my messmates, was in one of the houses. He had been sent to the rear the evening before, wounded. I soon found him, and seeing the condition of my dear old comrade, I made up my mind to stay and nurse him if I could obtain my captain's permission. Dear old fellow! how he thanked me when I said it. I had long ago made up my mind never to be taken prisoner, but could not leave my messmate. All our wagons and ambulances had long passed, our lieutenant had promised to send an ambulance back, the surgeon had also promised. I finally became so uneasy, that I went to all the town folks to see if I could get a vehicle of some kind to take him away, but could get nothing. All the infantry had now gone, even the stragglers had left the village. The cannon of the horse artillery, our rear guard, were near, having ceased its firing, and I could hear the exchange of carbine shots. I went to the door, and looked up the street for my long looked-for ambulance, but nothing was in sight. I looked down the street, and saw the horse artillery entering the village. I now made up my mind to ask the officer in command to take my friend on one of the caissons, and went into the street to meet him, when, taking another look up the street, I saw an ambulance coming on a run. We put my comrade into it in a hurry, pitched in his knapsack, etc., and off we went. We passed out of the village in time to get away, but the Yanks gave us a parting shot from a cannon as we left, the shot passing over without damage. The horses to the ambulance received some heavy whacks from the whip of the driver, and we were out of all danger.

I went along with my comrade, and before night had collected about half a dozen of the wounded of my company. I took care of them until we arrived at Staunton, and put them on the cars en route to their homes. I then returned to my company.

This was the first regular battle of the regiment, and it was said we displayed great gallantry. F Company had six wounded, Tucker Randolph, Ned Taylor, Charles Taylor, Henry Pecor, Charles Skinker, and Joe Nunnally.

This attack of Gen. Jackson on the enemy was a very daring one, and was the means of helping our army at Manassas, as the troops the enemy were sending away were recalled. The enemy were far superior to us in numbers, and although Jackson was whipped, Congress thought it did the cause so much good that it at once passed a resolution of thanks to Jackson and his army.

CHAPTER IX
THE RETREAT FROM KERNSTOWN

ON THE 24TH OF MARCH our brigade moved to the vicinity of Strasburg, where we halted about midday and camped. The enemy were in hot pursuit, we could hear firing in the rear all day, and from some high points could see the enemy during the march. We had built fires in our camp, drawn rations, and were busy cooking, when a shell came screaming over our heads, followed by another. In a few minutes the woods were full of shells from the enemy, who had driven our rear guard far enough to command our woods from one of the neighboring hills. We loaded our cooking utensils and baggage on the wagons, and they went off in a run; we soon followed in a slow march, and continued it until we reached the neighborhood of Woodstock, where we quietly went into camp out of hearing of the enemy. The next day we went into camp near Mt. Jackson. On the 26th, the second brigade was sent back to near Woodstock to meet the enemy, with whom we skirmished till the 28th, when we marched to Mt. Jackson; and on the 3d of April returned to near Edinburg to meet the enemy again. We were to coöperate with Col. Ashby in any

movement he made. F Company was ordered forward as
skirmishers through a wood, halting on its edge. A large
open field was in our front, and Edinburg in full view, and
the Yankee skirmish line on the opposite side of the creek.
We engaged them at once. Col. Ashby came along, riding
his white horse; he had the dwarf courier with him, and
told us not to fire unless the enemy attempted to cross the
creek, and if they should make the attempt, to give it to
them. He rode out in our front to a small hillock to see
what was going on, the little courier accompanying him.
The enemy immediately shot at them; as they reached the
hillock, the courier's horse fell dead. We could hear
Colonel Ashby tell him to take off his saddle, bridle and
accouterments, and carry them to the rear, which he did as
quickly as possible. Colonel A. sat his horse as quietly as if
he had been in camp, until the courier reached the woods,
when he quietly turned his horse and walked him off towards us, passing through our line going to the rear. Soon
afterwards he gave orders for our brigade to go back to
camp, as he would have nothing for us to do that day.

On the 5th we marched to Rude's Hill, and went into
camp. The next morning I was ordered to report, with
arms, to the brigade quartermaster. On arriving at his
quarters I saw two large wagons, four mules hitched to
each, and learned that a detail of six men had been made
to accompany the wagons on a trip to get corn. As soon as
all the men reported, a quartermaster sergeant who went
with us, ordered us to get into the wagons, three in each.
The wagons started at once, went to the valley pike and
turned down the pike. Reaching Rude's Hill we passed
some artillerymen who had a cannon trained on the bridge
over the Shenandoah. At the foot of the hill we passed the
cavalry outpost of about thirty or forty men, who were
dismounted and waiting events, their horses strung along
and fastened to the fence each side of the road. When they
learned our destination, all of them bade us good-by, say-

ing they would never see us again, as the Yankees would certainly capture us. Going about a half a mile farther we passed the cavalry vidette on the outpost. He said good-by too, and pointed out to us the Yankee vidette in his front, a little above the bridge and on the other side of the river. We went about a fourth of a mile farther, pulled down two panels of fence on the left of the road, entered a large corn field, and loaded those wagons more quickly than any were ever loaded before. When we had them about half full a Yankee cavalryman rode to his vidette in plain view of us, had a short talk, then rode off at full speed. That made us pull corn faster. The wagons were driven back to the road and headed for camp. A countryman who was with us said that was "the slickest job he ever saw." When we reached our vidette, he gave us a hearty welcome, and the outpost cavalry gave us a big cheer.

On the 7th we marched below Mt. Jackson and camped in our old place. On the 10th all of Jackson's force marched up the valley, and stopped near New Market. On the 13th our brigade marched to the gap of Massanuttin Mountain that leads into Luray Valley, it having been rumored that the enemy were making a demonstration from that direction. On the 17th all the force marched up the valley to Big Spring, staying there all night, and the next morning marched up the valley, leaving the valley pike near Harrisonburg towards Swift Run Gap, and crossed the Shenandoah river, going into camp next day. We were safe from pursuit now, with our backs to the Blue Ridge, and at this point our little force could keep off easily thrice as many as have been in pursuit of us.

This was the boldest retreat I ever saw. Gen. Jackson was defeated at Kernstown on the 25th of March, by an overwhelming force, and the next day retired up the valley more slowly than I ever saw him march; and when we went into camp at night we tarried as long as possible. If the enemy did not hunt for us, Gen. Jackson would hunt for

them. The regiments had orders to drill just as if no enemy
was within a hundred miles of us. It can be seen that our
movements were slow since it took us from March 24th to
April 18th to march about one hundred miles, although we
marched about half that distance in two days when we
advanced to Kernstown.

We rested at this camp and made ourselves as comfortable as we could in shelter of brush, oilcloths, etc. The day
we reached here Gen. Jackson ordered all the wagons containing tents and extra baggage to the rear and so far that
we never saw them again! This was a hard blow to us, since
we had gotten in the habit of smuggling many articles into
our tents to avoid carrying them, and when our tents left,
they had dress coats, underclothing, etc., in them. "Old
Jack" flanked us that time.

We had a snow storm while we were in this camp, but
as it did not turn cold, we got along very well. We first felt
in this place the strict hand of Jackson. Our regiment and
several others during the snow storm burned some of the
rail fencing. Gen. Jackson seeing it, gave orders for each
regiment to maul rails and put the fence up again, and if
we repeated the burning, he would punish every man.

While we were in this camp the reorganization of the
army took place. This was a great misfortune to us, as
many good officers were thrown out, and men who were
popular were elected in their stead; in many instances men
utterly unfit to fill the places to which they were elected.

F Company elected William H. Morgan, Captain; he was
adjutant of the regiment. W. Granville Gray, First Lieutenant; G. W. Peterkin, Second Lieutenant, and E. G. Rawlings, Jr., Second Lieutenant. The regiment elected John M.
Patton, Colonel; Richard H. Cunningham, Jr., Lieutenant
Colonel, and John B. Moseley, Major.

In one of the regiments of our army two men carried
each a game cock. On a march they perched on the shoulders of their owners, and seemed as well contented as if on
their roost, and their crowing and the flapping of their

wings always called forth a lusty cheer from the men. They, like everything else in the Confederate army, had their use. On a march passing a farmyard, one of those men would run out of ranks when he saw a lot of fowls, and his game cock would fly to the rooster at their head, and a battle would take place at once. The owner of the game cock would pick up both roosters, and quickly join his command. That night he would have stewed rooster for supper.

I must not forget to tell about our umbrella man. In one of the companies of our regiment there was a sergeant, who was an old country gentleman. When he left home he carried an umbrella. This he kept until he left us at this camp. During a march on a hot day one would see the old sergeant marching along at the head of his company with his umbrella hoisted; the boys would call to him, "Come out of that umbrella." He took it kindly, and would generally reply that he knew they wanted it. During a rain when he hoisted it, he always had numerous applications for a part of it. When it was not in use he carried it strapped to his knapsack.

We stayed in this camp until the 23d, when we moved into the cove, a large opening within the outer mountain, and camped. We marched from this camp on the 30th, towards Harrisonburg, across the Shenandoah a mile or two, returned and took a road on the right, and marched up the river to Port Republic, reaching it on May 2d, after one of the most severe marches we had undergone. The road on which we marched was an ordinary country road, and it had been raining and snowing so much that it had become very soft, and when the artillery and wagons came along they sank up to their axles, and there was no way to get them out, unless the men put their shoulders to the wheels. This Gen. Jackson had foreseen, as details of men were sent along with the wagons. As an evidence of Gen. Jackson's anxiety and solicitude, I saw him personally getting rocks, and putting them in the holes of this road.

We were now retreating and advancing at the same time, a condition an army never undertook before. We were retreating from Banks. In my next I will show how we were advancing. The Great Valley Campaign is opening.

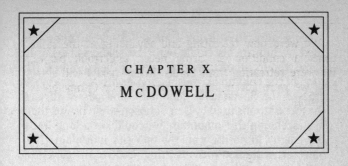

CHAPTER X
McDOWELL

O<small>N</small> M<small>AY</small> 3d we left Port Republic. This is the commencement of that great Valley campaign, the most brilliant of modern times, and I do not know that it was ever surpassed. We marched across the Blue Ridge to the Central Railroad near Meechum's Depot, and there we took the cars and went to Staunton, arriving on the 4th. On the 5th we were joined by the 10th Va. Reg. Inf., which was assigned to the third brigade, and by the cadets from the Va. Military Institute. On the 6th we left Staunton, marching towards Buffalo Gap, and about midday joined Gen. Edward Johnson's force, that had fallen back about six miles from Staunton. He had been in great danger before we arrived; a force in his front pressing him, and that of Banks threatening to march to his rear. With Jackson's coming all was changed. Near Buffalo Gap we went into camp for the night. The next morning the advance was continued, with Johnson's force in front. We encountered some of the enemy near Ryan's, and captured some stores, tents, etc., and a sutler's outfit. There was lying just outside of the sutler's store door about a bucketful of "sutler's" coin, used by him in his traffic with the soldiers, having his name, regiment, etc., and the value of the coin on it. The head of the column skirmished some with the enemy. We crossed the Shenandoah Mountain, and passed through the fortifications used by Gen. Johnson while he was there. In descending this mountain, we could see a long line of the enemy in position on the opposite mountain. They, however, withdrew without firing, and we halted for the night. On the 8th we marched in about the same order— Gen. Jackson's command in front, the second brigade next, then the third brigade, the Stonewall brigade in the rear, the cadets marching, I think, in front of the Stonewall brigade. The second brigade was ascending the Bull Pasture Mountain in the afternoon, marching a few yards and halting, then a few yards and another halt, a march that fatigued men more than one in which they take an even step and march for a length of time. We had been marching in this way for such a long time, that evening was approaching, and it was rumored that we could not cross the mountain that night; that we would return to the valley, or bottom, and camp for the night, that the remainder of Jackson's division would join us there. The men had begun to think that there was some truth in the report. Soon the idea was discarded, and the 21st Va. Regt. was hurried up, and on reaching the top of the mountain we could hear firing, and, going a little farther, we could hear that it was heavy. We were hurried along the road until we reached the 31st Va. Regt. of Johnson's command, who were ordered to join Gen. Johnson, who was heavily engaged on our left, and we were formed in line of battle across the pike. Gen. Jackson now arrived and gave orders in person to Lt. Col. Cunningham, who was in command of the regiment. He told him to protect his men as much as possible and to hold the position at all hazards, and ended by saying, in that sharp way of his, "Tell your men they must hold the road." This was the only road by which

Jackson could get his forces out if he should meet with disaster, and the road be taken, the enemy would be directly in his rear. This was therefore the key to Jackson's position, and if it were lost, all was lost. The men of the regiment now took their position behind trees and big rocks, the bottom in which we are being filled with them. As the men took their places it was with the determination that no enemy should drive them away. We were not called on for a test of our courage, a few skirmishers only appearing in our front, the enemy attacking us from our left, and next to the village of McDowell. It is said that Gen. Jackson had no idea of fighting this battle on the 8th; he and Gen. Johnson had ridden to the front and examined the situation of the enemy, and they decided to wait until morning to make an attack; as Jackson had obtained information that the enemy could be attacked in their rear, and he intended to send a force to that point as soon as it became dark. Some of his staff had actually gone to our rear, to direct those troops where to camp.

Milroy, who was in command of the enemy, received some reinforcements about noon, and thought best to make an attack at once on Gen. Johnson, not knowing of Jackson's presence. This was the cause of the battle.

The enemy made a gallant and spirited attack, but were promptly met, and, after some hard fighting, were driven back with loss. We lost a number of men and some valuable officers. Gen. Johnson was shot through the foot in the thickest of the fight. We had no artillery on our side, as we could get no position on the mountain side, and not more than two-thirds of Jackson's force was up in time to take part in the battle. The enemy used artillery from the other side of McDowell. When we passed through the town the next day, we could see the holes they made in the ground, in order to so elevate their guns as to shoot at us on the mountain side.

During the night the enemy retreated, burning some of their stores; some, however, falling into our hands. They threw a large quantity of ammunition into the creek from a bridge on the road.

We followed in hot pursuit as far as Franklin, Pendleton Co., overtaking them on the afternoon of the 11th. There the enemy took position in a narrow valley that ran between the mountain hills; these hills were covered with woods, and they had fired the woods on both sides of the valley in their front, and as soon as we came in sight, their artillery commenced firing at us. We could not locate the guns because of the smoke. Gen. Jackson sent a small force to the enemy's rear to obstruct the road at the mountain gaps; the small force was driven off before it accomplished the work. We remained in front of the enemy, trying to find their position by skirmishers, but the fire and smoke from the burning woods prevented.

Gen. Jackson, having other and more important plans, abandoned the place about 10 o'clock on the morning of the 13th, and retraced his march, going back through McDowell, marching about eleven miles, taking a road on the left leading to Harrisonburg. We stopped on the 15th, at Lebanon Springs, and remained there on the 16th to observe the national day of humiliation and prayer, ordered by the President of the Confederacy. On the 17th we resumed our march and stopped near Mossy Creek on Sunday, the 18th, where most of the command had religious worship. At early dawn on the 19th we resumed the march and reaching Bridgewater crossed the Shenandoah river on a bridge made of wagons, that were placed in a row across the river, and planks laid from one wagon to the other, thus making a very good footbridge. On the 20th we passed through Harrisonburg, and were joined by Brig. Gen. Taylor's brigade of Louisianians, of Ewell's division. This brigade made an unusually good appearance, as the men were more regularly uniformed than any we had seen.

When Gen. Jackson moved from Swift Run Gap, Gen. Ewell with his division and two regiments of cavalry occupied a position in Culpepper Co., on the Rappahannock river. He moved his command to Swift Run Gap, and occupied the position just vacated by Jackson. This was to prevent Banks from making an attack on Jackson's rear, while he was advancing on Milroy. After Jackson had disposed of Milroy, he turned to the Valley, and the junction with Taylor shows that he had reached that great country; and we went into camp on the Valley pike.

CHAPTER XI

THE VALLEY CAMPAIGN— FRONT ROYAL, MIDDLETOWN, WINCHESTER, CROSS KEYS, PORT REPUBLIC

O<small>N</small> M<small>AY</small> 21st Jackson marched down the Valley pike. When we reached New Market we took the road leading to the Luray valley, and formed a junction on the 22d, near Luray, with the balance of Gen. Ewell's command, which had marched down the Luray valley from Swift Run Gap. Jackson now had the largest army he had ever had. He had brought Gen. Edward Johnson's force of six regiments and some artillery with him from the Shenandoah mountain, and had Ewell's command, and his old command.

On the 23d Jackson's army left its bivouac near Luray, taking the road to Front Royal, the head of the column arriving about three or four o'clock in the afternoon. Gen. Jackson, as usual, made an immediate attack on the enemy, with the few men who were up. His eagerness all through this campaign was surprising, and his escape from death was almost a miracle. The enemy were found drawn up in line of battle in a strong position on the opposite side of the Shenandoah river. He had a line of skirmishers formed under his eye, and gave them the command to forward, and pushed them and some advance cavalry from the start. The Yanks finding things getting so hot, set fire to the two bridges, and were immediately charged by our cavalry and skirmishers, who saved the bridges in a damaged condition, crossed and were right in the midst of the enemy, Jackson along with them. The enemy made a bold stand and fought well, but they could not withstand Jackson's mode of warfare, and retreated to a farm orchard and buildings. Here they made a gallant stand; but our two regiments of cavalry from Ewell's command came up, were formed under Jackson's eye, and charged the protected enemy. The cavalry swept everything before them, and soon the entire force was killed and captured. In the charge at the bridge, the gallant Captain Sheets, Ashby's right hand, was killed. A large amount of stores and several hundred beef-cattle were captured. The second brigade did not come up until night, having marched twenty-seven miles.

On the next morning, as our brigade passed the prisoners that had been captured the evening before, one of them hallooed to us, "How are you, Tom?" Tom replied, "What are you doing in such bad company, Bob?" Tom, however, left ranks, and went inside the prison lines and had a hearty shake of the hand and a few minutes' conversation. Coming back he said it was his brother; literally is brother against brother. We kept up our march in the direction of Winchester until we reached Cedarville. Jackson's division with Taylor's brigade taking the road on the left, and the remainder of the army under Ewell's command keeping the direct road to Winchester.

Company B of Maryland, of our regiment, who were mustered into service for one year, having served out their term of enlistment, left us at this point; and the 21st Va. Regt. had only nine companies after that date.

The force of Jackson's command that left the road at Cedarville marched to Middletown on the Valley pike. When we came in sight of the pike, it was filled as far as we could see from one end to the other, with Yankees on their way to Winchester, and we had surprised them on the march. We attacked at once, and cut their marching column in two; one part keeping on towards Winchester, the other turning back towards Strasburg. This part of their command the second brigade, was ordered to pursue, and we followed them until they had crossed the bridge over Cedar Creek. Then we were recalled and joined in the general pursuit. In marching through Middletown, we found long lines of knapsacks behind the stone walls on the pike, as if whole regiments and brigades had unslung them in order to make a stand, and as soon as we attacked them, left in such a hurry as to leave them.

Near Newtown we came to a long wagon train of the enemy's, standing on the side of the road. Some of the wagons had been fired by them. As we passed, one thing struck the writer about the contents of those wagons as singular. In every one that had articles in sight, I could see portions of women's clothing; in one wagon a bonnet, in another a shawl, a dress in the next, and in some all of a woman's outfit. I never saw the Yankee soldiers wearing this kind of uniform, and why they carried it was beyond my knowledge. Some of our men suggested that it had been confiscated from citizens of the valley. Marching a little farther we halted, the enemy having some artillery on the opposite hill shelling our road. Our advance ran out some guns, and these, with our advanced skirmishers, soon had them retreating again. It was now dark, and we soon came to another long train of captured wagons and a pontoon-bridge train; the men looked at these with much interest, as they were the first we had seen. Marching a little farther we saw a string of fire along a stone wall, and the crack of muskets tells it was from the Yankee rear guard. They stopped at nearly every cross wall and gave us a volley. Gen. Jackson, who was always in front in an advance, came near being shot from one of these walls.

We captured over one hundred wagons during the night, keeping up the pursuit without intermission until about dawn, when we halted and were allowed to rest an hour or two in our places along the road. Soon after daybreak on the 25th, we were on the move again, and when we reached the mill about two miles from Winchester, we saw that the enemy had made a stand on the hill behind it. We were met by one of our men, wounded, who was hatless, and had been shot in the head, the blood streaming down his face so freely that the poor fellow could hardly see. The second brigade took the left road here, and marching a short distance, filed to the right, and formed line of battle under the foothills on the left of the Stonewall brigade, the 21st Va. Regt. supporting the Rockbridge battery.

We could see Ewell's command on the Front Royal road far away to our right, engaged, we locating his line by the smoke from his artillery and musketry; and could plainly see the Yankee shells bursting over his lines, and see his shells bursting over the Yankees'!

The enemy in our front were behind a stone wall that ran entirely across the open field, and a little way behind them were two batteries of artillery. A piece of the Rockbridge battery was run out on a knoll on our left, where they were met by grape and minie balls. Every man at the piece was killed or wounded. Nothing daunted, the battery ran forward another piece, but were more careful not to expose it, as in the case of the other gun. The men were soon picked off by the infantry behind the wall, and they were forced to abandon both pieces. The pieces were safe, however, as they were in our line, and if the enemy wanted them they must fight for them. About this time Gen. Jackson made his appearance, and rode to one of the hillocks in our front. Col. Campbell, commanding our brigade, accompanied him on horseback; Col. Patton of the 21st Va. Regt. and Col. Grigsby of the Stonewell brigade on foot. They were met by a hail of grape and

musket balls. Campbell was wounded, Grigsby had a hole
shot through his sleeve, and said some ugly words to the
Yankees for doing it. Gen. Jackson sat there, the enemy
continuing to fire grape and musketry at him. It is right
here that he issued his celebrated order to the commander
of the Stonewell brigade: "I expect the enemy to occupy
the hill in your front with artillery; keep your brigade well
in hand and a vigilant watch, and if such an attempt is
made,—it must not be done, sir! clamp them on the spot."
After satisfying himself as to the location of the enemy, he
quietly turned his horse and rode back in a walk. Arriving
at the road in our rear he called for Taylor's brigade, led
them in person to their position, and gave Gen. Taylor his
orders. Taylor says he replied, and added, "You had better
go to the rear; if you go along the front in this way, some
damned Yankee will shoot you!" He says that Gen. Jackson
rode back to him at once, and said, "General, I am afraid
you are a wicked fellow, but I know you will do your duty."
Taylor formed his brigade in the road about two or three
hundred yards to our left. We were on his flank, and could
see nearly the whole of his advance. His march was in an
open field, then up the steep foothill or high bank, then
on a gentle rise to the top. Near the top stood the same
stone wall that was in our front; the enemy's line of battle
extending beyond Taylor's left. As soon as Gen. Jackson
saw that Taylor had commenced the advance, he rode back
to the hillock in our front to watch the effect of Taylor's
attack. The enemy poured grape and musketry into
Taylor's line as soon as it came in sight. Gen. Taylor rode
in front of his brigade, drawn sword in hand, occasionally
turning his horse, at other times merely turning in his
saddle to see that his line was up. They marched up the
hill in perfect order, not firing a shot! About half way to
the Yankees he gave in a loud and commanding voice, that
I am sure the Yankees heard, the order to charge! and to
and over the stone wall they went! At the same time Gen.
Jackson gave the command in that sharp and crisp way of

his, "After the enemy, men!" Our whole line moved forward on a run, the enemy broke and ran in all directions. The Rockbridge artillerymen rushed to their two abandoned pieces, and gave them a parting salute. This charge of Taylor's was the grandest I saw during the war. There was all the pomp and circumstance of war about it, that was always lacking in our charges; but not more effective than ours which were inspired by the old rebel yell, in which most of the men raced to be foremost.

Near Winchester the advance artillery, which had been firing from every elevation over the heads of our infantry at the fleeing enemy, halted. A scene was witnessed that had no parallel in history that I know of. The men of several batteries unhitched the lead horses from cannons and caissons, threw the traces over the horses' backs, mounted and charged the enemy through the town, capturing and bringing back many prisoners! As we passed through Winchester the citizens were so glad to see us that men, women, and children ran into the streets to welcome us, wringing our hands with both of theirs, some even embracing the men, all crying for joy! The bullets from the enemy were flying through the streets, but this made no difference to these people. It seemed that joy had overcome fear. Such a scene I never witnessed.

The second brigade followed the enemy about five miles below Winchester, where they were ordered to halt, and go into camp, other troops following the fleeing enemy. Some of our men followed the enemy into Maryland, and were only stopped by Jackson, when he received notice of the effort of other forces of the enemy to get into his rear.

The enemy, on this occasion, was commanded by Gen. Banks, from whom Gen. Jackson captured vast stores: several hundred beef cattle, several hundred wagons with their teams, eleven thousand new muskets in boxes that had never been opened, a large amount of ammunition, and over three thousand prisoners. Jackson lost a very small number of men, but he had led us for three weeks as hard as men could march. In an order issued to his troops the next day, he thanked us for our conduct, and referred us to the result of the campaign as justification for our marching so hard. Every man was satisfied with his apology; to accomplish so much with so little loss, we would march six months! The reception at Winchester was worth a whole lifetime of service.

On the 28th the 21st Va. Regt. was ordered to Winchester to take charge of the prisoners; a job little relished by the men, since we had only about two hundred and fifty men to guard about three thousand prisoners!

The enemy had a large force in the valley of the South Fork of the Potomac under Fremont, and another on the Rappahannock river under McDowell. As soon as it was known that Jackson had routed Banks, the authorities in Washington gave these two commanders orders to march at once to Strasburg in the valley, which was twenty to thirty miles in Jackson's rear. There they were to form a junction, the united force of between thirty and thirty-five thousand to fall on Jackson, whip him, and capture his army. McDowell ordered Shields with his division to the valley. He moved promptly and rapidly, and actually burst into the Luray valley at Front Royal, before Jackson was advised of his movement! Learning that Fremont was moving on a road that led to Strasburg, Jackson divined their purpose, recalled his advance, and ordered the other troops to concentrate at Strasburg. The Stonewall brigade was the advance of Jackson's army at that time; they were in the neighborhood of Harper's Ferry, the Second Va. Reg. had crossed the Shenandoah, and gone to Loudoun Heights. They received the order on the 31st to march above Winchester before they stopped. The brigade marched over thirty-five miles, and the Second Regiment over forty to accomplish it.

On the 31st Jackson sent all his captured stores and his wagon train up the Valley pike, and our regiment with the prisoners followed in the afternoon. We marched to Cedar Creek, and stopped for the night; our guard line was around a large barn, in order to allow the prisoners to have the benefit of its shelter, as it was raining. Some amusing scenes were witnessed the next morning. The barn had a large quantity of hay in it; we went to the door and ordered all out; we then called for those that were concealed to come out, or they would be punished when found. None came; so some of our men were ordered to go in, and see if they could find any. Two or three were pulled out of the hay, amidst shouts from their comrades, as well as our men. Then we fixed bayonets and told them we were going to thrust the bayonets into the hay in the entire building. One or two came out; and presently the bayonets began to be used. A few strokes, and a man is struck, but fortunately for him not hard enough to hurt him; he and several others then came out.

We formed our line and commenced the march. At Strasburg we could see Ewell's division in line of battle on the right of the road, awaiting the advance of Fremont, whose skirmishers had made their appearance and were then engaged with Ewell's.

Our prisoners became very much excited by this, and declared loudly that Jackson had met his match now, and would be badly whipped; and it would be only a few hours before they would be retaken. After all the wagons and prisoners had passed, Jackson waited for the Stonewall brigade to arrive, and as soon as it had passed, Ewell was withdrawn and followed the column up the valley. Fremont made a big show at one time in Ewell's front, but hearing nothing from Shields, who for some reason had not made his appearance, he withdrew his men back into the mountain fastness, his skirmishers following Ewell a short distance.

The plan to bag Jackson at Strasburg had failed; "Old Jack" was too quick for them; besides, he had some plans of his own.

The next day, June 2d, Fremont followed us in hot pursuit, and so closely that our guard and the prisoners, from the tops of some of the hills in our march, could plainly see his advance.

Reaching the Shenandoah at Mt. Jackson, Jackson gave Col. Ashby orders to burn the bridge across that stream, after all our army had passed. Col. Ashby left this to one of his officers and his men to do, but they were driven off by the enemy before it was accomplished. Ashby learning this, took a few men with him, went back, drove off the Yanks, fired the bridge, and then retired; but as he rode off his famous white horse was shot! This beautiful and great horse, that was known by the enemy as well as it was known in our own army, was thought by the Yanks to be enchanted. I have heard their prisoners repeatedly say that they have often taken deadly aim, sometimes resting their guns on a fence or wall, at that horse and its rider, and the ball had no effect on either! He was a grand horse, and after being shot, carried Col. Ashby about a mile from the bridge before he fell dead. This was the first intimation he had of his horse being wounded.

Shields marched up the Luray valley with the intention of getting into Jackson's rear at New Market, but "Old Jack" defeated that by burning the White House bridge over the Shenandoah. Shields continued his march up that valley, expecting to force a fight with Jackson as soon as he and Fremont should unite, somewhere in the neighborhood of Port Republic. Again Jackson frustrated their plans by turning on Fremont at Cross Keys on June 7th, and easily whipped him. In the combat of the 6th we lost the great Ashby! He was killed while leading some infantry, who had been sent to the front to aid him. At this time he was the most gallant and conspicuous cavalry officer we had. Gen. Jackson thought a great deal of him, and said that he was a born soldier, and also seemed to have the faculty of knowing *what* the enemy were doing, and when they were doing it. The army and the

Confederacy could ill afford to lose him, and I think his loss was never repaired. In this short time his name was known all over the Confederacy, and amongst the enemy just as well. He was a tower of strength to us, as he was more feared by the enemy than any man on our side at that time. His remains were carried to the University of Virginia, and buried there.

After defeating Fremont on the 7th, Jackson sent some of his troops to Port Republic on that night, only leaving in Fremont's front Trimble's brigade and the Second brigade, both small, under command of Brig. Gen. Trimble. His orders from Jackson were to hold his position as long as he could, and at the same time to make as big a show as possible; if he were forced back, he should fight at every fence, wall, ditch, etc., and keep the enemy back as long as possible. If he could do this, until ten o'clock in the morning, Jackson would be back to reinforce him. If he were forced back to the bridge, he should burn it.

At the break of day on the 8th, Jackson commenced his movement against Shields. He crossed the bridge over Middle river with his troops, marched through the town to the South river, over which he made a bridge of wagons, like the one on which we crossed at Bridgewater, a few weeks before. About the middle of the stream, where the planks running from one wagon to the next should have overlapped, only one of the planks did so, the others lacking a few inches of meeting. When the men in the front reached this place in crossing, those planks tilted, and the men were thrown into the river. Those who followed seeing this, refused to cross on those planks, and waited for each other as they crossed on the one. This caused a great delay in the crossing. When Jackson found his troops did not come up as quickly as they usually did, and learned the cause, he ordered the men to ford the river. This was a serious delay for Jackson, as time was most important to him, and there is little doubt this little incident ruined Jackson's plans, and saved Fremont from utter rout. After getting his troops over this stream, he hastened them into position, and launched them against Shields; and after a severe battle Shields was utterly routed, Jackson taking many of his guns and many prisoners. But time that waits for no man had been lost!

Fremont, hearing the heavy firing in the direction of Shields, knew that he and Jackson were engaged, and thought that Jackson's force was divided. He made a demonstration in his front, then made an attack on Trimble, but could not drive him a foot. He now brought up more troops, lengthened his lines on both sides, and in this way forced him back. They fought all the way to the bridge, and it was late in the morning before they were driven to the bridge; after crossing that they burned it.

Jackson, recalling his troops from the pursuit of Shields, was hurrying across the battlefield to Trimble, whom he had not heard from, when his army was fiercely assailed by Fremont's artillery. He was on the other side of the river, and had placed his artillery on the high banks that overlooked the battlefield of Shields. Jackson withdrew his men behind the hills for protection and there heard of Trimble's inability to keep the enemy back for a longer time. Without the accident at the bridge of wagons, there is not the least doubt of Jackson being able to carry out his plan to the very letter, and Fremont would have been wiped off the face of the earth. As it *was*, the campaign ended in a blaze of glory that was sounded from one end of the world to the other!

Jackson's loss with Shields was heavy, and amounted to as much as he had previously lost in the campaign. The loss of Shields was also heavy, and Fremont's loss was largely in excess of Jackson's.

Jackson stayed behind the hills, in the neighborhood of Brown's Gap, until the 12th, when he marched up the Shenandoah to the neighborhood of Weyer's Cave, and camped in a beautiful country. In the meantime, Fremont had become frightened, and retreated towards Winchester. This ended the great Valley Campaign.

One of the Yankee prisoners marched at my side daily, talking about what he was going to do with me when they were retaken, and how he would take care of my gun. While we were uneasy all the time, for fear they might make a break for liberty, we never had a thought of their being rescued except on one occasion. On the 5th, after marching a short distance past Port Republic, we halted, and were told that we would camp there for the night. While our lieutenant colonel was looking over the ground, an order came from Gen. Jackson for us to move on, and a few cavalry were ordered to report to Col. Cunningham. This did not excite suspicion amongst the guard, but about nine o'clock one of our officers came to me and whispered in my ear that the enemy were in Port Republic, and I must keep the strictest watch, and under no circumstances let a prisoner escape. I did not know what to think. The enemy in Port Republic meant that they were between us and Jackson, and the prisoners' expectation of release might be realized. We marched until about midnight, and went into camp near New Hope for a few hours' rest. The next morning we were up early, and marched to Waynesboro.

The report of the enemy being in Port Republic on the 5th was untrue, but the advance of Shields did enter the village soon on the morning of the 6th, and came near capturing Gen. Jackson. There are several versions of his escape, but all agree that it was by the merest chance. Most of his staff, that were with him at the time, were captured. This body of the enemy, it is said, learned the direction the prisoners had been sent, and part of them made an attempt to follow us, but were driven back by some of our artillery, supported by a small body of infantry.

We remained in Waynesboro, and heard the cannonading at Cross Keys and Port Republic. The

prisoners were very excited, it would have taken very little
to stampede them: every man was on duty, and it was a
great strain on our men; and when more prisoners were
brought us, with the information that Jackson had
defeated Fremont, the relief was almost overpowering.
Amongst a small squad of prisoners, brought us here by
some cavalry, was an Englishman, captured on the 6th,
calling himself Sir Percy Wyndham. He was a colonel in
the Yankee army, and, it is said, requested to be sent to
the valley, as he would capture the rebel Ashby the first
time he got within striking distance of him. Ashby with
some of his cavalry met Sir Percy near Harrisonburg and
almost the first man taken by Ashby was this same Sir
Percy. He was made to march on foot with other prisoners
from the place of his capture to Waynesboro, and when he
reached us, was the most exasperated man I had seen for
a long time. He said that in his army (the English), when
an officer of his rank was captured, he was taken charge
of by an officer of like rank, and treated accordingly, until
exchanged or paroled. Here he was marched through mud
and mire, and that, too, by a rebel private; it was enough
to make a saint swear. We treated him as other prisoners,
making no distinction in his favor as he thought we
ought, as he had come all the way across the ocean to
capture Ashby!

On the evening of the 8th we conducted our prisoners
from Waynesboro, crossing the Blue Ridge at Rockfish
Gap. They did not give up hope of being retaken until they
had crossed the mountain, when they became as meek as
lambs, and gave us very little trouble. We reached North
Garden depot, on the Orange and Alexandria R. R., on the
9th, and went into camp. Here one of the prisoners made
a break for liberty; the guard fired at him, but missed, so
he got away.

We took the cars on the 11th, and went to Lynchburg,
marched our prisoners through the town to the fair
grounds, where we guarded them until the 18th. We

turned them over to the city guard, and went by rail to Charlottesville, leaving the train, however, about a mile from the town. We camped on the side of the railroad, staying there until Jackson marched by on his way to Richmond, when we rejoined our brigade. It was the unanimous desire of the regiment never to have charge of prisoners again.

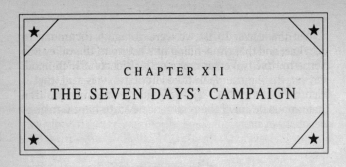

CHAPTER XII
THE SEVEN DAYS' CAMPAIGN

O<small>N</small> J<small>UNE</small> 17, 1862, Jackson broke camp in the valley, and marched towards Gordonsville. As he passed through Charlottesville on the 21st, our regiment rejoined its brigade. We were plied with many questions as to the destination of the army, and we made as many inquiries of our comrades in the brigade, but all agreed that we knew nothing. We guessed that on reaching Gordonsville we would file to the left, and fall upon the enemy under McDowell at Fredericksburg, or our destination was Washington, and this circuitous route was taken to mystify the enemy. None of us had a single thought of Richmond. Why then send Whiting's division to the valley to join Jackson? When we reached Gordonsville, we kept the same road, and when we arrived at Louisa C. H., some cars came along on the Central R. R. and took up the troops that were marching in the rear, and carried them to Beaver Dam depot. These cars returned, and took up those in the rear again, and carried them to the same place. In this way Jackson would help his men with cars on a march.

We now decided that we were going to Richmond to help Lee; and that the sending of Whiting to the valley was a ruse to have two effects, one on McClellan at Richmond, and one on the enemy in the valley; and, it is said, that it was successful in both directions. Jackson's men realized that we would have to do some desperate fighting, since we knew we could not stay in Richmond; and the only way for us to leave was to attack McClellan, and drive him away.

We reached Ashland on the 25th, and received orders to cook three days' rations. The next morning we marched as soon as the column could be formed, leaving the road we had been following, and taking one on the left, going in the direction of the Central R. R. crossing near Peak's turnout; marching to the neighborhood of Pole Green Church, we stacked arms and rested for the night. We saw the first signs of the Yankees' presence in our march to-day: the telegraph wires were cut not far from Ashland. In the evening, Gen. Stuart's cavalry, which had joined us, had a brisk skirmish in our front, killing, wounding, and capturing some of the enemy. Those prisoners were the first of McClellan's army that we saw.

We were up and moving early the next morning. At Pole Green Church we found that Stuart's men needed the assistance of our infantry, in order to clear the way. Some regiments were ordered forward, and soon captured nearly all the Bucktail regiment of Pennsylvanians at Hundley's corner. We did not know whether McClellan had learned that Jackson was in the neighborhood, or thought the column was a part of Lee's force. We continued the march now without any obstruction, and soon we heard the musketry and artillery of Longstreet and Hill, commencing the attack on McClellan at Gaines' Mill; and we learned that we were about to unite with them in an attack. We had thought until now that they were on the south side of the Chickahominy, and that we were to make the attack from the north side alone.

Our march was kept up in quick time, the firing

becoming heavier in our front, and was the heaviest musketry I heard during the war. We marched on, and towards evening halted and retraced our steps until we came to a road we had passed some time before. This road was to the east, and we kept it until our division halted, was ordered to load, and a line of battle was formed and ordered forward through a pine thicket so dense that a man ten yards in front could not be seen.

The Second Brigade was on the right of the division, the Stonewall next, and the Third Brigade on the left. The division was about the center of Gen. Lee's line of battle, and in going through the thicket the division, having no guides, lost its way; our orders being to press forward to the firing in front. The division obeyed; but, very singularly, the Stonewall Brigade crossed the line of march, and when it reached the firing line, it was on the left, coming up just in time to help D. H. Hill, whose line was giving way. The united force swept everything before it. The Third Brigade, maintaining nearly a straight line, came up to Whiting's line as it was falling back, and their united efforts drove the enemy at that point. When the Second Brigade emerged from the thicket, they had, like the Stonewall, taken a long swing, but towards the right, and we entered an open field. Not far ahead we saw two men on horseback, who seemed to be in a consultation, and, as we approached them, we recognized at once our beloved leader, Gen. Lee, on his well remembered gray, and President Davis. We passed them with a cheer, and they recognized it by raising their hats. Here are two of the most notable men of the Confederacy in close consultation on the battlefield, and, from their appearance, no one would imagine that the fortunes of the war were on their shoulders.

President Davis looked calm and self-possessed, and seemed to look on us with interest, it being the first time he had seen our brigade.

Gen. Lee was as calm and dignified as ever in giving us the salute.

We went straight ahead, and not long afterwards we came in sight of some of our troops, who seemed in confusion, and giving ground. Our brigade commander, Lt. Col. Cunningham of the 21st Regt., rode forward to the brigade commanded by Brig. Gen. Anderson of Longstreet's division, on the extreme right of our line. I was told he said to Gen. Anderson that his brigade was coming, and he would take the front. Gen. Anderson thanked him, and said, that because of the arrival of Jackson's men, he could finish what his brigade had commenced. He moved his men to the right, and made an attack on the enemy's flank, while the Second Brigade kept them busy in front; and when Anderson's men gave the yell, we went forward on a run, and the works were carried by Anderson in gallant style.

This was the strongest point I saw occupied by either army during the war. In the enemy's front for half a mile was an open field, with a hill gently sloping towards them, at the foot of which a creek ran that had washed its banks perpendicular, about six to eight feet deep; it was eight to ten feet wide. When we jumped in, we could not get out without assistance. We threw our guns on the side next the enemy. One comrade then helped another out, and when he had scaled the bank, he stooped or lay down and pulled another out. It was almost level from this creek for about fifty to one hundred yards, where there was a steep and high hill. This hill was covered by a large and open wood. At its foot a rail fence ran, which had been converted into an excellent breastwork. This was the enemy's first line of battle. About twenty-five yards up the hill was a second line of breastworks, made of logs and dirt, and about the same distance in its rear, on top of the hill, was another line behind similar breastworks, and behind this was their artillery, which had a full sweep at us as soon as we entered the clearing in their front. Charging this point, Anderson on the flank, we in front, we drove the enemy out, and, on top of the hill, we entered a field that was filled with Yanks and

Confederates. The line on the left of us having been carried too, every man was yelling and shooting into the mass of the enemy as fast as he could load; this was continued until it was so dark that we could not see.

The position taken by Jackson's division in this battle is rather remarkable. Our orders were to march right ahead to the firing, as before stated. Not having guides, in our moving about in the thicket, the brigades finally emerged apart, and in going to the front, each brigade moved, as was thought, in a straight line; but one went to the extreme right, another near the center, and the other to the extreme left, yet each reached its destination when assistance was greatly needed. Thus it seems that the old division, which had such a bad start, put itself into a better place than "Old Jack" himself had ordered, and played no small part in the success of this great battle.

Late in the night we lay down on the hard-won field to take some rest, but the cries and groans of the wounded kept many of us awake all night. In the morning we could see the result of the battle: the greatest slaughter of the enemy in the field, the dead and wounded numbering thousands. A large number of cannon were captured in this field; I don't know how many. I counted fifteen on one hill, standing just as the enemy left them: on this same hill I saw the first machine gun, with its handle to turn out a bullet at every revolution. I saw another, which was captured during the seven days' fight, the only ones seen by the writer during the war.

During the night the enemy made good their escape across the Chickahominy, destroying the bridge in our front. Replacing this, so that we could cross, delayed Jackson's command all day. The enemy sent up a large balloon for observation during the day, and some of our guns fired at it. Whether it had any effect towards making its occupants retire or not, I cannot say, but they were up only a short time.

Longstreet and A. P. Hill crossed higher up the stream,

and went in pursuit of the enemy, and Magruder's troops made an attack on the enemy in the evening near Savage Station.

The bridge being ready on the morning of June 30, Jackson's command crossed early to the south side of the stream, passing in our march the house McClellan had used as his headquarters, and thence on to the Williamsburg turnpike. Here we passed some of Gen. Lee's troops, who had halted for us to take the front. We created much excitement and enthusiasm, as we were just from Jackson's brilliant valley campaign, and many remarks and cheers greeted us. I remember that our captain had a saber but no scabbard, and the remark was made several times along the march, "See there, the officers don't even carry scabbards for their swords." "No wonder they march so, the men carry no baggage." As a general thing, our knapsacks had been discarded long ago. We passed the field on which Magruder made the attack on the enemy the evening before, and saw many of the enemy's dead along the road, and it was strange that nearly every one was shot near the heart. Reaching the toll gate, we saw a man sitting on a box leaning against the gate post, and soon discovered that he was dead. We passed Savage farm, and saw hundreds of tents standing, which were used by the enemy for hospitals, and nearly all were full of sick and wounded of the enemy.

We marched to the vicinity of White Oak Swamp, where skirmishers were thrown forward; some of our artillery was brought into position, and firing commenced. Gen. Jackson ascertained that the enemy had made a stand here. We were moved from place to place, looking for a place to cross; at night we lay down on the ground for a little rest. Early in the morning we resumed the march, as the enemy had left during the night. Crossing the swamp on a bridge of logs, we followed in hot pursuit, and found the enemy in position at Malvern Hill. Gen. Jackson promptly formed his line of battle; our division in a wood on the right of the road, in three lines, the second brigade being in the third line. The enemy shelled us terribly the whole time. Just about dark the second brigade was ordered to march by the left flank, and entering the road, we marched towards Malvern Hill, crossed a creek, and soon were in a field at the edge of which we halted, staying there the remainder of the night. I sat down in a fence corner to get a little rest, and had not been there long before one of our men, wounded, came along, and was begging for water. Having some in my canteen, I stopped him and gave him a drink. He sat down and complained very much of being weak. I gave him something to eat from my scanty rations; he seemed very thankful, and revived a little, but soon complained of being cold. I unrolled my blanket, and made him lie down, and covered him with it; a little while after I got cold too, so crept under the blanket with the wounded man, fell asleep, and did not wake until morning. I then crawled from under the blanket as carefully as I could, to avoid disturbing him, went to the creek, took a wash, filled my canteen, and brought it to my friend, tried to arouse him, but he was dead.

The enemy fled during the night, and my division was ordered back, stopping at Willis' Church the remainder of the day. It had commenced to rain, and was very disagreeable. While we were here, I went to the spring for water, but found a dead Yankee lying with his face in the spring. I suppose the poor fellow had been wounded in the fight two days before with Longstreet's command, and going to the spring, had leaned down to drink, and death overtook him. The next morning we moved in pursuit of the enemy, and found them at Harrison's Landing on James river, busily fortifying. Jackson's command remained there, most of the time in line of battle, until the 8th, when our division was moved back one and one-half miles to a creek, where Gen. Jackson said he would like all of us to take a bath, and would give us several hours to do it. This was much needed; because of the constant duty and scarcity of water, some of the men had not washed their faces and hands for five or six days.

We marched from this place to White Oak Swamp, where we rested for the night; and the next morning Jackson's command took up its march for Richmond, marching around the city on its northeast side. During this march we moved along the York River Railroad some distance. We saw many large warehouses in which the enemy had stores. Some were burning, others were partially burned, and some were captured before they were fired.

Jackson's division was marched to Morris farm on the Mechanicsville turnpike and there went into camp on the 11th. Gen. Jackson on the next day gave F Company permission to spend the day in Richmond. To most of the company that was a great day, many of them not having been in the city since they left it a year ago. What changes had taken place in one year. We left Richmond a year ago in new uniforms, with the fair complexion of city men, some frail and spare, none of us with one exception having seen anything of real war. We returned now ruddy and brown, with the health and hardness that outdoor living creates, and were veterans. Our welcome was an ovation, and it made us feel our standing in public esteem. The only thing we regretted as our time closed was that the day did not last forever.

We stayed at Morris farm several days, taking a much needed rest, the first we had had since April 30th. During the time that ended now at Morris farm, Jackson's men had marched over five hundred and fifty miles, fought nine battles, many skirmishes, captured several thousand prisoners, large quantities of small arms and cannon, wagons, and stores.

At the commencement of the war, the Southern army was as poorly armed as any body of men ever had been. In the infantry, my own regiment as an example, one company had Springfield muskets, one had Enfield, one had Mississippi rifles, the remainder the old smooth bore flint-lock musket that had been altered to a percussion gun. The cavalry was so badly equipped that hardly a company was uniform in that particular; some had sabers, nothing more, some had double-barrel guns, some had nothing but lances, while others had something of all. One man with a saber, another with a pistol, another with a musket, another a shotgun, not half a dozen men in the company armed alike. The artillery was better, but the guns were mostly smooth bore, and some of the horses had wagon and plow harness. It did not take long for the army of Northern Va. to arm itself with better material. When Jackson's troops marched from the valley for Richmond to join Lee in his attack on McClellan, they had captured enough arms from the enemy to replace all that were inferior, and after the battles around Richmond, all departments of Lee's army were as well armed. After that time, the captures from the enemy kept us up to their standard. Our ammunition was always inferior to theirs.

Towards the close of the war, nearly all equipments in the army of Northern Va. were articles captured from the Yankees. All the wagons were captured, and to look at them on a march, one would not know that they belonged to the Confederacy, many of them having the name of the brigade, division and corps of the Yankee army branded on them. Nearly all the mules and horses had U.S. branded on them; our ambulances were from the same generous provider, our tents also, many of them having the name of the company, etc., branded on them; most of the blankets were those marked U.S., also the rubber blankets or cloths; the very clothing that the men wore was mostly captured, as we were allowed to wear their pants, underclothing and overcoats. As for myself, I purchased only one hat, one pair of shoes, and one jacket after 1861. We captured immense quantities of provisions, and nearly all the "hard tack" and pork issued to us was captured.

On the 16th we received orders to march to Richmond, where we took cars of the Richmond, Fredericksburg and Potomac R. R., and on reaching the junction, were transferred to the Central Railroad and conveyed to Louisa C. H. This route was necessitated by the enemy having destroyed a portion of the Central Railroad between Richmond and the junction, now known as Doswells, and it had not been repaired at that time.

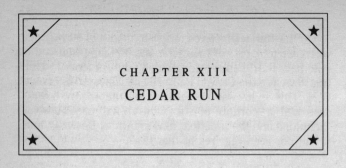

WE REMAINED at Louisa C. H. a day, and marched to Gordonsville, then to Liberty Mills, then to Mechanicsville, not far from Louisa C. H., staying two or three days at each place. On August 4th we marched again to Liberty Mills. These movements were occasioned by reports from the enemy in our front, who had raised a new army, "The Army of Virginia," commanded by Gen. Pope, who said he had been doing great things in the Western army. In his order to his troops on taking command he said he had never seen anything "but the backs of the rebels, his headquarters were in the saddle, and he wanted the talk of guarding the rear of his army stopped, as an invading army had no rear, it was useless to make provision to look after communications in that direction." In less than a month he found out that his army did not have any rear, as Jackson had quietly slipped into Manassas, and gobbled it up. Gen. Stuart with his cavalry had previously raided his headquarters at Catlett's Station, capturing his official papers and his military dress coat.

92

On August 7th we left Liberty Mills and marched to Orange C. H. We were up early the next morning and on the march. During the day we were joined by A. P. Hill's division and Stafford's Louisiana Brigade. Our advance guard reaching Barnett's Ford on the Rapidan river, found the enemy in their front, and offering some resistance to our crossing. Near the ford we passed a "Quaker cannon," which our advance had rigged up. It was the hind part of a wagon with a black log on it. Our men ran this out on a hill in full sight of the Yanks, and advanced at the same time with a cheer. The enemy left the ford in a hurry. They could not stand the sight of the cannon. Soon after crossing the river, I saw one of our cavalrymen with a saber wound; his ear was nearly severed from his head.

On crossing the river, we took the direct road to Culpeper C. H., forded Robertson river in the afternoon, and about sunset went into camp in a wood near the road. About midnight we were awakened by the firing of musketry, and the ting of balls falling amongst us. Each man rose up and took his place in ranks more quickly than I ever saw it done; and when the order was given to "take arms," every man had his gun ready for action. We marched to the road and halted, to await orders from headquarters. The firing soon ceased. It resulted from the surprise of some Yankee cavalry on their way from Madison C. H. to Culpeper C. H. They were ignorant of our advance, and, being halted by our guard, they began to retreat, and after a brisk skirmish made off as soon as they could extricate themselves. In this affair my regiment got into ranks directly from their beds, and when we marched back to our camp, the laugh began; and those old Confederates made the woods ring with shouts. Some of the men were in their shirt sleeves, some having on them nothing but shirts, some with one shoe on, etc., hardly one with a hat, but every man was in his place.

On the next morning, August 9th, we resumed the march, Ewell's division in front, Jackson's next, and Hill

bringing up the rear. About one o'clock we heard the
boom of cannon in our front, and we knew that Pope had
made a stand. The column hurried up, Ewell filing to the
right, and sending the first line of skirmishers forward.

"Peace and beauty all around us, death and danger just
  ahead,
On our faces careless courage, in our hearts a sombre
  dread.

"Then the skirmish line went forward, and the only sounds
  we heard
Were the hum of droning insects and the carol of a bird;
Till, far off, a flash of fire, and a little cloud went by,
Like an angel's mantle floating down from out an azure
  sky.

"Then a shell went screaming o'er us, and the air at once
  was rife
With a million whispering hornets, swiftly searching for
  a life;
And the birds and insects fled away before the 'rebel yell,'
The thunder of the battle, and the furious flames of hell."

Our division was hurried along the road some distance,
the Second Brigade marched to the front of the column
and halted, the roll was called, we were ordered to load,
and, after a few minutes of rest, we resumed the hurried
march. Going a short distance, the men on the left of the
road cleared the way for a cannon ball that came bounding
along like a boy's ball. The force with which it was traveling
is indicated by its striking the stump of a tree, glancing up,
and going out of sight. A little farther on we came to four
of our men lying in the road dead, killed by this same ball.
The road was fairly alive now with shot and shell from the
enemy, and we filed to the left into the wood, went about
one hundred yards, filed to the right, and continued our
march, parallel to the road. We passed an old Confederate
standing beside a small sapling, with one hand resting on
it, and we asked him, "What is the matter?" He said, "I

don't want to fight. I ain't mad with anybody." This put all in a good humor, and amidst laughter and cheers we continued the march. After going several hundred yards we halted and were ordered to lie down. The enemy were shelling this wood terribly, and our Captain Morgan was killed by them. After a short stay we were ordered forward, and halted on the edge of the wood, beside the main road that ran north and south. The woods we occupied extended north about one hundred and fifty yards to a field. This field continued along the road for about two hundred yards to another wood.

The Second Brigade formed a line of battle in the corner or angle of the wood, the 21st Va. Regt. on the right, the 48th Va. next, both facing east, the 42d Va. next, and, at right angles to the road and facing north, the Irish battalion next, forming the left. The brigade thus formed a right angle. In front of the 21st and 48th there was a large field surrounded by a rail fence, the road running between the wood and fence. In the open about three or four hundred yards obliquely on our left there was a corn field, full of Yankees, well concealed. Another line had formed at right angles to the main road and across it, its right concealed in the second wood, which was beyond the small field in front of the 42d Regt. and the Irish battalion. As soon as we reached the road, we saw a line of Yankees advancing from the corn field, the 21st and 48th opened fire on them at once; and the battle of Cedar Run had commenced in earnest. We caused the advancing line to halt, and the fighting was terrific. The Second Brigade was alone at this point, since Jackson had not had time to extend his line. The Yankees now made an advance with the line that had been concealed, in front of the Irish battalion and the 42d Regt. Their line being longer than ours, they swung around the Irish battalion in our rear, and occupied the position from which we had advanced only a few minutes before. The 21st and 48th were fighting the force at and near the corn field, although it had been strengthened by

the second line; still we were fighting with such effect that
we kept this force back. A part of the force, advancing
against the left of the brigade, were firing directly into the
flank of the 48th and 21st Regiments, and were making
terrible havoc in their ranks. Col. Cunningham of the 21st,
who was sick, came along the line, walking and leading his
horse, and said to the men as he passed that the enemy
were in our rear and he desired to get us out of the position
we were in, and we must follow him. His voice was one of
loud compass and great command, but he could hardly
speak, and as he passed me he said, "John, help me get the
men out of this, I can't talk loudly." I induced all the men
near me to face down (southward) the road, and we started.
After a few steps, I saw a Yankee sergeant step into the road
about fifty or seventy-five yards ahead (south) of us, and at
the same time heard the firing of rapidly approaching enemy in our rear. A great dread filled me for Jackson, because I had seen him at this spot only a moment before.
The sergeant, having his gun in his left hand, his drawn
sword in his right, turned up the road towards us, and
approached. A Yankee private stepped into the road just
ahead of him; this being the road on which we marched to
get to our position, it showed that the enemy were not only
in our front, flank, and rear, but actually had the second
brigade surrounded. The Yankee sergeant did not stop his
advance towards us until he actually took hold of one of the
men of our regiment and pulled him out of ranks, and
started towards the rear with his prisoner. One of our men,
who was in the act of capping his gun, raised it to his
shoulder, fired, and the sergeant fell dead not ten feet
away. By this time the road was full of Yankees, and there
was such a fight as was not witnessed during the war; guns,
bayonets, swords, pistols, fence rails, rocks, etc., were used
all along the line. I have heard of a "hell spot" in some
battles, this surely was one. Our color bearer knocked
down a Yankee with his flag staff, and was shot to death at
once. One of the color guard took the flag, and he also was

killed; another, Roswell S. Lindsay of F Company, bayo-neted a Yankee, and was immediately riddled with balls, three going through him. Four color bearers were killed with the colors in their hands, the fifth man flung the riddled flag to the breeze, and went through the terrible battle unhurt. Col. Cunningham had crossed the road leading his horse, pulled down the fence, passed through the gap into the field, started to mount his horse, his foot in the stirrup, when he was struck by a bullet, and fell back dead, his horse receiving his death wound at the same time. It was a terrible time, the Second Brigade was overwhelmed, nearly half of the 21st Va. Regt. lay on the ground, dead and wounded. F Company of Richmond carried eighteen men into action, twelve of them were lying on the ground, six dead and six wounded, and many of the regiment were prisoners. The remnant was still fighting hand to hand. Jackson hurried men to our relief, the Stonewall Brigade coming in on our left, and the Third Brigade on the right. They succeeded in surrounding a part of the command who had surrounded us, and took nearly all of them prisoners, including their brigadier general; and released those of our men who had been captured in time for them to join the little band in the advance. Just at this moment the enemy hurled a line of cavalry against us, from the corn field, but our fire on them was so hot that those not unhorsed, wheeled, and off to the rear they went on a run. Our whole line now advanced, and the enemy were in full retreat. We could plainly see Ewell, with a part of his division on Slaughter Mountain, way off to the right of our line, advancing too; as the mountain at this point was free of woods, we could see his skirmish line in front advancing down the mountain, his line of battle following, and his cannon belching forth fire and smoke, and we could see the enemy's shell bursting on the mountain side. It was a magnificent and inspiring sight.

We kept up the pursuit until 9 or 10 o'clock at night, when we halted, and were allowed to rest for the night.

The Battle of Cedar Run

The battle was fought and won, the 21st Va. Regt. had written its name high on the scroll of honor, but at what cost. They went into battle with two hundred and eighty-four men; thirty-nine of them lay dead on the field, and ninety-two were wounded. Old F Company of Richmond lost Capt. Morgan, shot through the body by a piece of shell. He was a splendid soldier, and the best informed man on military matters that I knew during the war. Henry Anderson, Joe Nunnally, John Powell, William Pollard, and Roswell Lindsay were killed, Bob Gilliam was shot through the leg, Clarence Redd through both wrists, Ned Tompkins through one arm and in the body, Porter Wren in the arm, Harrison Watkins through the body, and Clarence Taylor through the hip.

Nearly half of Jackson's loss in this battle was in the Second Brigade. Amongst the killed were Brig. Gen. Charles Winder of the Stonewall Brigade, who commanded the division, and Lieut. Col. Richard H. Cunningham (an old F), who commanded the 21st Va. Regt., two as gallant men as the cause ever lost, a great loss to our command and the army. Both were conspicuous on every battlefield for brave deeds, and they gave promise of being great soldiers. I have always thought there was a similarity in their deaths. Both were on the sick list, each had been riding in an ambulance during the day, but, at the sound of the guns, each mounted his horse, came to the front, and took command of his men. Winder was posting his advance artillery in the open field just to our right when he was killed, and Cunningham was killed a few minutes later near the same place. I also think if they had lived each would have been promoted, Winder to be a major general, and Cunningham to be a brigadier general, both commissions dating from this battle.

Here is what Major Dabney, on Jackson's staff, says in his life of Stonewall Jackson. After describing the position of the brigades that were already in line of battle to our right, he comes to that occupied by the Second Brigade and says:

"The whole angle of forest was now filled with clamor and horrid rout. The left regiments of the Second Brigade were taken in reverse, intermingled with the enemy, broken and massacred from front to rear. The regiments of the right and especially the 21st Virginia, commanded by that brave Christian soldier, Colonel Cunningham, stood firm, and fought the enemy before them like lions, until the invading line had penetrated within twenty yards of their rear, for the terrific din of the musketry, the smoke, and the dense foliage concealed friend from foe, until they were separated from each other by this narrow interval. Their heroic colonel was slain, the orders of officers was unheard amidst the shouts of the assailants, and all the vast uproar; yet the remnant of the Second Brigade fought on, man to man, without rank or method, with bayonet thrust and musket clubbed, but borne back like the angry foam on a mighty wave, towards the high road."

Lt. Col. Garnett, commanding the Second Brigade, gives the 21st Virginia special mention in his report of this battle. Likewise does Brig. Gen. Taliaferro of the Third Brigade. Brig. Gen. Early of Ewell's division says in his report that his attention was directed, especially in the general advance, towards a small band of the 21st Virginia with their colors; as every few minutes the color bearer would shake out his colors, seemingly in defiance to the enemy.

We remained on the battlefield all the next day, gathering the wounded and burying the dead. Gen. Jackson was joined during the day by Gen. J. E. B. Stuart, whom he ordered to take command of a reconnoitering expedition. On Stuart's return, he reported to Jackson that Pope had been heavily reinforced. In consequence, Jackson would not renew the advance, and Pope, being so much surprised at seeing the *front* of a rebel, had not recovered sufficiently to attack Jackson.

About midday, Pope asked permission of Gen. Jackson to succor such of his wounded as had not already been treated by us, and to bury his dead; this Gen. Jackson granted, and put the field of battle under the command of Brig. Gen. Early. Soon the Yank and Confederate were engaged in friendly converse, trading papers, tobacco, etc.

When night came on, Gen. Jackson thought it best to fall back behind the Rapidan, and we crossed that stream the next day, and went into camp between that river and Gordonsville. While we were there, Stark's Louisiana Brigade was added to Jackson's division; the division consisting of the First (Stonewall), Second, Third, Fourth, or Louisiana, brigades. We remained in this camp until August 16th, when we marched a few miles, and prepared for another advance against Pope.

CHAPTER XIV
SECOND MANASSAS

Longstreet having joined Jackson and Gen. Lee having completed his plans, the army broke camp on August 20th and marched in the direction of Pope's army. Jackson crossed the Rapidan river at Summerville Ford. Pope had retreated behind the Rappahannock river, and we made that river our objective point. After trying several fords with the seeming intention of crossing, the morning of the 25th found us near the village of Jeffersonton in Culpeper county. Here we received orders to cook three days' rations, and be ready to move as soon as possible. Soon afterwards, orders were given to fall in; but many of the men had not prepared their rations for want of time,—the half baked biscuit and the raw dough were left. This for many was nothing to eat for some time, probably days! The wagon train having remained behind, and everything being in light marching trim, indicated that something of importance was on hand.

As soon as the column was formed, we were hurried off on the march, passing through the village of Amissville, and crossing the Rappahannock at Hinson's Mill; thence several miles right through the country, through fields, over ditches and fences, through woods until we came to a public road. This we took, passing the village of Orleans and marching steadily until we passed Salem, about 8 or 9 o'clock at night. Here we halted in the road, stacked arms, and were told we could lie down and rest, having marched about twenty-six miles. Early the next morning we were up and on the march again, passing through Bull Run Mountain at Thoroughfare Gap, thence through Hay Market and Gainsville, not stopping until ten or eleven o'clock at night; marching about the same distance as the day before, and again stopping in the road. Many of the men lay down right where they stopped in the road, being so completely used up from the march and heat as not to have energy to move to one side. We were near Bristow Station, and not far from Manassas Junction, and far in Pope's rear, "the man that had no rear." (?) Gen. Jackson now sent a force ahead to capture Manassas, which was done during the night with small loss to us. Immense quantities of stores were captured with several trains of railroad cars, eight pieces of artillery with caissons and horses, etc., complete, a number of wagons, several hundred prisoners, and several hundred negroes, who had been persuaded to run away from their owners. Early the next morning Ewell's division marched in the direction of Bristow, the remainder of the corps to Manassas Junction, which place our division reached about 7 or 8 o'clock in the morning. The Second Brigade was filed by regiments to the right of the road, in an open field and near the storehouses, where arms were stacked, and we were ordered to rest and remain near our guns.

Not long after this it was rumored that a force from Washington was approaching to drive us away. A. P. Hill's division was sent forward to meet them, and soon put them to rout. They consisted of a brigade of infantry with some artillery, sent down to brush away a small raiding force, as they supposed us to be.

A scene around the storehouses was now witnessed, but cannot be described. Were you, when a boy, on some special occasion allowed to eat as much of everything you wanted? Were you ever a soldier, who had eaten nothing but roasting ears for two days? Well, if you have ever been either, you may probably have some conception of what followed. Only those who participated can ever appreciate it. Remember, that many of those men were hurried off on the march on the morning of the 25th with nothing to eat, that it was now the 27th, and we had marched in this time about sixty miles. The men who had prepared their rations did not have enough for two days, much less for three, and, after dividing with such comrades as had none, everything had long been eaten. Now here are vast storehouses filled with everything to eat, and sutler's stores filled with all the delicacies, potted ham, lobster, tongue, candy, cakes, nuts, oranges, lemons, pickles, catsup, mustard, etc. It makes an old soldier's mouth water now, to think of the good things captured there. A guard was placed over everything in the early part of the day, rations were issued to the men, but not by weight and measure to each man. A package or two of each article was given to each company. These are some of the articles issued to F Company. The first thing brought us was a barrel of cakes, next, a bag of hams. We secured a camp kettle, made a fire, and put a ham on to boil; and we had hardly gotten it underway before a barrel of sugar and coffee, the Yanks had it mixed, and a bag of beans were sent us. After a consultation, we decided to empty the ham out of the kettle, as we could take that along raw, and in its place put the beans on the fire, as they were something we were fond of and had not had for a long time. About the time they commenced to get warm, a bag of potatoes was brought us;—over the kettle goes, and the potatoes take the place of the beans. We now think our kettle is all right, as potatoes cook in a short time, but here comes a package of desiccated vegetables, and the kettle is again emptied, and the vegetables are placed on the fire, as soup is so good. We were also given a barrel of syrup. This was a liberal and varied bill of fare for our company, which was small then.

Gen. Jackson's idea was that he could care for the stores until Gen. Lee came up, and turn the remainder over to him, hence he placed the guard over them. The enemy began to make such demonstrations that he decided he could not hold the place, therefore the houses were thrown open, and every man was told to help himself. Our kettle of soup was left to take care of itself. Men who were starving a few hours before, and did not know when they would get another mouthful, were told to help themselves. Well, what do you think they did? Begin to eat. Oh, no. They discussed what they should eat, and what they should take with them, as orders were issued for us to take four days' rations with us. It was hard to decide what to take, some filled their haversacks with cakes, some with candy, others oranges, lemons, canned goods, etc. I know one who took nothing but French mustard, filled his haversack and was so greedy that he put one more bottle in his pocket. This was his four days' rations, and it turned out to be the best thing taken, because he traded it for meat and bread, and it lasted him until we reached Frederick City. All good times have an end, and, as night approached, preparations were made to burn everything that we could not carry; and not long after sunset the stores were set on fire. Our division, taking up our march as soon as the fires got well under way, marched several hours, when our brigade was ordered to a road on our left for picket duty. At daybreak we found ourselves on the Warrenton and Alexander pike near Groveton.

There was only one field officer in our brigade at this time, and Gen. Jackson had assigned Col. Bradley T. Johnson temporarily to command it. The Irish battalion was commanded by a major, the 48th Va. Regt. by a

lieutenant, the 42d by a captain, and the 21st by a captain.
The Second Brigade remained about Groveton until late in
the evening. Col. Johnson had orders to make
demonstrations and the biggest show he could, so as to
delay the enemy as long as possible from any advance in
this direction; and well did he do it. At one time he had
one regiment on top of a hill, with its colors under the
next hill, just high enough to show over its top; a
regiment with its colors on the next hill, etc., thus making
the appearance of a long line of battle. We had two pieces
of artillery, and as one body of the enemy was seen, one
or both pieces of artillery were brought into view, and
when the enemy moved, the cannons were limbered up
and moved also to some far hill, and the movement was
repeated.

Early in the morning, while the 21st Va. Regt. was on
one of these hills lying down in line, the enemy ran a
cannon out on a hill, unlimbered, and fired a shot at us,
hitting one of the men of Company K, tearing the heel of
his shoe off, but not injuring him. This was the first
cannon shot from either side at Second Manassas, and the
only one fired at that time, as the piece limbered up and
withdrew in a trot. When the 21st regiment soon
afterwards was deployed as skirmishers, and stationed
across the Warrenton pike, a Yankee artilleryman rode
into our line, thinking it was his. He was the first prisoner
taken.

The inmates of the Groveton house now abandoned
it,—a lady, bareheaded, and her servant woman, running
out of the front door, having a little girl between them,
each holding her by one of her hands, the child crying
loudly. They crossed the pike, climbed over the fence, and
went directly south through the fields, and were soon lost
to sight. In their excitement they did not even close the
door to their deserted home.

The Yankee wagon train was seen on a road south of us,
on its way to Washington; the two pieces of artillery were

run out and commenced to fire at them, causing a big stampede. It was now about eleven or twelve o'clock, and we retired to a wood north of the pike, formed the brigade into line of battle, stacked arms, and lay down in position.

None of the men had seen or heard anything of the remainder of our corps, and we had no idea as to where they were, and it was singular that "Old Jack" had not made his accustomed appearance along the front, the artillery fire not even bringing him. The men were much puzzled and mystified by this. Col. Johnson sent to the 21st Va. Regt. for a lieutenant and six men to report with arms, etc., at once to him; one of the men from F Company, the writer, was designated by name. On reporting, they were ordered to drive a squad of Yankees away from a house in sight. This they did in quick order, although they had to cross an open field and get over three fences before reaching the house. We remained at the house a while, and seeing that we were about to be cut off, we retired to the brigade without loss. This was the first musket fire of Second Manassas, and it may be said that the battle had commenced, the enemy being seen in several directions towards our front. The officer returning to Col. Johnson made his report, when the colonel retained the "F" man, the writer, and ordered him to go out to the front as far as possible without being seen by the enemy, and keep a lookout, reporting to him any body of the enemy seen approaching, and, in order to get along the better, to leave his arms. I crept to the front until I reached a bush on top of a slight elevation, where I lay down for several hours, observing the movements of several small bodies of the enemy, mostly cavalry. While I was lying down behind the bush, an incident occurred that has always puzzled me. I heard the quick step of a horse to my right and rear, and looking around I saw a horseman in full gallop, coming from the north and going along a small country road that joined the Warrenton pike at Groveton house. Arriving at the gap in the fence along

the road, he wheeled his horse and rode directly towards
me as I lay down in the field; and it was done in such a
deliberate way as to impress the vidette that his presence
was known before the horseman came along the road. He
did not draw rein until he was almost on the vidette, when
he asked if the vidette knew where Gen. Jackson was.
Receiving a negative reply, he wheeled his horse and rode
back to the gap, turned into the road, and was off at full
gallop towards Groveton house. This man was riding a
black mare, and wore a long linen duster and dark pants;
there was something so suspicious about his movements
and dress, that the vidette would have taken him to Col.
Johnson if he had had his gun. There was a squad of
Yankees at the Groveton house, and when the rider
reached it, several of them ran from the front of the house
and surrounded him. He dismounted and went with them
to the front of the house while one of their number led the
horse into the back yard and tied him. This was hardly
done before a body of our cavalry charged up the
Warrenton pike, and captured the party. The vidette had
seen that detachment coming along the road a few
minutes before, and could have warned the man riding the
horse of the Yankees' presence, but a distrust came over
him as soon as I saw him.

About 4 o'clock in the afternoon the vidette was
startled by a long line of skirmishers stepping out of the
wood in his front and advancing. Jumping to my feet, I
started towards Col. Johnson and having gone only a short
distance, I saw their line of battle following. Now that
fellow just "dusted" made his report to Col. Johnson, who
called the line to attention, and gave the command,
"Right face! double quick! march!" and away we went
northward through the woods. All of us were wondering
what had become of Jackson, but when we were through
the woods, the first man we saw was "Old Jack," and
looking beyond, we could see that his command was
massed in a large field, arms stacked, batteries parked, and
everything resting. Col. Johnson rode up to him and made

his report. Gen. Jackson turned at once to his staff, gave each an order, and, in a minute, the field was in a perfect hubbub,—men riding in all directions, infantry rushing to arms, cannoneers to their guns and the drivers mounting. We saw the master hand now. In the time I am taking to tell this, one heard the sharp command of an officer, "Right face, forward march," and saw a body of skirmishers march out of that confused mass right up to "Old Jack," where the officer gave the command, "File right," and the next instant the command to deploy. The movement was done in the twinkling of an eye. Forward they went to meet the enemy. Gen. Jackson had waited to see this; he now turned to Col. Johnson and told him to let his men stack arms and rest, as they had been on duty since the day before; he would not call on them if he could avoid it; and off he went with the advance skirmishers. Another body of them had, in the meantime, marched out and filed to the left, and gone forward. A column of infantry unwound itself out of that mass, marched up to the point where the skirmishers had been filed to the right, fronted, and went forward. Another was now filing to the left, while the third column moved straight ahead, a part of the artillery following each column of infantry. This was the most perfect movement of troops I saw during the war. The crack of muskets and the bang of artillery told us that the lines had met, and the fire in a few minutes was terrific. An officer soon came, however, ordering the Second Brigade to report on the extreme left of Jackson's line, where the whole brigade was formed as skirmishers, ordered forward and, after going a certain distance, halted, and ordered to lie down. We stayed there all night, sleeping on our arms. The enemy did not appear in our front; but our right had a hard fight, in which the enemy were defeated, retreating during the night. Brig. Gen. Taliaferro, commanding Jackson's division, and Maj. Gen. Ewell were amongst our wounded.

The next morning, August 29th, the Second Brigade marched to the right of Jackson's line, on top of a large hill, where there were several pieces of artillery. We stayed there about an hour, and were shelled severely by the enemy, who had made their appearance from another direction than that of the evening before.

Jackson now took position behind an unfinished railroad, which ran parallel to and north of the Warrenton pike, and, I suppose, about a mile from it. Jackson's division was on the right, Ewell's next, and A. P. Hill's on the left. The Second Brigade marched from the hill to the left about half a mile, where we joined our division and formed two lines of battle, in a wood and near its edge, facing south. In our front there was a narrow neck of open land, about three hundred yards wide; on the west, the wood ran along this field about three hundred yards to a point where the field joined a larger field. A short distance around the angle of the wood was the hill which we occupied early in the morning, and Jackson had now several batteries of artillery on it. On the east, the woods ran along the field for six hundred yards to a point where the field joined a large field; this large field ran east and west and at its far side the Warrenton pike ran. About two hundred yards in our front was a part of the abandoned railroad, running across the open neck from the wood on the east to near that of the west. The eastern end of the road was in a valley, where there was a fill for about one hundred yards, extending to a hill through which a cut ran out on the level ground just before it reached the west wood. The reader will notice now that in front of the railroad there was a short strip of wood on the west side and a long strip on the east. Our skirmishers were stationed at the railroad; we were ordered to lie down in line, guns in hand, and directed to rush for the railroad as soon as an order to forward should be given.

Col. Johnson came along the line, stopped about ten yards in front of F Company, took out his pipe, filled it and lighted it, and quietly sat on the ground, leaning against a small sapling.

Everything was perfectly quiet, but this did not last long. The stillness in our front was broken by a shot, and almost in the same instant a shell went crashing through the trees overhead. This was the signal for a severe shelling of our woods; a man was wounded. Col. Johnson immediately arose, went to him, sent him to the rear, and stopped long enough to talk to the men around him, and quiet their uneasiness. He came back and resumed his seat. This was repeated several times. The enemy now advanced and engaged our skirmishers at the railroad, some of the balls aimed at them occasionally reached our line, and wounded some of the men. Col. Johnson invited several of the men who were becoming uneasy to come and sit by him, and he had about a dozen around him, talking and laughing. Our skirmishers were now being driven from the railroad, and soon they retired to the line of battle. The enemy were now some distance north of the railroad in our front. The brigade being called to attention, instantly was on its feet, and when the order was given to forward, it rushed to the front. Reaching the field, we emptied our guns into the enemy, and charged them with empty guns. They turned and ran, leaving many dead and wounded on our side of the railroad. Approaching these men, lying on the ground about one hundred yards from us, I noticed one of them on his back, gesticulating with his hands, raising them up, moving them violently backward and forward. I thought he was trying to attract our attention, so that we might not injure him in our advance. When I reached him, I recognized by his shoulder straps that he was a Yankee captain, and one of our captains, who was running on my left, said he was making the masonic sign of distress. Arriving at the railroad, the 21st Va. Regt. occupied the bank, and the remainder of the Second Brigade occupied the cut on our right. We loaded and fired at the retreating enemy, and soon cleared the field.

Expecting a renewal of the attack by the enemy, we

remained at the railroad, and, after a short halt, the announcement "Here they come!" was heard. A line of battle marched out of the far end of the east wood into the field, halted, dressed the line, and moved forward. They were allowed to come within about one hundred yards of us, when we opened fire. We could see them stagger, halt, stand a short time, break, and run. At this time, another line made its appearance, coming from the same point. It came a little nearer. They, too, broke and ran. Still another line came nearer, broke, and ran. The whole field seemed to be full of Yankees and some of them advanced nearly to the railroad. We went over the bank at them, the remainder of the brigade following our example. The enemy now broke and ran, and we pursued, firing as fast as we could. We followed them into the woods, and drove them out on the other side, where we halted and were ordered back to the railroad. We captured two pieces of artillery in the woods, and carried them back with us. As we returned a Yankee battery of eight guns had full play on us in the field, and our line became a little confused; we halted, every man instantly turned and faced the battery. As we did so, I heard a thud on my right, as if one had been struck with a heavy fist. Looking around I saw a man at my side standing erect, with his head off, a stream of blood spurting a foot or more from his neck. As I turned farther around, I saw three others lying on the ground, all killed by this cannon shot. The man standing was a captain in the 42d Va. Regt., and his brains and blood bespattered the face and clothing of one of my company, who was standing in my rear. This was the second time I saw four men killed by one shot. The other occurred in the battle of Cedar Run, a few weeks earlier. Each time the shot struck as it was descending,—the first man had his head taken off, the next was shot through the breast, the next through the stomach, and the fourth had all his bowels torn out.

We went back to our position in the woods, formed our

old line of battle in two lines, and lay down as before. Immediately our attention was called to a line of battle filing into position in our front, but nearly at right angles to us. What did this mean? Were the enemy making preparations to storm us again? General Starke, our division commander, arrived, his attention was called to the line, he used his glass, and, after a careful survey, called a courier, and directed him to go to the right around the hill in our front, and find out who they were. The Yankees were shelling our woods heavily, but the excitement was so great that the men, who had orders to lie down for protection, were all standing up watching the line form, which grew longer each moment. Our courier, after a short stay, was seen coming as fast as his horse could run, and before he reached General Starke, cried out, "It is Longstreet!" A great cry that Longstreet had come was taken up by the men all down the line. The courier now told General Starke that the man sitting on a stump, whom we had noticed before, was General Lee; and that Longstreet said he had gotten up in time to witness our charge, which, he said, was splendid!

This put new life into Jackson's men, who had heard nothing of Longstreet. They knew that if Pope with his large army would put forth energy, he could greatly damage us; but every thought was changed now. We only wished for a renewal of the attack, but were afraid he would not attack us after his repulse on the morning and the presence of Longstreet! He did attack A. P. Hill's division on the left, and met with the same kind of repulse that we had given him. A part of Longstreet's command became heavily engaged also. This ended the second day's fighting, and the Second Brigade was jubilant over its share of Second Manassas so far.

The cannonading commenced early on the morning of the 30th with skirmishing in front that at times became active. About noon, expecting an attack, the Second Brigade moved to the railroad, taking position as on the

The Battle of Second Manassas

day before. About 2 or 3 o'clock we heard on our right, the sound of "Here they come!" and almost instantly we saw a column of the enemy march into the field from the point at which they appeared the day before, dressing the line and advancing on us. Every man in our line shifted his cartridge box to the front, unstrapped it and his cap box, gave his gun a second look, and took his position to meet the coming enemy, who were rapidly approaching. We allowed them to come about the same distance as on the day before, and then opened fire, with about the same result. Other lines advanced, each getting nearer us; the field was filled with Yanks as on the day before, but in much greater numbers, and their advance continued. Every man in the Second Brigade at this moment remembered Cedar Run, each one loaded his gun with care, raised it deliberately to his shoulder, took deadly aim, and pulled the trigger! We were fighting now as I never saw it done, we behind the railroad bank and in the cut, which made a splendid breastwork, the enemy crowded in the field, their men falling fast, as we could plainly see. Our ammunition was failing, our men taking it from the boxes of dead and wounded comrades. The advance of the enemy continued; by this time they were at the bank, they mounting it, our men mounting too, some with guns loaded, some with bayonets fixed, some with muskets clubbed, and some with large rocks in their hands. (Col. Johnson in his official report says he saw a man's skull crushed by a rock in the hands of one of his brigade.) A short struggle on top of the bank, and in front of the cut, and the battle was ours! The enemy were running! and then went up that yell that only Confederates could make! Some men were wild with excitement, hats were off, some up in the air! It was right here that Lieut. Rawlings, commanding F Company, was killed!—his hat in one hand, his sword in the other, cheering his men to victory! He was struck in the head by a rifle ball, and fell dead.

After the flying enemy we went, through the field in

our front, to the woods on the left, through that into the next field, where we could see our line advancing in all directions, our artillery firing over our heads! Some of the artillery following in the pursuit, and nearing a hill, ran up, unlimbered, and fired rapidly through openings in our advancing line, thousands of muskets fired, the men giving the old yell! It was one of those inspiring scenes, which its actors will never forget, and made a staunch soldier of a recruit!

We kept up the pursuit until eight or nine o'clock in the night, when we halted, and were allowed to rest until morning. The man, "with headquarters in the saddle," who "had no rear," was taught the second lesson of Jackson's tactics. He wished now that he had a rear, as he was putting forth all his efforts to find Washington with its fortifications, which was forty-five or fifty miles in his rear, when we commenced our movement.

The loss in our brigade was small. Among the killed was Lieut. Edward G. Rawlings, commanding F Company. He was as good a soldier as the war produced, a magnificent specimen of manhood, tall and erect, over six feet in his stockings, weighing about two hundred pounds, with endurance in proportion to his size. I have often heard him say he could march forever, if his feet would not become sore. He was kind and gentle, always at his post doing his duty.

To Jackson belongs the chief honor of Second Manassas, as in the first battle of Manassas, and the position held by the Second Brigade was one of the points on which the enemy made many desperate and repeated assaults; in all of which they were repulsed with great loss. I saw more of their dead lying on the ground in our front than I saw in the same space during the war.

One of our company wrote home that he was shot all to pieces, having twenty-seven holes shot through his blanket. In his next letter he explained that his blanket was folded, and one shot going through it, made the twenty-seven holes!

I take pleasure in adding my mite of praise to our division and brigade commanders. Brig. Gen. Taliaferro, commanding the division the first evening, was wounded. Brig. Gen. Starke of the Louisiana Brigade succeeded him. This was his first experience in handling a division, but he did it with great skill; he was conspicuous for gallantry, and seemed to be at the right spot at the right moment! His conduct was such as to endear him to this old command, and when he was killed at its head, a few weeks later, many an eye was dimmed by a tear!

It was the unanimous sentiment of the Second Brigade that they were never handled as well as they were by Colonel Bradley T. Johnson, during this battle and the rest of the time he was with us. His personal interest in the men went right to their hearts, and they showed their appreciation by obeying every order with cheerfulness and alacrity. And we made him a Brigadier General. Here is an extract from a letter written to the Secretary of War by Lieut. Gen. Jackson, in which he speaks of Col. Johnson and the Second Brigade at Second Manassas: "The heroism with which the brigade fought, and its success in battle, but brightened my opinion of its commander."

It is not generally known that the ground occupied by the enemy in the battle of First and Second Manassas was almost the same. The junction of the Warrenton pike and the Sudley road was an important point in both battles. In the first battle, they marched southward along the Sudley road to the Stone House at the junction of the Warrenton pike and thence moved to the Southeast. In the second battle, they marched Northward along the same road to the Stone House, and from that point Northwest. Some of their guns occupied the same hills during both battles. In the first, firing to the Southeast, and in the second, reversing and firing to the Northwest.

CHAPTER XV

THE MARYLAND CAMPAIGN— HARPER'S FERRY AND SHARPSBURG

T HE MORNING AFTER the battle of Second Manassas, the pursuit of the enemy was resumed, and continued all day. The next morning, Sept. 1st, Jackson advanced by the Little River Turnpike, and about noon learned that the enemy had made a stand near Chantily, or Ox Hill. He immediately made arrangements to attack them. When we were ready to advance, it commenced to rain, lasting a short time, but coming down in torrents! At its height, the Yanks made an attack on us, which was as sudden and almost as furious as the rainstorm! We repulsed this attack and advanced, but night came on and put a stop to the fight. The enemy lost two generals, killed in this battle; one of them being Phil Kearney. It is said that Gen. Jackson was told by one of his officers that the rain had wet and ruined all the ammunition of his men, and the officer desired to know what he must do about it. Gen. Jackson replied that the rain had ruined the enemy's, too! We lay down in our wet clothes on the wet ground for rest, and arose early in the morning, feeling stiff and sore. We marched in pursuit of the enemy a short distance, and heard that during the night they had retreated, and sought protection in their fortifications around Washington. As night approached we made preparations for a good rest, as it was the first we had had for a week out of sight of the enemy, and we made good use of it, feeling the next morning like new men. We started on the march early in the morning. Soon it was passed from lip to lip along the line that we were going into Maryland. This created great excitement among the men, and they stepped off so briskly as to give no suggestion that these men had had only one night's rest and none during the day, for more than a week! At night we halted, and were allowed another good rest. Our wagons joined us during the night, and the next morning we were given time to cook rations, the first that the men had cooked since Aug. 25th. It would have done one good to sit down by one of the fires and watch the men! As one "spider" of biscuits and one frying pan of meat was cooked, it was immediately divided and eaten, then another was cooked and eaten, most of the rations for the twenty-four hours being thus disposed of. After the cooking was done and wagons were loaded, we resumed our march, and halted at night in the neighborhood of Leesburg. The next morning, Sept. 5th, we marched again, and about 9 or 10 o'clock in the morning the Second Brigade reached the Potomac river, and forded it at White's Ford, with great enthusiasm, —bands playing, men singing and cheering! Reaching Maryland, we marched up the tow path of the Washington Canal a short distance to the locks, where we crossed the canal on a bridge, then took a road and continued our march until night; camping in the neighborhood of the Three Springs, resuming the march the next morning. The Second Brigade, Col. Bradley T. Johnson commanding, was given the advance of the army, and late in the evening we came to the Baltimore & Ohio R. R. depot near Frederick City, and saw several cars loaded with watermelons. The men broke ranks as they passed and many secured a melon, and hurried back to his place.

Soon afterwards we entered Frederick City, many of the men having watermelons in their arms. We marched to the Fair Grounds, which had been fitted up as a large hospital for the enemy. Our brigade stacked arms, and were told to make themselves comfortable for the night. A guard was placed around our camp, in order to prevent the men from straggling through the town. A friend and I succeeded in passing the guard, and took a stroll through the town. We were invited into several houses and entertained handsomely at supper, eating enough for half a dozen men. After being absent for some time, we returned to our quarters. Reaching my company I was told to report to brigade headquarters at once. I thought something terrible was to pay now, did not know whether I was to be shot or sent to prison, but I knew something was to be done with me. I was soon ready, found headquarters, and reported to the adjutant general. He greeted me cheerfully, and told me to go at once to the enemy's hospital, ask for the surgeon in charge, get a list from him of the names of all the inmates, and write a parole for each, according to a copy he furnished me. He said the surgeon in charge would give me all the information wanted, and render me any assistance that was needed.

I went back to my company with a light heart, made disposition of my gun and ammunition, and took my baggage with me. I will take occasion to tell what that consisted of, and at same time will say that it was rather above the average in our army, as to quality as well as quantity. I had a very good oilcloth haversack to carry my rations in, a tin cup, a splendid rubber cloth, a blanket, a pair of jeans drawers, and a pair of woolen socks; every article captured from the enemy! The socks and drawers were placed in the blanket, the blanket was rolled up with the rubber cloth on the outside, the ends drawn together and fastened with a short strap. To carry this we put it over the head and let it hang from the shoulder. Thus equipped, I reported to the surgeon. He treated me very politely, gave me a list of about seven hundred men who were in the hospital, conducted me into one of the dining-rooms, gave me a lamp, pen, ink, and paper, and told me to use one of the tables. He thought it the best place, because I would have plenty of room, and no one to disturb me. I cleaned the table and prepared for action, sat down and commenced to write at once. I tell you it was a job, as I had to write every word of the paroles for those men in duplicate, one for the prisoner and one for us. I wrote until about twelve at night, when the doctor came in and brought me a nice lunch. He sat down, and we had a pleasant talk for about an hour, he leaving and I continuing my writing until nearly day, when I lay down on one of the benches, and had a good nap. I arose, went to the pump, washed myself, looked up my company, had a little chat with them, and went back to my dining-room, keeping at my work until it was finished, the doctor sending me my meals. After I had finished, I reported at headquarters to the adjutant general, who told me to stay there, that I was wanted for special duty, as Col. Johnson was in command of the town, and had the Second Brigade on guard duty. I stayed at headquarters until Sept. 10th, when Jackson's corps left the city, taking the road to Hagerstown, and camping that night near Boonsboro.

I was marching at the head of the column, and reaching Boonsboro the next morning, saw the advance cavalry enter and pass through the village. Gen. Jackson followed a short distance after them, and at a house near the corner of a cross street, dismounted, and tying his horse, entered the house. He had hardly entered the house before a body of cavalry charged through the village on the cross street, in full sight of the head of our column. When we reached the village, we learned that they were a body of Yanks, who had made a dash through our line. This was a narrow escape for Jackson, as he surely would have been captured if he had ridden on, or delayed his going into the house! The god of battle took care of him; it was not destined that the Yanks should get him!

We turned to the left and marched to Williamsport, crossing the Potomac into Virginia. I made a big speculation at Williamsport; my messmates asked me to get some soda, as we needed it to make our biscuits. I went to a drug store to get it, asked the salesman for a pound, and the price was only eight cents. I gave him a Confederate note, which he took without hesitation, and gave me change. I then asked what he would sell a keg for; his reply, six cents per pound. I paid him at once, shouldered the keg, one hundred and twenty pounds, carried it to the river, where I induced a wagon to carry it to camp for me. I sold it that night for twenty-five cents per pound! We marched to the neighborhood of North Mountain depot on the B. & O. R. R., and camped for the night.

The next morning we continued our march, passing through Martinsburg, where we captured from the enemy a good lot of stores, they retreating to Harper's Ferry, and we going into camp for the night not far from Martinsburg.

In the morning we marched to Harper's Ferry, where the enemy were fortified, and were awaiting us. We skirmished some, driving the enemy in, and locating their position, we rested in our places for the night, and the next morning a line of battle was formed, Jackson's division on the left, its left resting on the Potomac river, Ewell's division next, and A. P. Hill's on the right, and their right resting on the Shenandoah river. Our skirmishers drove those of the enemy all along the line, and the artillery from each side commenced firing. We were joined in the afternoon by artillery from Maryland and Shenandoah Heights, and learned, through this, that we had help from McLaws, who occupied the former, and Walker the latter position. Both of these commands were sending shot into the doomed enemy. Firing was kept up in this way until late in the evening, when we made several attacks on different positions of the enemy, capturing them, gaining much advantage, and bringing our line closer to their fortifications. Night coming on, we rested in our places. Early the next morning the guns all along our line opened, and the infantry was preparing for a general charge, when the white flag was seen in several places along the enemy's fortifications. In a little while firing ceased and soon after it was announced that the enemy had surrendered!

Some of the headquarters folks had offered to feed a horse for me, if I would get one. My opportunity had come. Making my way to the fortifications, I clambered over them, saw the Yankees had stacked their arms, and were parking their artillery and wagons. I was surrounded at once and plied with all kinds of questions as to what Jackson would do with them. Since I did not know anything about the terms of surrender, I could tell them nothing. I took a Colt's army pistol from one of them, and buckling it around my waist, went on my way looking for a horse. McLaws had not ceased firing; every now and then a shot from his guns would drop near me. A Yankee major rode up to me and in a very rough manner wanted to know "why your people kept firing on us, after we had surrendered?" I told him very politely to ask Gen. Jackson. I approached a line of tents that looked as if they were abandoned; going among these, I was delighted by the sight of as fine a horse with equipment as I had ever seen. He was tied to a stake near a tent, and my heart fairly leaped to my throat as I went to him, untied and mounted him! As I started off a Yankee colonel came from a tent, spoke to me very politely, and inquired what I intended to do with his horse. I replied that I was very much obliged to him and would take good care of him for Harper's Ferry's sake. He asked me to stop, which I did, and he came forward and told me that probably I did not know the terms of the surrender; then he told me that Gen. Jackson had allowed the officers to retain their arms, horses, equipments and private baggage, and added that he had no fear of my taking his horse after learning the terms. I sadly turned the horse's head toward the stake, rode him to it, and fastened him. The colonel invited me into his tent to take a lunch, as he called it, which was a big dinner for an old Confederate; he also placed several bottles on the table, from which I might help myself. I disliked the losing of the horse, but could not take him after the terms were made known to me; indeed, the behavior of the officer so impressed me, that it would have saved the horse to him, if the terms had not been known!

I walked around and looked at the long lines of stacked muskets, the park of artillery and wagons, gave up my notion of a horse, and soon wended my way back to our line over the route I had come. While I was inside of the enemy's fortification, I did not see a Confederate. We captured over eleven thousand prisoners, seventy-two pieces of artillery with caissons, horses, etc., about ten thousand muskets, several hundred wagons with mules, and a large quantity of stores. Gen. A. P. Hill and his division attended to the surrender. Jackson's and Ewell's divisions were withdrawn from the line, and, stacking arms, were allowed to rest. In the afternoon we were ordered to cook rations, and be ready to move as soon as possible; and, as night approached, we were under arms and marched, taking the road to Shepherdstown.

SHARPSBURG

Jackson's division marched all night, passed through Shepherdstown the next morning, and forded the Potomac at Boteler's Ford, a little below the town. We were in Maryland the second time. Marching a short distance from the river, we came to the town of Sharpsburg, and passing through it, marched about a mile, halted near the Tunker or Dunkard church, stacked arms, and were told that we could rest. We remained there several hours and were much refreshed. We marched up the Hagerstown road about half a mile, when, in passing through a field, we were heavily assailed by shot and shell from the enemy. We marched a short distance and formed a line of battle; Jackson's division occupied the left of our line of battle, and was formed in two lines on the left or west of the Hagerstown road, and at nearly right angles to the road. The Second and Stonewall Brigades were formed in the front line, in a field, the Stonewall Brigade resting on the Hagerstown road and connecting with Ewell's division, the line under the command of Lt. Col. A. J. Grigsby of the Stonewall Brigade. Starke's and the Third Brigade were formed in a wood about two or three hundred yards in our rear, and were commanded by Brig. Gen. Starke. We had been in position only a short time, when the enemy opened a heavy fire on us from guns in front and on our right. This was continued until late in the night. We went to sleep in line!

On the morning of the 17th we saw that McClellan had decidedly the advantage in position. His artillery in our front was on higher ground, and on the right his guns on high hills beyond the Antietam could enfilade us, and farther up the mountain side we saw his signal flags at work. They seemed to overlook our entire line. We were not allowed to make much of an observation before the enemy's shells dropped in our midst from batteries in front and flank, and this soon became the fiercest artillery fire of the war. It seemed that the air was alive with shells! This fire continued a short time, when their infantry in dense masses attacked us. After stubborn fighting, they were driven back with heavy loss, and the artillery commenced again, a fiercer fusilade than before! Gen. Jones, commanding the division, left the field on account of injuries received from this fire! Brig. Gen. Starke, our commander in battle of Second Manassas, assumed command of the division, and ordered a charge by the entire division, which was promptly obeyed; and while he was leading the division, received three musket balls, and fell dead! We retired to a lane on the edge of the field, where the fighting was terrific! We were finally forced back by overwhelming numbers into the woods, and here succeeded in driving the enemy back; we finally retired through the woods into a field, and were allowed by the enemy to rest a short time.

Old F Company had reached low water mark! After Second Manassas there were only three men to answer roll call,—Malcolm L. Hudgins, Reuben J. Jordan, and John H. Worsham. As we had no officer, we were ordered to report to Capt. Page of Company D, and when we did so, he called us young gentlemen, and told us we might march and camp anywhere we chose in the regiment, reporting to him once daily, and in the event of a fight, reporting at once; and ended by saying we might call the roll as often as we chose! This gallant and good man had to pay the penalty of commanding F Company, losing a leg in this battle. We were known during the Maryland campaign as the guerrillas of the 21st. At Harper's Ferry the company had Hudgins and Jordan to stand up for them, and at Sharpsburg Hudgins got sick, and Jordan was the only man with the company in that terrible battle. By a singular circumstance, Jordan was detailed as a skirmisher, sent out to the front and, when the line was deployed, was on the left of that line, and was the soldier that held the left of Gen. Lee's line of battle. His position was on the edge of a wood, and when the line on his right in the field was driven back; Jordan gathered a few of his comrades from the right, and held back the line until he found he was outflanked on his left; and that the enemy's line was far in his rear. He made a run for safety, going back to our line of battle, and found that it had retired, and that he and his few comrades had been left! Hurrah for Jordan! Hurrah for F Company! in having such a representative! He passed along the lane and saw the great slaughter of friend and foe, then to the woods and through them to a field. Here he noticed a body of men in the field to his right, but kept on until he reached the other side of the field where he found Gen. Jackson and staff. Inquiring of one of the staff for his division, he was told that the body of men he had passed was the remnant.

At this moment Jackson was in the most critical position of his military career! His entire line had been driven back beyond the Dunkard church, and they were holding on now by a mere thread, but succor was at hand! Brig. Gen. Early with his brigade which had been detached to assist Gen. J. E. B. Stuart's cavalry on the extreme left, arrived, and McLaws' division was expected every minute!

Jordan, who had been retracing his steps in order to get to his command, now saw the first brigade of McLaws arrive on the field, and heard the commanding officer give his sharp command, "On the right by file into line! Double quick! March!" In a run and under fire the line was formed. Jordan stopped long enough to inquire who they were and to see the line grow every moment, and then hurried to his command with the good news. Arriving, he saw Gen. Early and Col. Grigsby, commander of our division, in consultation. It is said that Early directed Grigsby with his division to make an attack on the enemy who were again advancing with a large force. That he would take his brigade to the left, pass swiftly around the brow of a hill and attack the enemy in flank and rear. This attack was a great success, in which McLaws' troops joined, and the enemy were driven back at this point with great slaughter!

Old Jack, who had been riding along his line, got his mettle up with this success, and ordered an advance along his entire line; the men replied with the old yell, and the bayonet! The enemy were hurriedly driven out of the woods and across the Hagerstown road; and Jackson's old line was reëstablished. The firing soon was confined to that of the sharpshooters; the enemy having suffered so much that they made no more attacks on Jackson's line.

Oh, for a few more men! With one good division we could have routed the enemy; but alas! Gen. Lee had fought every man he had, except one division on his right! This was soon attacked and driven back, but A. P. Hill, who had just marched upon the field from Harper's Ferry, seeing the situation, wheeled his division into line, and attacked the enemy with such vigor that they were driven across the Antietam!

At night we lay down on our arms, and the next morning were up bright and early, expecting a renewal of the battle, but the enemy were badly whipped, and did not make any demonstration during the day. The skirmish fire, which was feeble, and occasionally a shelling from his far off guns, were all he attempted.

The loss in Jackson's command was larger, in proportion to the men he had engaged, than in any battle he fought during the war.

Col. Penn, commanding the Second Brigade, lost a leg; Capt. Page of the 21st Va. Regt., commanding the skirmishers of the brigade, lost a leg also; men and officers were killed and wounded by hundreds! Our brigade came out of the fight in command of Lieut. John A. Booker, of the 21st Va. Regt., and the division under command of Lieut. Col. Grigsby. It was no larger than a good regiment!

The little Tunker or Dunkard church, situated in the nice grove on the Hagerstown road, had become famous. Around this church some of the fiercest fighting of the war had just taken place. Dead and wounded men lay in sight of it by thousands.

During the night of the 18th we marched from our position towards the Potomac river, which all of Lee's army forded into Virginia, my brigade crossing after sunrise on the morning of the 19th.

All our army crossed in safety, and without molestation. The enemy, however, attempted to follow us on the 20th. After a corps had crossed, Gen. Jackson ordered A. P. Hill to attack them, and drive them back. Hill attacked with his division and drove them back with great slaughter; driving them into the river, where most of them were drowned, very few reaching the Maryland shore. This ended the Maryland campaign.

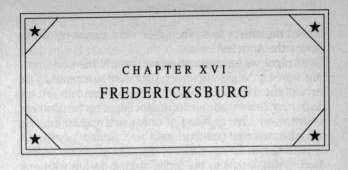

AFTER LEAVING MARYLAND, Jackson's Corps marched to the neighborhood of Martinsburg; here they were busy several days in the work of destroying the B. & O. R. R., tearing up the track for about forty miles. We took up the rails, laid them aside, pulled up and stacked the ties, then set them on fire, and placed the rails on them. When the rails became hot they bent. Whenever there were trees or telegraph poles convenient, we twisted the rails around them, while they were hot in the center, which could easily be done.

We stayed several weeks in the lower valley, mostly in Jefferson County, every few days moving our camp; sometimes because of an alarm from the enemy, sometimes merely to be in a fresh place. Gen. Jackson did not allow his men to camp in one place too long. New camps were more healthy, in consequence of which, we rarely stayed two weeks in the same place. It was very easy for the men to move, because by this time we had learned to live without tents. The only shelter the men had was oil or rubber cloths and cotton flies. The latter were pieces of cotton about four by six feet in size, hemmed around the borders. Button holes were worked around these borders and buttons sewed on at certain places; they were so arranged that three of them buttoned together made a very comfortable shelter for three men. We were dependent on the Yankees for them, as I never heard of our quartermaster issuing any. The men who could not get these, made a "shebang," by putting two forked sticks in the ground, about six feet apart, laying a pole in the forks, placing bushes with one end on the ground, the other inclined to the pole, enclosing in this way one side and the ends, and leaving the other side open. This would accommodate three or four men. The men with care could make them impervious to rain. They were very comfortable in warm weather. In moving, all that was needed was to roll up our fly or oilcloth and take it with us, put our small lot of cooking utensils in the wagons, put on our accouterments, and take arms. Then we were ready for a march to another camp, or to meet the enemy.

While we were in one of these camps, one evening at regimental dress parade, one of the soldiers was conducted under guard along the front of the regiment with a large placard attached to him, on which "Thief" was written, two soldiers marching behind him with guns at charge bayonet! This was the first and only man I saw punished in that way during the war. We punished some by making them ride a wooden horse, by standing on a stump, or by putting a barrel over them, with the inscription on it, showing what they had been guilty of.

On Nov. 21st we took up our march to join Gen. Lee at Fredericksburg, it being reported that he thought he would soon need us. We marched up the Valley pike, to New Market, left the Valley pike, crossed the Massanutta Mountain, and crossed the Blue Ridge at Fisher's Gap. My brigade was in front while we were crossing the Blue Ridge, and we enjoyed one of the most inspiring views I saw during the war. It is said that the road leading over the mountain at this gap is six miles long from the valley to the top, and seven miles from the top to the foot in Madison County. Near the top, as we were marching, there was a large rock on the side of the road. Stepping on this rock, and looking back and down the road, we could see six lines of our army; in one place infantry, in another artillery, in another ambulances and wagons. Some seemed to be coming towards us, some going to the right, some to the left, and some going away from us. They were all, however, climbing the winding mountain road, and following us. We passed Madison C. H., Orange C. H., through the Wilderness and by Chancellorsville,—which became famous and full of grief before we left it!—and on to the neighborhood of Guinea's Station on the R. F. & P. R. R. There we went into camp on Dec. 2d, having marched from fifteen to twenty-three miles each day since we left Winchester.

Winter had come, and many of the men were shoeless. They could not obtain them, and finally orders were issued in Jackson's division, that the men should get the hides of the cattle we daily killed, and make moccasins of them. It became such a serious matter that a list of shoemakers in the division was made, a member of F Company was sent to Richmond to get leather, etc., in order to enable these men to make shoes in camp for their comrades! This man went to Richmond, attending to his orders, and on the morning of Dec. 11th read a telegram that the enemy, now under Gen. Burnside, were crossing at Fredericksburg. He, at once, went to the Provost Marshal's office to get a pass to leave the city (no one could leave without this permission) by the first train, but was told that he must report to Sergeant Crow, who would carry him up under guard, and turn him over to his proper command. This indignity he did not intend to submit to, and so informed the officer, explaining to him how he was sent to Richmond, and showing him his papers. He did not ask for transportation, as he was willing to pay his railroad fare; he only wanted the necessary permission to leave the city, in order to join his command and take his post in the expected battle! The only answer he received was, "You must report to Sergeant Crow." He left, and went back three times during the day, with hope that he would find another man in command, who would be more civil and accommodating; but without success. The next morning he went again very early, and one of the men there threatened to take him into custody; but he left very quickly. He returned about an hour later, when an old comrade, who had witnessed the way in which his friend was treated the day before, quietly slipped a pass into his hand. This comrade was an old member of our regiment, who had lost a leg in battle, when he was with us, and was at this time employed in the provost office. This is mentioned to show how far red tape goes!

Going at once to the depot, he boarded a train that was pulling out, and reached Guinea's about one or two o'clock on the 12th. Making inquiries, he learned that Jackson's corps had gone to the front, and after tiresome walking found his command at Hamilton's Crossing, awaiting orders to take its place in line of battle. On the morning of Dec. 13th, Jackson's division was assigned to Jackson's second line of battle and was lying down on the ground, awaiting the movements of the enemy. Gen. Jackson soon made his appearance along the line with a cavalcade of officers following him. He was dressed in a brand-new uniform, with the usual gold lace trimmings for a lieutenant general. He even had exchanged the old gray cap for a new bespangled one, and looked so unlike our "Old Jack" that very few noticed him, and none recognized him until after he had passed. Then the old accustomed cheer to him went up with unusual vigor! About ten o'clock the fog lifted, and the cannonading from the enemy commenced; it was awfully terrific, as, it is said, they had two hundred and fifty or three hundred guns, sending shot and shell at us! Soon afterwards the Yankees in our front made their advance. We were in the woods on a slight hill, that over-looked an immense open field. The number of the enemy visible to us gave the impression that the whole of the Yankee army was in our front! A battery to our right and front was pouring shot and shell into them as they advanced. We learned after the fight that it was Pelham's! What a grand and heroic stand he maintained during the battle! Jackson's artillery was posted along our front, but did not fire a shot at the advancing lines until they got within easy range, when all of it opened at once, and sent its hail of iron into the dense masses, making them stagger, then stop, and then retreat to a road, where they were protected by its banks and fences! An hour or so afterwards they made another advance, and this time with so much determination that they broke the first of our lines, and commenced the advance more vigorously; when our second line was ordered forward, and charged! After some stubborn fighting at several points, they were driven back along their entire line with great loss. They continued their retreat to the road and river bank. Their skirmishers and batteries kept up a fire during the whole day.

A splendid line of breastworks had been made around Marye's Hill, extending along the line of Generals Hill and Longstreet. They did not extend as far east as the position occupied by Jackson during the battle of Fredericksburg on Dec. 13. The fight in Jackson's front was a regular stand-up one; the only protection we had was such as the woods afforded. As evening advanced, Jackson arranged his lines; the second brigade occupying the railroad in the first line of battle. Here we awaited the expected advance of the enemy, and only wished they would come. Skirmish fire and fire from their far guns was kept up at intervals during the 14th. The next day the enemy asked permission to look after their wounded, who were in the field in Jackson's front. This was granted, and the pickets or sharpshooters of each army ceased firing, and entered into friendly converse, traded tobacco, coffee, and sugar. Night approached, and put a stop to this; and each man took his place in line, ready to shoot the man in his front on sight! The next morning we learned that the enemy had taken advantage of the night, and had crossed the Rappahannock. The fight on the left of Lee's line, at Marye's Hill, had been terrific, and the enemy had been slaughtered by thousands. The loss in Jackson's corps was not large, Brig. Gen. Gregg being amongst the killed. There was a larger number of cannon used in this battle than in any previous battle, the situation being such as to give them fine positions.

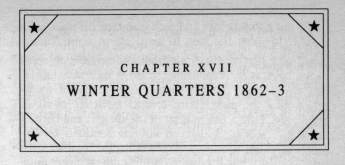

On Dec.17 Jackson's Corps left the battle field of Fredericksburg, and marched down the Rappahannock river to be better located for protection against the weather and observation of the enemy. About this time the First Va., or Irish Battalion, was detached from our brigade and made provost guard for the Army of Northern Virginia, and the 44th and 50th Va. regiments were added to our brigade.

About Jan. 1st, 1863, Maj. Gen. J. R. Trimble was assigned to the command of Jackson's division. He remained with us until about March 1st, when he was ordered to another command. About this time Brig. Gen. J. R. Jones left the Second Brigade.

Jackson's division went into camp at Moss Neck, where we made our winter quarters. These were huts made of any material that could be gotten, and in any way the architect of the party thought best. The greater number were of logs. A few men had tents. The men soon made themselves very comfortable. A large picket was required along the river, which was several miles from our camp; a brigade was sent, staying there several days. The picket guard was sent to the front from the brigade by companies, and, as each company arrived at its destination, it was divided into squads. These squads stationed themselves near the picket post, erected a shelter of cloth, brush, etc., built a fire in front of the shelter, and tried to be comfortable while not on duty as sentinels on the picket line. But in snow and cold rains, the weather tried men's souls! While they were on this outpost picket duty, a soldier's nerves, too, were tried! Far to the front he stood on his lonely beat, only occasionally moving because he feared he might attract the attention of the enemy's sentinel on similar duty, who might shoot him from a distance, or creep up later and shoot him!

A party of the enemy may steal up on him, and take him prisoner! Knowledge of this created an uneasy feeling that could not be gotten rid of, and the man on outpost guard was uneasy until he was again in camp with his comrades!

Occasionally some of the men went down to the river's edge, and had a talk with the Yanks on the other side. Sometimes a little boat was made of bark or a piece of rail, which, with the assistance of the wind and tide, now and then crossed to the other shore; and in this manner papers and tobacco were exchanged.

After getting back to camp, the brigade had its daily drills, camp guard duty, inspections, etc. The daily roll calls and cooking left very little idle time for the Confederate soldier. Notwithstanding this, one could always hear someone singing, laughing, whistling, or in some way indicating that the camp was not dead. We indulged in games of all kinds, ball, marbles, drafts, chess, cards, etc., and when the snow was on the ground we had great fun snowballing! I have seen several times more than twenty-five hundred men engaged in a game of snowball!

No one who has not had the experience, knows what a soldier undergoes on a march. We start off on a march some beautiful morning in spring, at midday slight clouds are seen floating about, which thicken with the appearance of a heavy storm soon to come; the instinct of home comes over us, and, instead of the merry chatter of the morning, stillness pervades the ranks. Each man is thinking of home and some place to shelter himself from the storm. The command, "Close up!" awakens him from his reverie, and he is made to think of his place in ranks. A flash of lightning and a loud peal of thunder, causes him to realize his position all the more, and now the rain commences and soon pours down! Poor fellow! he pulls down his hat, buttons up his jacket, pulls up his collar, and tries to protect his gun. In a short while he feels the water running down his arms and legs, but he is defiant yet, and the same good old Confederate! Now the water is slowly feeling its way down his back, and, as it gradually covers him, the courage goes out, and when his back gets *completely* wet, he, for a few minutes, forgets that he is a Confederate soldier! The thought only lasts a few minutes, and the storm within him breaks loose, resulting in his cursing the Confederacy, the generals, and everything in the army, and even himself! Then, with a new inspiration, he commences on the Yankees, is himself carried away, and is once more the good old Confederate soldier, marching along at a brisk rate, in the pelting rain! He is all right now, conversation commences, and when he reaches camp he builds his fire, and has something to eat. It makes very little difference, when he lies down to rest, whether it is raining or not!

We went through equal trials in very *dusty* marches; when our eyes, our noses, our mouths, our ears, and, in fact, our whole person became soiled with dirt, and dust finding its way all over one. Besides, we had muddy days to march in! We soon got our shoes full, our pants wet to the knees, and some comrade, stepping into a mud hole, would throw it all over one! Ask Tom Ellett what he thinks of marching in the mud, and be sure to do so when he is in a good humor! Then think of the marches in hot weather, when we became so hot and tired that we could hardly put one foot before the other, but on we went, the word, "Close up!" being always in our ears! In winter, too, amid sleet and snow, and sometimes when it was so cold that with an overcoat on we could not keep warm, indeed, any season, makes no difference to the soldier; when he is ordered to fall in, he takes his place in ranks, ready to face whatever may come!

At the commencement of the war, soon after starting on a march we were given the route step, on passing a village or town we were called to attention, and marched through with military precision; but towards the close of the war, we generally kept the route step throughout the march, as all had learned that the men got along so much better and could march much farther, by being allowed to carry their guns as they chose, and take their natural step.

One thing the government managed well, and that was the mail for the soldiers. In my brigade we had a man who was the mail carrier, the government furnishing a horse for this purpose. The letters written by the soldiers were delivered at regimental headquarters, where our carrier came for them, taking all that were handed him by the soldiers, too, whence he would start for the nearest post office at some depot or village. There he delivered his mail, and if he found there any mail directed to the men of his command, he brought it to us at once. If there were none, he would go to the next place, and to the next, until he found it; and brought it to us. His arrival was a great event in camp. Because he had no regular hour for returning, some of the men were always on the lookout for him, both day and night, and heralded his coming. On his arrival, there was a gathering of men from each company at regimental headquarters, who got their company's mail, took it to company's quarters, looked over it, and called out the names of the men to whom it was addressed. It made no difference as to hour, whether it was day, or one or two o'clock at night, when a man's name was called for a letter, he was generally on hand to get it in person, unless on duty. It was interesting to watch those fellows as they gathered for their mail. Those who received letters went off with radiant countenances, and, if it was night, each built a fire to himself, for light, and, sitting down on the ground, read his letter over and over; while those unfortunates who got none, went off looking as if they had not a friend on earth! In the beginning of the war, postage was not required to be prepaid on letters from soldiers in the field, the postage being collected on the delivery of the mail. In directing the letter to soldiers it was only necessary to write name, company, regiment, brigade, division and command. This was the rule in Jackson's command, and I suppose in the army generally. There was no post office or location mentioned, because we moved about so much our post office was continually changing. Notwithstanding this roundabout way for letters to travel, I never heard of one being lost either going to or from the army! Regularly sometimes for two or three weeks, we would receive a mail daily, then it would be several days, and sometimes a week before another came, but the letters always turned up. If the carrier overtook us while we were on a march, the mail was distributed and collected. I have seen it delivered in this way just before a battle.

It is surprising how the Confederacy got along with such a small variety of medicines, which consisted, in the field, almost entirely of blue powders, one kind of pills, and quinine. Go with me to the "sick or doctor's call," this morning. Reaching the surgeon's quarters, the sick were lined up, and the surgeon with the hospital steward passed along. The first man accosted was asked, "What is the matter with you?" The answer is something like this: "I don't know, doctor, but I have a terrible misery here," designating the locality by placing his hands on his stomach. "Put out your tongue," says the doctor. After an examination, the doctor says to Blunt, the hospital steward of my regiment, "Give him a blue powder." The next is examined in about the same manner, with instructions to Blunt to give him two pills; the next is given 10 grains of quinine. Then the treatment is varied by giving to the next one pill and 5 grains of quinine, to the next a blue powder and quinine, the treatment varying as the supply of pills, blue powder and quinine holds out. Occasionally some favored one was given a gill of whiskey; nearly every man thereafter developed the same symptoms! Probably one of the men has an aching tooth; the doctor tells him to take a seat on some log near by, that he will make an examination presently. The poor fellow seats himself and waits his turn. When the doctor comes to him, he looks his mouth over and says, "It must come out," goes to his tent, gets a pair of forceps, and, on his return, straddles the log, inserts the instrument in the man's mouth, takes holds of a tooth, and by main strength, after a lengthy struggle, succeeds in pulling an excellent tooth!—but he cures the ache.

This was about the daily routine in camp, and it was surprising how many cures were effected with this limited supply of medicines. The surgeon and hospital steward of my regiment were always kind and considerate to the sick, and did all in their power for them. I will mention the treatment used on the first man of my company, whom I saw after he was wounded. The surgeon gave the nurse a bottle of whiskey, with instructions to put a spoonful in the water used, each time he dressed the wound.

Old "F" Company of Richmond had become so small, that the three or four men with it were ordered, in January, 1863, to Camp Lee, Richmond, to recruit. They enlisted a few men as soon as they reached the camp, and commenced squad drill; and subsequently, company drill, as soon as they enlisted enough to call it a company, entering upon camp guard duty, policing, and other duties at once. The old members of the company did all in their power to make efficient soldiers of the recruits, who were conscripts of boyhood and middle age and some old substitutes. On June 21st we received orders to get ready to leave Camp Lee the next day, to join our regiment which was with Lee's army.

All the old members were allowed to go into the city to bid family and friends good-by, and to take a last look at some bright eyes, it somehow taking longer to bid that pair of eyes farewell than it did to take leave of a whole family. This consumed the larger part of the day; the remainder we diligently devoted to preparations for moving promptly the next morning. As night came on, instead of going to bed, each man stole off quietly to the city to look once again into those eyes to which he had already bidden farewell, returning in time to get a short nap before day. After breakfast we marched out of Camp Lee to the Central depot, where we took the cars for Staunton.

The following are the names of the members of F Company who left for Staunton, June 22, 1863:

*Captain, William A. Pegram.
*Second Lieut., Reuben J. Jordan.
*Jr. Second Lieut., Malcolm L. Hudgins.
*First Sergeant, William S. Archer.
*Second Sergeant, John H. Worsham.
*Third Sergeant, J. Porter Wren.
Fourth Sergeant, T. Walker.
First Corporal, E. Gouldman.
Second Corporal, W. C. Tiney.
Third Corporal, George J. Floyd.
Fourth Corporal, Henry F. Munt.
Anderson, Joseph H.
Barber, N.
Bates, W.
Bowe, H. C.
Brown, A. D.

Brown, A. H.
Brown, George W.
Brown, Henry.
Brown, James R.
Callis, G.
Coleman, N.
Couch, J. M.
Cumbia, W. S.
Dillard, R. H.
Divers, W. H.
Dowdy, Nathaniel A.
Fox, Henry C.
Gentry, M. G.
Griffin, J.
Hawkins, L. A.
Houston, George W.

*Old members.

Johnston, J. W.	Seay, M.
Kayton, P. W.	Simpson, F. J.
Kidd, J. A.	Smith, J. T.
Mason, J. M.	Smith, Thomas.
Merriman, J. T.	Soles, P. D.
Nance, J. L.	Trainum, C.
Richeson, P. S.	Tyree, William C.
Richeson, William R.	Wallace, R. H.
Rutledge, William.	Wilkins, J. M.
Searles, S.	Wood, S. E.

We were joined afterwards by a few of the old members and the following new ones:

Bates, Edward.	Seay, W. C.
Legg, A. C.	Smith, Henry.

And W. E. Cumbie, who was transferred to our company from the 24th Va. Battalion in exchange for R. H. Wallace.

During the summer of 1862, Col. John M. Patton of the 21st Regt. had been transferred to Maj. Gen. Anderson's division of Longstreet's corps. Lt.-Col. Cunningham had been killed, and during the fall Major John B. Moseley left the regiment. This left the regiment without a field officer. While the regiment was in camp at Moss Neck, the following appointments were made to fill vacancies:

William A. Witcher, Colonel.	William P. Moseley, Major.
William R. Berkeley, Lt. Col.	

Lt.-Col. Berkeley remained with the regiment only a short time, when Major William P. Moseley was made lieutenant-colonel, and A. D. Kelley, major. Those three remained with the regiment until the surrender.

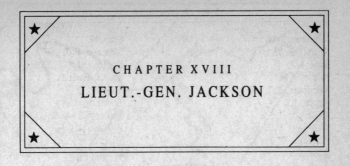

THE BATTLE of Chancellorsville was fought May 2d, 1863. Gen. Jackson's great flank movement against Hooker was managed with skill and success. Jackson was wounded and unfortunately by his own men, and died on the 10th, in the height of his fame. It was soon known in the army of Northern Virginia. The men of his old division were prostrated with grief, nearly every man in it shedding tears.

Gen. Lee's conduct when he heard of the wounding of Jackson and afterwards at his death, caused the old division to love him more than ever. What a loss to the Confederacy. What a loss to the army of Northern Virginia, and to Lee, its commander, who said he had "lost his right arm," and what a loss to his corps. Never more will his sword flash in the enemy's rear, nor will he see his banner floating in one of his fierce attacks on their flank, nor will he hear the wild cheers of his men as they drive everything before them. In my humble opinion, the army never recovered from the loss of Jackson.

There was something about Jackson that always

143

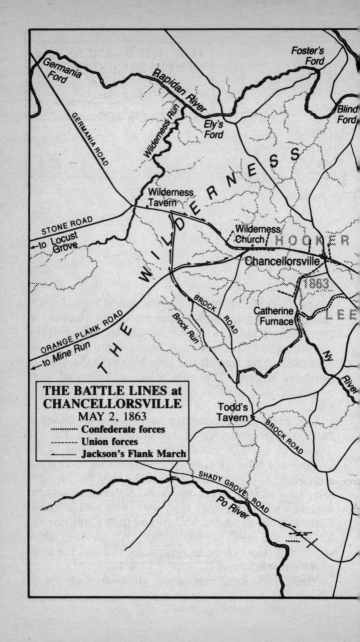

Foster's
Ford

Germania
Ford

Rapidan River

Blind
Ford

GERMANIA ROAD

Wilderness Run

Ely's
Ford

T H E   W I L D E R N E S S

Wilderness
Tavern

STONE ROAD
to Locust
Grove

Wilderness
Church

HOOKER

Chancellorsville

1863

LEE

BROCK ROAD

Catherine
Furnace

ORANGE PLANK ROAD
to Mine Run

Brock Run

Ny

River

**THE BATTLE LINES at
CHANCELLORSVILLE**
MAY 2, 1863

.... Confederate forces

-------- Union forces

Jackson's Flank March

Todd's
Tavern

BROCK ROAD

SHADY GROVE ROAD

Po River

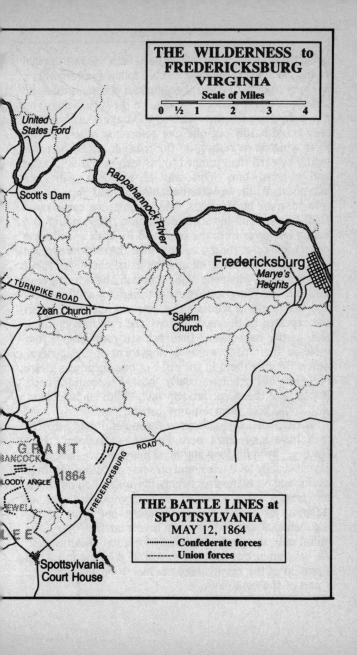

THE WILDERNESS to
FREDERICKSBURG
VIRGINIA
Scale of Miles
0   ½   1   2   3   4

United
States Ford

Rappahannock River

Scott's Dam

Fredericksburg
Marye's
Heights

TURNPIKE ROAD

Zoan Church

Salem
Church

GRANT

HANCOCK

1864

BLOODY ANGLE

FREDERICKSBURG ROAD

EWELL

LEE

Spottsylvania
Court House

THE BATTLE LINES at
SPOTTSYLVANIA
MAY 12, 1864
·········· Confederate forces
-------- Union forces

attracted his men. It must have been faith. He was the idol of his old soldiers, and they would follow him anywhere; the very sight of him was the signal for cheers. It made no difference where he was, in camp, on the battlefield, or on a march, when the men were so thoroughly used up that they could hardly put one foot before the other, or they were lying down resting on the roadside, when he came riding by each man jumped to his feet, pulled off his hat and cheered him. This was always done with one exception. While we were marching around Pope, to get into his rear at Manassas, one evening, we came upon Gen. Jackson and his staff dismounted and standing in a field a few yards from the road, and the little sorrel lying down nibbling at the grass. As soon as the men recognized "Old Jack," hats came off and the usual cheer was about to break forth, when one of his staff standing near the road said to them, "No cheering, men; the enemy will hear you, and Gen. Jackson requests that you will not cheer." This was repeated by the men all down the marching column, and, as the men passed their beloved commander, they took off their hats, some waving them at the general, others flinging them in the air. Not one cheer was given, but some of the fellows nearly "busted" keeping it back. It was here that Gen. Jackson said, "With such soldiers, who could keep from winning battles."

What shall I say of Jackson's wonderful marches? His men have long since been known as "Jackson's Foot Cavalry," from his long and rapid marches. We have often marched daily for a week, and on some occasions for three weeks, and on many days twenty-five miles. I do not think my brigade ever marched over thirty miles without stopping for a rest of several hours; but some of the regiments of the old division have marched over forty miles, only stopping occasionally for a ten minutes' rest. We have often marched and fought all day, and in case of a pursuit of the enemy, kept the march up all night, and a part of the next day.

It was in battle that the men showed their great love for and confidence in Gen. Jackson, his old soldiers having implicit confidence in him. How many times his old command wished him back, to lead in one of his furious attacks on the enemy.

The South produced many generals of great ability, but for brilliancy and dash, the world never saw Stonewall Jackson's equal.

"Let us pass over the river, and rest under the shade of the trees."

O<small>N THE ARRIVAL</small> of our company at Staunton on June 22, 1863, we met orders to take charge of about one hundred stragglers of Lee's army, who had been collected there, in order to march with us to the army of Northern Virginia, and be delivered to the provost guard.

We left Staunton on the 24th with stragglers and nothing else; no baggage wagon, no cooking utensils, no rations, as the men expressed it, "No nothing." On account of those stragglers, who gave us a great deal of trouble, we made short marches, and stopped at a barn on the way at night. It was necessary to guard our stragglers, and the company could do it better by having them in a house. We induced someone in the neighborhood of our stopping place to let us have rations, generally to cook them also; and in this manner we reached the Potomac river opposite Williamsport, Md., on the morning of July 4, without rations or cooking utensils. After a visit to Williamsport by some of the officers who found no rations there, a detail was made and sent to a mill not far off to

148

"press" flour, if it could not be gotten otherwise. This detail went to the mill and seized two barrels of flour, secured a wagon to haul it, and then went to a hog pen in the neighborhood for a hog. They were told by its owner that bacon could be gotten at a certain store in Williamsport, where they found as much as they wanted. Having no cooking utensils, and having a baker in the company, they decided to bring into service one of the "Dutch ovens" found in that part of the country at nearly all the houses. It was now late in the evening; we decided to do the best we could for the night, and use the oven in the morning. A sergeant with a file of men went into town early the next morning, took possession of an excellent oven, and went to work. During the day of the 5th, F Company disposed of the stragglers, and crossed the Potomac into Williamsport, marched through the town to the northeast side, stacked arms, and there received the cooked rations.

An officer was found in the town who said he had orders from Gen. Lee to stop all men here, as the battle of Gettysburg had been fought, and Gen. Lee intended to fall back into Virginia by this route. Many of his wagons had already arrived, and others were coming in every moment in large numbers. As the river was too high to be forded, because of recent rains, they were being parked along the river under the bluff near the town. This officer asked our captain to remain with his company, as it was thought that a raiding party of the Yankees might make an attempt to capture or destroy the train; and, as there was only one organized regiment at the place, he thought it the duty of our company to stay. During the afternoon and night of the 5th there was much talk of Yankee cavalry coming.

On the morning of the 6th of July, the company formed a line, and stacked arms in a field overlooking two roads that ran into the town. The men were ordered to stay near their arms, a picket under a sergeant was sent out on the road that the enemy would use, with orders to allow no one to go outside. Soon after the picket was posted, a young lady and a boy on horseback passed the picket going into the town. She was a fine looking woman, and, as she passed, gave me a bow and a smile. She stayed in town an hour or two, then started to go out, but was stopped by the sentinel. I was called, and she stated that she was returning home, and had no idea we would prevent her return; that she had been in town on business, and told me what it was. Although I told her my orders, she tried to induce me to let her pass, but without success. I told her I would go with her to see our captain, and probably he might let her pass. I did this, and the officers consulted and agreed to it; but a little Georgian, who overheard the conversation, said to the captain, "You ain't going to let that woman pass, are you? She is a spy, come in here to find out all she can, and now she is going back to tell the Yankees." It was then decided not to let her pass. She asked me where the commanding officer was. I told her who he was and where his office was located in town, and she asked me to go with her to see the officer. I could not leave my picket post, and turned the duty over to our handsome orderly sergeant, Willie Archer. She did not get the permission, and from what we heard afterwards, it was well she did not.

The day passed quietly. The wheat and hay recently cut was shocked in the fields around the town, most of it, however, on the two roads in our front and beyond our picket post. The teamsters were quietly getting both for feed, some in wagons and others on the backs of mules. About four or five o'clock in the afternoon a pistol shot was heard and a great commotion was seen amongst the teamsters farthest from us. Soon the field was full of Yankee cavalry, whooping, yelling and firing pistols; riding up to the wagons that had hay or wheat, ordering them to halt, and, instead of injuring or detaining them, quietly pulling out matches and firing the provender, and then letting them go. Mules were seen flying across the field with a flame of fire leaping from them, which would last only a few seconds before the rider would have it off, and in many instances himself off too, in his efforts to remove the burning hay or wheat. Many wagons were burned.

During the day all the broken down artillery that had been sent along with the wagon train was placed on some prominent place around the town, the guns making a formidable appearance. I have been told there were twenty-two pieces, and all in view; that some had no ammunition, some had no chests, some a few shot, and some of the pieces were disabled, but they made a show.

The enemy had now brought out of the woods into the field in full view of us, eight pieces of artillery and a large body of mounted cavalry, which had formed a line of battle. A body of dismounted men with mounted officers were busy leveling fences. The dismounted men had approached a lot of farm buildings about four hundred yards from our company. Our picket post had been called in, guns loaded, and our company formed as skirmishers. Captain Pegram took in the situation at once, and acted promptly. He knew we could not hold our position in the open field against these large odds, and remarked to some of the old members of the company that there were only two things for him to do: attack or retreat; and that he was going to charge the enemy. He gave the order, "Forward! double quick!" and to the farm buildings we went in a run.

We had fifty-two men present in our company, nearly all of whom were substitutes and conscripts; one of them even fainted when he saw the enemy, another had a terrible ache and had to lie down on the ground, where we could hear him groaning after firing commenced. This reduced us to fifty. A few stragglers, including the little Georgian, named Ward, of Wright's brigade, wearing a red Zouave cap, volunteered to go with us. This made about sixty, all told, who went into action.

About fifty yards in our front it was necessary to climb over the first fence, and there the Yankees opened fire on us. About half way to the farm buildings we encountered the second fence. There was a lane from the buildings towards the town, with a fence on each side of it, and at its end a gate that opened into the barn yard. Our advance was oblique to this lane. Soon after we passed the second fence, the left of our line came to the lane fence. I was on the left and went over the fence into the lane, requiring three or four men to follow me, amongst whom was the little Georgian. We ran up the lane to the gate which I threw open, and rushed into the barn yard, the little Georgian following, and I think old man Callis next. A mounted officer was in the yard, "cursing" and flourishing a pistol. As I entered the yard, I told the men to shoot him, but he leveled his pistol at us and fired, and the little Georgian fell dead—as gallant a little fellow as I ever saw. I cannot say that the officer killed him, since the enemy were firing briskly from several points in the yard at us. My men fired at the officer, who rode off bowed down on his horse. I was told a few days afterwards by a citizen, that he was a major and was wounded. I can truly say he was a gallant man. A small house in the barn yard and on the right of the lane, with its rear towards us, was occupied by some of the enemy, who were firing at us. As I ran around to the door, I met some of my company who had by this time gotten into the yard from the other side, and we brought out five Yankee cavalrymen, and sent them to the rear.

We had now cleared the yard and buildings of all opponents; but the fight was on in earnest, the enemy having opened with their artillery, some firing at us, others at our guns on the hills. We took up a position along a rail fence beyond the buildings, and about half way between the two roads before mentioned and parallel to them, keeping up our fire on any of the enemy we could see to be within range. Our right had suffered more than the left. Inside the barn yard were lying Sergeant Walker and Corporal Tinney, both dead, and both splendid soldiers—in all, three of our men killed, including the Georgian. We captured, wounded, and killed fifteen of the enemy in the barn yard. We now found that the enemy were advancing on the road in our rear, and we fell back to that road, and were joined there by a company of about thirty, mostly stragglers. Placing a few of our company along a cross fence to protect our flank, we kept up a fierce fire in front. Soon Capt. Pegram was killed, another one of old F to join Jackson "under the shade of the trees." The Yankees were shelling us very heavily, and, their dismounted men largely increased, had possession of the fence which we had relinquished, and were firing heavily at us. A regiment of our men, that was at the river with our train, now made its appearance, drove the Yanks from the fence. Our line was lengthened on the left by a large body of armed wagoners, so that our company moved farther to the right. We kept up our fire until night, when the enemy disappeared.

This I consider the best fight of F Company during the war. With nearly all new men, only six or eight of the old company, we attacked and drove the enemy and held the position against tremendous odds. Buford, who made the attack, had present twelve regiments of cavalry and twelve pieces of artillery. When he made his appearance in front of our company, there was no armed body of men between him and Gen. Lee's entire wagon train, except this small company. We had been fighting nearly half an hour before the company of thirty men, and three-quarters of an hour before the regiment, came to our assistance; and I repeat, it was the best fight the company ever made, and, in its results, one of the best of the war. The new men, except those noted, behaved like veterans, and every one did his duty, and they covered themselves with glory.

Our loss as before stated was four killed, including the Georgian. One of the substitutes became frightened when

the enemy opened their artillery, and ran towards the
wagons. As he approached a fence, one of the enemy's
shells burst in front of him, tearing the fence to pieces;
this so "conflumuxed" him that he ran back to us saying,
"No whar was safe." He stayed with us during the
remainder of the fight, and with the loss of a piece of skin
knocked from his shin, was the only one wounded.

In the death of Capt. William A. Pegram we suffered a
great loss. Young, unassuming, but a true soldier, by his
gallantry he was notable on many a battlefield. We buried
him the next day in the cemetery at Williamsport, and the
three men on the field, which they gave their lives to win.
We marched in the afternoon to Hagerstown, sleeping
that night on the brick pavement at the market house,
resuming our march early the next morning, July 8, 1863,
and joining our regiment in their bivouac two miles from
Hagerstown.

During the absence of F Company from the army,
several changes were made in officers. Lt.-Gen. Richard S.
Ewell was made commander of the Second Corps,
Maj.-Gen. Edward Johnson was made commander of
Jackson's Division, and Brig.-Gen. J. M. Jones commander
of the Second Brigade. The battles of Chancellorsville,
Winchester and Gettysburg had been fought, and on our
uniting with our regiment they told us of those battles
and we told them of Williamsport.

When Gen. Lee arrived in the neighborhood of
Williamsport and found that his army could not cross the
Potomac on account of a rise in the river, he promptly
turned his army back, and formed a line of battle near
Hagerstown. Here he awaited an attack from Meade, who
marched his army up in front of Lee's, had some
skirmishing, and began to fortify; we following his
example. Gen. Lee had thrown a pontoon bridge across the
Potomac at Falling Waters, about four or five miles below
Williamsport. This had been partially destroyed after
Gettysburg by a raiding party of the enemy's from

Harper's Ferry. While we were in line at Hagerstown, Gen. Lee had this bridge repaired, and the wagons passed over it; in the meantime the river had fallen enough for the men to ford it. Gen. Ewell withdrew his corps from the line on the night of the 13th, marching all night, and reaching the Potomac a short distance above Williamsport about daybreak. We marched at once into the river and forded, the water taking us up to our breasts. It was necessary that a comrade and myself should help little Bates, and every time we stumbled on some of the large rocks at the bottom of the stream, his head went under the water. The remainder of our army crossed at the same time on the pontoon bridge.

Our army at this time was in a sad plight as to clothing. Hundreds had no shoes, thousands were as ragged as they could be, some with the bottom of their pants in long frazzles, others with their knees out, others out at their elbows, and their hair sticking through holes in their hats. Some of the men patched their clothing, and it was usually done with any material they could get; one man having the seat of his pants patched with bright red, his knees patched with black; another with a piece of gray or brown blanket; in fact, with anything one could get. There were so few patches, however, and so many holes, that it was not surprising that one of the Pennsylvania girls in a party on the side of the road looking at us pass, when she was asked by her mother how the officers were distinguished from the privates, replied that it was easy enough, because the officers' pants were patched, and the privates' pants were not.

THE 14th of July found the army of Northern Virginia back in Virginia from the Pennsylvania campaign. Gen. Lee crossed the Blue Ridge into Orange County with all his troops except Ewell's Corps, which was left in the valley, engaged in destroying the B. & O. R. R. On the 20th Ewell's corps took up our march to join Gen. Lee, and marched through Winchester to Manassas Gap. Here we learned that the enemy had advanced into the Gap from the other side of the Blue Ridge, and were trying to effect an entrance into the Luray Valley. We had some heavy skirmishing with them, which lasted until late in the night, when they withdrew. In the morning we marched up the Luray Valley to Thornton's Gap, where we crossed the mountain and marched to Orange County, joined Gen. Lee on August 1st, and went into camp at Montpelier, the old home of President Madison. This last day's march was the hottest I ever experienced; more than half the men falling out of ranks on the march, overcome by the heat. Every tree we came to along the road side had a squad of men under its shade, officers as well as privates. While in this camp that splendid regiment, the 25th Va., was added to our brigade. We remained in camp at Montpelier until the 14th, when we marched to Liberty Mills to meet some movement of the enemy; remained there until the 16th, at which time we returned to Montpelier. It was reported one evening, while we were at Liberty Mills, that a small body of Yankees was at the Madison County poor house. A detail of men and an officer were sent there to capture them. I was one of the party. We started as soon as we could get ready, which was a little after sunset. Soon after we left camp a severe thunder storm arose. I do not know that I ever saw one more severe. It rained in torrents, the thunder roared, the lightning flashed, and in the midst of it all we trudged along an unknown road without a guide. No one in the party had ever been over the road before. It was at times so dark that we could not see our hands before us. We halted several times to let a passing cloud empty itself on us, and the sky clear up some, so that we might see how to march. The dogs along the road proved to be great friends that night, it being so dark that we could not see the houses. When we heard a dog bark, someone would go towards him, and thus find the house, awake the inmates, and get directions for our march. The little branches and creeks running across the road had by this time become small rivers, and the water of some came up to our waists as we forded. Just before reaching the poor house village, the moon came out, and we entered the village about midnight; no lights were visible and not a soul was stirring. We, however, surrounded the largest and best looking house, and knocked at the door. After some delay, an old man with a veritable nightcap on, poked his head out of an upper window and informed us that a squad of Yankee cavalry had been there that afternoon, and left about sunset. We then marched to the church which was open, went in, and, after posting a sentinel, lay down on the benches in our wet clothes, thoroughly broken down, and slept the rest of the night. On our return next morning, one of the streams we crossed the night before had risen so high that we could not cross; while we were waiting, an old gentleman in the neighborhood gave us a breakfast which was so good that it paid us for our trip. This march, during the night, was as trying an experience as I had during the war. We reached camp about ten in the morning, having marched about twenty-four miles.

Soon after we returned to Montpelier a detail of men was made to make soap. These men gathered the ashes from our fires, put them into several barrels, and commenced making lye; they also gathered the offal from the slaughter pens, and with the use of several old-fashioned dinner pots, in which the soap was made, they soon had some excellent and pure soap. This was issued at once, and the men of our brigade soon presented a very clean appearance. All the work of these men was done out of doors. They were so successful in their work, that we carried a large quantity with us when we left camp.

This was a very busy week: first, our regiment, the 21st Va. Inft., was presented with a battle flag; the next day, we had a brigade inspection; the next day, a brigade review; and the next day, a division review.

Quite a charming story is connected with this flag. At the battle of Chancellorsville our color bearer was shot down; one of the color guard caught the flag, and waving it aloft, was in a few minutes shot, taken off the field, and his left arm amputated above the elbow. When he recovered, he reported at this camp for duty, saying he could carry the flag with one arm as well as before. Gen. Johnson, our division commander, hearing this, determined to present the flag in person to our one-armed color bearer. It was received at division headquarters, and Friday, the 20th of August, was the day announced for the presentation. On that day the Second Brigade was drawn up in line, and in the presence of many spectators, including a number of ladies, Gen. Johnson, in patriotic and thrilling words, presented to our regiment its first battle flag. The occasion was very impressive and enthusiastic. Our flag had the following battles inscribed on it: Kernstown, McDowell, Winchester, Second Manassas, Harper's Ferry, Sharpsburg, Fredericksburg, Chancellorsville, and Gettysburg. Through an oversight these were omitted, viz.: Cold Harbor, Malvern Hill, and Cedar Run. This flag was carried with distinction in all our battles to the end.

On September 3d we received orders to clean our arms and accouterments and cook one day's rations, and be ready to march early the next morning, when a grand review of the Second Corps would take place. This created a great stir in our regiment, since we had never been to a review on such a grand scale, and all wanted to participate in it. We were up betimes on the morning of the 4th, and soon had our breakfast, and were ordered to fall in. We marched through Orange C. H. to a large field about one mile east of that village, reaching it about 10 A.M. Our division formed a line facing east, about midway of this field, stacked arms, and rested. We were soon joined by Early's and Rode's divisions, the former taking position about two hundred yards in our front, and the latter about the same distance in our rear, making three lines each about half a mile long.

About a quarter of a mile in our front was the reviewing stand, where the corps headquarters' flag was waving. As the officers, who were to witness the review, and the visitors arrived, they took their positions near that flag. Many ladies were present on horseback and carriages, among whom were two of Gen. Lee's daughters, who received much attention from every one. The scene was very gay and brilliant around the flag.

We were to be reviewed by Gen. Lee in person; and about noon he made his appearance mounted on Traveler,

and joined the throng around the flag, where he seemed
to enjoy himself highly with the visitors. Soon the bugle
sounded, and announced that all was ready. Gen. Lee rode
to the front, accompanied by his staff, then Gen. Ewell and
staff, followed by the generals of the several divisions and
their staffs, in their respective order of rank. Gen. Lee rode
to the right of the front division, which had taken its
place, and, with bands playing and drums beating, the
general dashed along the front of the line, followed by the
large cavalcade of generals and their staffs. The men
presented arms, flags were lowered, the officers saluted
with their swords, and all the pomp of war that could be
shown by these old Confederates was brought into view.
Reaching the left of the line, the generals wheeled to the
left and passed in rear of the same line, until they reached
its end; when they wheeled to the right, going to the
second line, reviewing them in same manner as the first;
and then to the third line; and back to the flag, and took
their respective positions near it. The three lines now
marched forward several hundred yards, with bands
playing, then left-wheeled into column of regiments, the
regiment at the head guiding us to a line with the flag,
where the corps marched past the stand in column of
regiments. As each regiment arrived in front of Gen. Lee,
the men came to a shoulder arms, the flags dipped, the
officers saluted, the bands played; Gen. Lee raised his hat
in recognition, the ladies waved their handkerchiefs and
clapped their hands and cheered us, we answering with a
Confederate yell. The regiments, after passing the
reviewing stand some distance, filed to the right, and
again forming line, waited until the review was ended. We
then took up our march for camp, which we reached
about nine or ten o'clock at night.

This was said to be the grandest review of our troops
during the war, the movements of the men were excellent
and our marching splendid. Johnson's (Jackson's old

division) attracted special attention, and the one-armed color bearer of the 21st Va. Regt. was loudly cheered by all the officers and visitors as he passed the reviewing stand.

It was at Montpelier that the great religious revival commenced, which spread so rapidly over the entire army; and the converts were so numerous that they were numbered not by tens and hundreds, but by thousands. The place selected for preaching in our camp was on a hillside, in a large wood, the road running on one side of the place, and a small branch on the other. The ground was slightly inclined; trees were cut from the adjoining woods, rolled to this spot, and arranged for seating at least two thousand people. At the lower end, a platform was raised with logs, rough boards were placed on them, and a bench was made at the far side for the seating of the preachers. In front was a pulpit or desk, made of a box. Around this platform and around the seats, stakes or poles were driven in the ground about ten or fifteen feet apart, on top of which were baskets made of iron wire, iron hoops, etc. In these baskets chunks of lightwood were placed, and at night they were lighted, throwing a red glare far beyond the confines of the place of worship. The gathering, each night, of the bronzed and grizzly warriors, devoutly worshiping, was a wonderful picture in the army; and when some old familiar hymn was given out, those thousands of warriors would make hill and dell ring. In this rude place of worship thousands gathered several weeks. The interest manifested was so great that the seats were taken in the afternoon by such men as were not on duty; and when night relieved from duty those who had been drilling, etc., the men stood up in immense numbers around those who were seated. I think I can say that the order was perfect, no disturbance of any kind was ever known to occur, and the attention to the words of the preacher was never more faithful.

We enjoyed in this camp the longest rest of the war; and it was much needed. After the review we were disturbed only by regular drills and the usual camp duties. The men enjoyed this rest more than any we ever had. The camp was located in one of the healthiest sites to be found. In full view of the Blue Ridge and Monticello, it was a beautiful place and it was, too, a magnificent farm.

Our rest ended on September 16th, when we commenced a series of marches and movements, which culminated in Gen. Lee's crossing the Rapidan river, and offering battle to the enemy. They, however, preferred to retire; and we followed as far as Bristow Station, where their rear guard was overtaken and promptly attacked by a part of A P. Hill's division, which suffered some loss. When our division arrived on the field, the Second Brigade was formed in line of battle near the railroad, and perpendicular to it, and skirmishers thrown forward, and we were ordered forward about half a mile through a thin pine thicket. The men were cautioned to keep perfectly quiet, as the enemy were supposed to be in this thicket. We halted, and were ordered to lie down in place, with guns in hand. Everything so far had been done very quietly; but when an old hare came running to our line, the boys could not restrain themselves—some sprang to their feet, catching at the hare as it went by the line of battle. It was captured by one of the men who was lying down. A wild yell burst from the men, and the silence for that day was broken. Our skirmishers pushed on to Broad Run, and it was soon reported that Meade had taken refuge in the fortifications around Centreville. We quietly took up our march and returned to camp. The Second Corps followed the Orange & Alexander R. R., destroying the track from the bridge over Broad Run to the Rappahannock river, and, crossing that river, Johnson's division went into camp about three miles from it, a part of the corps staying at the river. We remained in this camp until the night of November 7th, when we marched to Kelly's Ford, to meet the enemy, who, it was reported, had crossed there. Near the ford, about two or three o'clock in the night, we halted and sent scouts ahead, who learned that a large body of the enemy had crossed, staying only a short time and recrossing about night. One of our regiment captured a prisoner, who was the only enemy seen by my corps as far as I know. This man stayed with the regiment two or three days before he was turned over to the provost guard. On the following morning we marched to Culpeper C. H., going around the town to the Rapidan river, which we crossed at Raccoon Ford about eight or nine o'clock at night. It was the coldest water I ever forded. Oh, how cold! I can feel it now. As the water at this time was about knee deep, we were ordered to take off our shoes and roll up our breeches; and, as we stepped into the water, it was so cold it felt as if a knife had taken one's foot off; and at each step the depth of the water increased. This feeling continued until we reached the middle of the river, where the water came to the knee, and one felt as if the leg was off from the knee down. Reaching the shore and halting to put on shoes and let pants down, many of the men were so cold they could not do it. This was true of myself: I had put on one shoe, but could not tie it, nor could I roll my pants down. In this way we marched about a mile, when we halted in a large wood, where we soon built immense fires and became warm. The next morning we marched and went into camp at Mt. Pisgah Church in Orange County. Thence our division went on picket at Morton's Ford on the Rappahannock, a distance of eight miles; a brigade going to the ford, staying three days, and relieved by another brigade, returning to camp at Mt. Pisgah.

During the winter of 1863–4 the subject of taking care of the widows and orphans of the soldiers who were killed, was agitated by some of the prominent citizens of the Confederacy; an organization was formed for that purpose, committees were appointed to make collections, etc., and agents of the society were sent to the armies in the field, to ask assistance from the soldiers. One of these agents visited our company while we were in this camp. He was received most cordially, as the cause was one that appealed to the sympathy of every soldier. When the company was assembled, the following sums were subscribed by its members, to be paid at the next pay day, or as soon thereafter as the collector could visit us:

Lt. R. J. Jordan...$20.00
Sergt. J. H. Worsham...................................... 10.00
Sergt. W. S. Robertson.................................... 10.00
Sergt. E. Gouldman.. 2.00
Corporal H. F. Munt 5.00
Corporal N. A. Dowdy 2.00
Corporal H. C. Tyree 5.00
Privates: N. Barber....................................... 2.50
          A. D. Brown..................................... 2.00
          G. W. Brown 2.50
          J. R. Brown 2.50
          J. M. Couch..................................... 2.00
          W. E. Cumbia 5.00
          W. S. Cumbia 1.00
          W. B. Edmonds 5.00
          H. C. Fox....................................... 5.00
          J. Griffin 2.00
          J. W. Johnston.................................. 2.00
          P. W. Kayton 5.00
          A. C. Legg 2.00
          J. M. Mason 2.00
          J. T. Merriman.................................. 2.00
          H. Peaster 5.00
          P. S. Richeson.................................. 2.00
          W. R. Richeson 2.00
          S. Searles...................................... 5.00
          W. C. Seay 2.00
          J. T. Smith..................................... 5.00
          S. E. Wood...................................... 5.00
          J. A. Kidd...................................... 5.00

                                                        $127.50

This was a liberal contribution from men whose pay was eleven dollars a month, the majority of whom had families who needed all their income. It is a pleasure to me to add that when the collector came, every one present paid his subscription; and some who were absent left the amount with me, which was duly handed over. Every man present at the first visit subscribed, and a few who were not present then but were present when the collector came, gave him what they could spare; they are included in the list.

Gen. Bradley T. Johnson was commanding our brigade again and his wife visited him here. The first day of her arrival she visited the camp of the brigade, and went to each company asking after the health of the men, and how we were getting along, etc. This she continued to do daily as long as we were in this camp. She was a beautiful woman with charming manners and always had a pleasant word and good cheer for the sick. The personal interest she took in us, so impressed the men that they looked forward to her daily visits with great pleasure. The good she did in this camp was never forgotten.

CHAPTER XXI
PAYNE'S FARM AND MINE RUN

O<small>N</small> N<small>OVEMBER</small> 27th it was reported that Meade had crossed the Rappahannock and was advancing. We broke camp, and Johnson's division marched towards Mine Run on a road north of that taken by the remainder of the Second Corps. We were quietly marching along a road which runs through a wood, listening to the distant cannon in our front and speculating as to the location of the expected battle. Suddenly a part of our column was assailed on the flank by a Yankee skirmish line. It was a complete surprise to us, since no one thought the enemy was in the vicinity. Regimental officers cut off companies from their regiments, formed them as skirmishers right in the road, and ordered them forward. I must say this was the promptest movement I saw during the war. Our skirmishers drove the enemy back on their line of battle, and by this time Gen. Johnson had formed the division in line of battle, and it was moving forward. The left of our line became heavily engaged at once. The Second Brigade was on the right, and swung around until we came to a field, where we could see the enemy behind a rail fence on the edge of a wood at the far side of this field. Continuing our wheeling, we soon came to a swamp in a bottom, the most miry place I ever entered. How the men crossed it I don't know. Many left one or both shoes in the mud, the horses could not cross, the officers were compelled to dismount and take the mud too. We, however, crossed, halted a few moments under the hill, reformed our line, and went forward. As soon as we advanced up the hill sufficiently for the enemy to see us, the action became general and heavy; we fought until night put an end to the battle.

I will mention a gallant action which I saw here. Capt. Johnson of the 50th Va. Regt., a man about fifty years of age, large and stout, thinking that some of his men were not doing as well as they ought, walked out to the brow of the hill, lay down on its top, broadside to the enemy, and then called to some of his men to come up; and if they were afraid, they could use him as a breastwork. Several of them very promptly accepted his challenge, lying down behind him, resting their guns on him, firing steadily from this position until the fight was over. I am happy to say that the gallant captain was not injured. The division suffered greatly; of F Company, L. M. Couch, J. A. Kidd, Henry Peaster and Porter Wren were wounded.

This action was known as the battle of Payne's Farm; it was fought by Johnson's division alone, against one of the wings of the Army of the Potomac that had crossed the river at a small ford to make the flank attack on Lee's army, and, but for the promptness with which the attack was met, it might have been very disastrous to his army. During the night we withdrew across Mine Run.

On the next morning we joined Lee, and took our position in line of battle with our corps, along the hills of Mine Run, and threw up breastworks. Meade occupied the hills in our front. Skirmishers had been thrown out in our front all along the run, we heard the continuous crack of their guns, occasionally a brisk cannonade would be indulged in; and thus matters went on all day. At night all became still, and we lay down in the breastworks to rest. When we arose the next morning we saw that the hills in our front had a line of fortifications from one end to the other of the enemy's line, and more formidable than our own. The skirmishing was as heavy as on the day before, and at one time we endured heavy cannonading from the enemy. Night put an end to the firing. In the morning we saw that Meade had strengthened his works and brought up additional cannon. I went back of our fortifications a few yards, built a small fire of twigs, put my cup on it to warm something for breakfast, and quietly took a seat on the ground near by to wait until it was heated. Two of the regiment joined me and put their cups beside mine, the enemy's shells from a battery on our right occasionally dropping in our vicinity. Soon after my friends put their cups on the fire, a shell dropped in it, burst, wounding one of them on the head, and when the smoke and ashes cleared up, our cups and fire too had disappeared. I sadly went back and took my place in line, without breakfast. Once during this day the cannonading from the enemy was the most severe we had from them. Anticipating an attack, a sergeant from F Company and two men were detailed from the 21st Va. Regt., ordered to go back to our rear, find the ammunition wagon, get two boxes of ammunition, bring them to the line of battle, keep them within one hundred yards of the regiment, and, if attacked, issue them to the men as fast as they might need them.

At night A. P. Hill's corps, which occupied the right of Lee's line, moved out of the breastworks and took a position on the flank and rear of Meade, in order to attack him at daybreak. Our corps remained in the breastworks, and extended its line so as to occupy the whole fortification, and in my regiment the men were not much closer together than in a skirmish line. Orders were given the men in case of an attack to hold the line at all hazards.

About midnight the men lay down in their places for some rest, and were aroused at break of day, sprang to their feet promptly, and listened for the expected attack by Hill. Not a gun was heard, so we became very anxious because we had no tidings from him. Soon after sunrise, Johnson's division formed in column and marched along the breastworks until we reached a country road, where we filed to the left, and marched over the run into the Yankee fortifications. Everything was perfectly still, not a Yankee to be seen, they having left during the night. We followed till we knew they had crossed the Rapidan.

Johnson's division then marched to Morton's Ford, and, on the next day, to Raccoon Ford, where we remained until December 19th, when we marched to the neighborhood of Orange C. H., and then back to our old camp near Mt. Pisgah Church on December 24th. The next day we had a regular old-time Christmas, since a good many boxes had been received from home, in some of which were the ingredients for egg-nog.

The men suffered a great deal at Mine Run from the cold winds. We were on a high hill, and were kept in the breastworks all the time, and not allowed to make fires.

CHAPTER XXII

WINTER 1863-4—CAMP NEAR MT. PISGAH CHURCH

BEFORE LEAVING our camp near Mt. Pisgah Church to march to Mine Run, some of the men had built huts. When we returned to camp huts were built for all, and soon we were comfortable. The Second Brigade also built of logs a commodious church. There we gathered every Sunday for regular religious services, sometimes having a preacher to expound the gospel, and at other times a soldier would lead the meetings, which were largely attended and much enjoyed by the men.

The whole division was ordered out one afternoon to witness the execution of three Confederate soldiers from another division, who were to die by being shot for some violation of the laws of the army. The division was formed on three sides of a hollow square, the fourth side being open. Three stakes were fixed in the ground about the center of this open side, and soon after our formation an officer and a guard with the prisoners appeared. The prisoners were made to kneel with their backs to the stakes, to which they were securely tied and a cloth was fastened over their eyes. Twelve men were ordered to take up the twelve guns lying on the ground in front of the prisoners. The guns had already been loaded, it is said six with and six without balls, so that no man would know that he killed one of the prisoners. The twelve men took their places about thirty feet in front of each man, the order to fire was given, and, at the report of the guns, two men were killed, the balls going through each; the third man, while shot, was not killed. One of the detail was ordered to place another gun against the man's breast and fire; this killed him instantly. This was the only execution I witnessed, and, if I live a thousand years, I will never be willing to see another.

We remained in this camp a long time, drilling, etc., during good weather, and going regularly on picket to Morton's Ford. On February 5th the whole corps was called to the ford, the indications being that the enemy were moving and were marching a column to the ford with the intention of crossing. They did not make their appearance on the other side of the river, but sent skirmishers to the ford, who became engaged with ours, and some of their artillery was in action and shelled our lines. We remained at the ford until the 8th, and then returned to camp, leaving a brigade as usual on picket. The enemy had disappeared and gone back to their camps before we moved. This was known in the Yankee army as the "Mud Campaign," and they said that if their artillery and wagons had not stuck in the mud they would have made things lively for us.

On March 1st the enemy made a movement in our front and sent a body of cavalry on a raid in our rear. About sunset of the 2nd the long roll was sounded in the camp of Johnson's division, we were ordered to fall in, and, as soon as we did so, we were ordered to march to the stone road. There the division was formed, and we marched at a quick step in the direction of Fredericksburg. Arriving at Mine Run, we camped for the remainder of the night. The roads were full of mud and the marching was bad; at one place we forded a branch and the road ascended a steep clay hill, the wet shoes of the soldier after coming out of the branch and treading on the clay had made it perfectly slick, and many a fall was the consequence. We had a boy recruit just from his home and this was his first march. He wore wooden bottom shoes, and, poor fellow, he slipped back into the branch, getting out a step or two, so often that some of his comrades finally undertook to help him. Frequently they went with him two or three yards from the branch, when he would commence to slip, pulling them all back together into the water. He was finally told to sit down on the road side until daybreak, when he would be able to see his way, and could then join us. This he did; but some of the boys, to have a little fun, told him that the Yankee cavalry were marching behind us, and as soon as we got a little way from him, they would come along and take him prisoner. Poor little fellow, he commenced to cry as if his heart would break. This little fellow, however, made his mark at the Wilderness battle a few weeks later. I saw him blow a hole through a Yankee, who was at the muzzle of his gun, during the attack they made on us.

Early the next morning we continued the march, halted at the crossing of the Germania Road, formed a line of battle across the road, stacked arms, and were told that we might rest; but must remain near our guns. It was rumored that the Yankee cavalry raiders were expected to return this way to their army, and we were there to intercept them. We remained several hours, marched to Chancellorsville, and, forming a line across a road leading to one of the fords, stayed there several hours; we marched back to the Germania Road, where we remained all night. The next morning we again marched to Chancellorsville, remaining there all day and night. We were called out of camp very suddenly on the afternoon of the 2nd on this expedition, and we did not carry any rations with us. (Some of the men were left behind in camp to cook them and then bring them to us.) We had eaten up everything in camp during the day, and were drawing rations for supper when we were ordered off on the march, and we left without it. The men with the cooked rations joined us at Chancellorsville on the morning of the 4th, and during all this time very few of us had anything to eat. I had nothing, and it was the longest time I went without eating during the war. As soon as we finished eating what the men brought, we took our places in line, and the next morning returned to Mt. Pisgah; the raiders having returned to their army by another route. We saw at Chancellorsville that a year's time had not healed the scars of the bloody battle fought there, the ground where we were being literally covered with human bones that had been scattered about since the shallow burial of those who fell there. It was an awful experience, even for soldiers, to lie down for rest at night, after scraping the bones away.

The night of the 5th found us back in our old quarters, and we were glad, very glad, to return to them, and were soon comfortable.

For a long time short rations were issued to us, and it being hard to divide them equally among the members of the messes, the majority of the messes adopted a system that gave general satisfaction. After the rations were cooked, they were divided into as many parts as there were members of the mess. Each of these parts was piled on a log or on the ground in a row, and one member of the mess was selected to turn his back to the piles of rations, while another member pointed his finger towards one of the piles and asked, "Who has this?" The man with his back towards the piles designated one of the mess by name, who immediately took it; and then another pile was disposed of in a similar way, until all the piles were taken. Coffee was not included in this method of distribution, because it was given us in the grain and in quantity so small that the grains were counted out to each man. None but the Confederate soldier knows how they lived. For months we had not had a full ration, and the rations became more scanty as the war continued, and after this time we never received as much as we wanted to eat, unless we captured it from the enemy.

The regular rations allowed by army regulations were not sufficient, but we did not get the regular allowance even at the beginning of the war, when everything was plentiful. Here is the allowance of rations for men in the field—for each man:

½ lb. bacon or beef—daily.
1½ lbs. flour or corn meal—daily, or 1 lb. hard bread.
For one hundred men:
8 qts. of pease or 10 lbs. of rice.
4 qts. of vinegar.
1½ lbs. tallow candles.
4 lbs. soap.
2 qts. salt.
6 lbs. sugar.

While we were in this camp we received some of the Telescope rifles, which were entrusted to a select body of men. On suitable occasions the men practiced shooting with them. At one of those practices they stood on one hill and shot at a target about half a mile off on another hill. The bottom between those hills was used as a grazing place for horses and mules belonging to our wagon train, and during the shooting, they accidentally killed one of the mules. That mule was very fat, and not long after it was killed some of the men cut chunks of meat from him and carried them into camp to be cooked and eaten. Some officer learning of this, had a guard stationed during the day near the mule to prevent it. That night many had mule steak for supper. We are now in a bad plight for cooking utensils; spiders are scarce, also frying pans; hardly a boiler and all the pans to make the bread in are gone; we make the bread in the spiders and frying pans, oilcloths, and during the time of year that the bark of the trees would slip we get an excellent tray by peeling the bark from a tree. We enjoyed this camp, as the quarters were the most comfortable we had during the war. The men really enjoyed the rest and the longest ever spent. There was more sociability here than I ever saw in camp. I enjoyed visiting Clark's Mountain, a mound rising several hundred feet above the surrounding country, and immediately on the Rapidan river. From its top, which was about three miles from our camp, I could see the camps of many of the enemy in Culpeper County; also I had an extensive view of the surrounding country. We had a signal station on its top, and sometimes I had an opportunity to look through the glass at the Yankee camps.

One of the incidents I witnessed while in this camp was changing the clothing of one of our men confined in the guard house, who was handcuffed. He desired to put on a clean shirt, and as he was not allowed to take off the cuffs, he went to work, took off his soiled shirt, and then put on the clean one, the handcuffs not being removed. It, however, took him about two hours to do it.

The negroes who accompanied their masters during the war were a source of much merriment as well as comfort to us. I recollect the experience of two of our negro cooks in battle. On one occasion we were in line of battle when Archer, a cook in one of our companies, came to the front with his master's haversack of rations. We were taking things easy at the time, some lying on the ground, others sitting or standing up engaged in talking over the impending battle, and at the sight of Archer we gave him a hurrah as a welcome. He had been with us only a few minutes, when the enemy made an advance along our front and turned our flank. Fighting became warm, and we had a hot time before we succeeded in driving them back; but following up our success, we drove the enemy from the field of battle. Archer was caught in the fight, and when night came and we were joined by the cooks, he had a splendid account to tell his companions of the part he took in the battle. He told them he took the gun of one of our dead, and fought side by side with "Marse Jim," and he "knows I killed a dozen Yankees. Oh, you ought just to have see me in the charge! Me and 'Marse Jim' just whipped them clean out!" This account of Archer's made a hero of him in the estimation of his friends, and so impressed them that one of their number, Ned, made up his mind then and there to go into the next battle, and see if he could eclipse Archer's account! Ned did not have long to wait, as we met our old enemy again some weeks later, when a line of battle was formed in a wood. Ned was in it, with gun in hand. He had a large knapsack strapped to his back, filled to overflowing with articles from many a battlefield, which he had been carrying for a month or more, with the hope of sending it to his wife by some soldier who was going to his neighborhood. Besides the knapsack he had one or more haversacks filled in same manner, and his canteen!

When we received orders to move forward, Ned marched boldly in our midst, and when we reached the edge of the woods the enemy opened on us,—a spent ball hitting Ned squarely in the forehead, raising a knot as large as a hen's egg in a few minutes! As soon as Ned was struck he was seen to halt, his mouth flew open, his eyes bulged, and he made a movement as if he was going to run, but the men steadied him by telling him that Archer was knocked down several times by balls, and he got up and killed the man who had shot him! In our advance we crossed a fence and started across a field. A man at Ned's side was shot down. Ned started and stopped at the sight, his gun fell from his hand, a ball went over his shoulder, cut the strap on his knapsack, and, as it turned, Ned slipped out of it, letting it fall to the ground; at the same time disengaging his haversack and canteen, pulled off his coat, dropped it, too, brushed off his hat, wheeled and broke for the rear like a quarter horse, amidst the yells of our men! This was a sore subject ever after for Ned. Not that he ran away,—but losing all those things he had been saving to send to Sally! And he would not believe a word of Archer's tale!

Here is another tale of the negro, showing the feeling the southerner had for him. My mess, of about half a dozen, had built for winter quarters a log pen about two feet high; on this they erected their tent, and at one end we had an excellent log chimney. This made us very comfortable. We had a negro slave as cook, who stayed about our tent during the day, but slept in a cabin with other negroes. He was taken sick with measles; we made him leave his quarters and come and stay in our tent, where we cooked for him and nursed him until he was well.

I tried to keep clean while in the army, and made it a rule to take a bath once a week and oftener when convenient; this included winter as well as summer. It looked very formidable to take a bath on some of those cold and stormy days which we had in the army, but it was more in looks than in the reality. Here is a winter's day experience in this camp. One day about noon the sun shining brightly and little wind stirring, I thought I would take my bath. I walked over to Madison Run, a large stream about half a mile from camp. I found the stream frozen over solid. I got a large rock, walked to the middle of the stream, raised the rock over my head, and hurled it with all my force on the ice, but it made no impression. I repeated this eight or ten times without breaking the ice. I then returned to camp, got an ax, went back to the run, cut a large hole in the ice, which was about seven inches thick, cleared the hole of all floating ice, undressed, took a good bath, dressed, and when I returned to camp was in fine condition.

It had been rumored in camp for several weeks that Gen. Grant had command of the army of the Potomac, our old enemy, and from indications in his camp it was supposed he intended to make a move soon. In anticipation of this, Johnson's division broke up winter quarters on May 2, and marched to Bartley's Mill on the Rapidan for better observation, and to be in better place to guard our line.

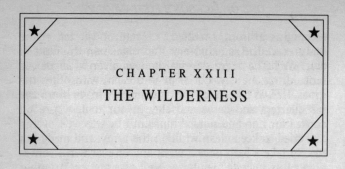

On the morning of May 4th, 1864, Johnson's division left Bartley's Mill and marched to Locust Grove and proceeded along the Stone road towards Fredericksburg nearly all night, then halted, and rested on the side of the road. Gen. Ewell, who had been riding at the head of the column, lay down beside a log not more than ten yards from me.

As the streaks of day were just beginning to show themselves, we were ordered to fall in, and resumed our march. We had gone only a short distance when the stillness in our front was broken by the sound of a drum, and the sweet notes of music from a band. Every man clutched his gun more tightly, as the direction of the music told him that the enemy were in front. There was no need of urging us to hurry, no need to inquire what it meant. All knew now that Grant had crossed the Rapidan, and soon the tumult of battle would begin. The march continued, the command was "Close up," soon the order, "Halt! Load your guns!" then "Shoulder arms! March!" Soon a line of battle was formed by the Second Brigade which was in front, the 21st Va. Regt. on the left of the Stone road, the remainder of the brigade on the right of that road. The order "Forward!" was given,—we moved forward through wood and brush! We were in the wilderness! With a tumult that seemed to come from the infernal regions, we were assailed by the enemy! As soon as the lifting of the smoke enabled us to see, we discovered that the portion of our brigade which was on the right of the road had been swept away; there were no Confederates in sight except our regiment. We broke the enemy's line in our front, and made no halt in our advance,—on we went, shooting as fast as we could load! Suddenly I was confronted by a gun, resting on a big stump, and behind the stump we saw a Yank! We hallooed to him to throw his gun down, several of us took aim at him; he started to rise, but before he could do so, a little boy on my left who had also taken aim at him, pulled the trigger, and at the crack of his gun the Yankee fell dead! This was the little fellow who was wearing wooden bottom shoes, whom we left on the road one night a few weeks before crying, because he could not keep up with us on the march. We captured many prisoners; behind every tree and stump were several who seemed to remain there in preference to running the gauntlet of our fire. We advanced to a dense pine thicket and halted, every man falling flat on the ground at once for protection! We could see troops coming to our assistance, and the line on our left was extended by the Third Brigade, one of its regiments halting directly in our rear, where they lay down, too! On our right the woods were large and open, and for some reason the enemy had disappeared from it. An explanation of this was given in the report of Maj. Meret C. Walsh, "7 Indiana Inf., in Vol. 34, page 617, War Records." He says, "We charged the rebel line, capturing the colors of the 50th Va. Regt., and nearly two hundred prisoners, but being flanked on the right, were forced to retire from the field, and return to the breastworks."

The force on the right was the 21st Va. Regt! It will be

seen that we not only drove those in front, but cleared the
enemy from the field on the right of the road.

The pine thicket in our front was so dense that we
could not see into it twenty feet, but we heard the enemy
talking. My company was near the road and I, wishing to
see what was going on in front, ran across the road to the
top of the elevation, and to the front. What a sight met my
gaze! Obliquely across the road and just behind the pine
thicket, the enemy was massed in a small field. I looked
down the road and saw two pieces of artillery coming up
in a run, and at this time I perceived that I in turn was
seen, and guns were leveled at me! I took shelter behind
a big tree, just as Cumbia of our company came running
to me! They fired a hundred shots, and Cumbia fell shot
through the body! He was as gallant a soldier as any in our
army.

I ran back to my company, and seeing the colonel of
the regiment of the Third Brigade who was with us, I
informed him of the position of affairs in front. He gave
the order at once, "Forward, men!"—the two regiments
jumped to their feet and advanced, the whole of the Third
Brigade taking part. Through the thicket we went, coming
upon the mass of the enemy, the battle raging again more
fiercely than before! With a yell we were on them, front
and flank! They gave ground and then ran! Such a yell
then went up as fairly shook the ground! Hurrah! the
cannon are ours, we capturing both pieces. The enemy in
their flight had crossed to the right of the road, and we
followed through the field about two hundred yards into
the woods; here we halted and were ordered back. In
retiring through the field, we discovered a body of the
enemy in the woods on our left; the 21st Va. Regt.
immediately wheeled and poured a hot fire into them!
They disappeared in great disorder, we resuming our
march across the field, and halting as soon as we reached
the wood on the east side. The 21st Va. Regt. taking
position there and on the right of the Stone road,

commenced to fire slowly at the enemy, who had taken position on the west side of this field. Here we were joined by the remainder of the Second Brigade.

We were then treated to a rare sight! Running midway across the little field was a gully that had been washed by the rains. In their retreat, many of the enemy went into this gully for a protection from our fire, and when we advanced to it, we ordered them out and to the rear; all came out except one, who had hidden under an overhanging bank, and was overlooked. When we fell back across the field the Yankees, who followed us to the edge of the woods, shot at us as we crossed. One of our men, thinking the fire too warm, dropped into the gully for protection. It will be noticed that there were then a Yankee and a Confederate in the gully, and each was ignorant of the presence of the other! After a while they commenced to move about in the gully, there being no danger as long as they did not show themselves. Soon they came in view of each other, and commenced to banter one another. Then they decided that they would go into the road and have a regular fist and skull fight, the best man to have the other as his prisoner. When the two men came into the road about midway between the lines of battle, in full view of both sides around the field, one a Yankee, the other "a Johnny," while both sides were firing, they surely created a commotion! This was true in our line and I suppose in the enemy's line, because both sides ceased firing! When the two men took off their coats and commenced to fight with their fists, a yell went up along each line, and men rushed to the edge of the opening for a better view! The "Johnny" soon had the "Yank" down, who surrendered, and both quietly rolled into the gully, where they remained until night, when "the Johnny" brought "the Yank" into our line. The disappearance of the two men was the signal for the resumption of firing! Such is war!

We remained in this position two or three hours, and

marched across the road and took position immediately on its left, and about two hundred yards in the rear of the line of breastworks that was occupied by the Third Brigade. Slight firing continued all day, and as night approached everything became quiet. We were ordered to rest for the night on our arms.

I was aroused about midnight to take a verbal order to the officer in our front on the skirmish line, which was on the outskirts of the pine thicket. I was instructed to leave my arms, etc., take my time, and make as little noise as possible. The night was dark and the pine thicket so dark that I could almost feel the darkness. Moving carefully, and thinking that I was getting on splendidly in perfect silence, I was thrown down with such a rattling noise as to awaken everybody in the neighborhood! Shooting commenced from the Yankees at once! They fired hundreds of shots in the thicket, and I lay perfectly still until quiet was restored. When I sat up and felt around to see what caused me to fall, my hand came into contact with a saber which I found belted to a dead man; this saber caught between my legs, threw me; it rattling against the man's canteen, as well as my falling amongst the pine twigs, was the big noise in the night. Fully reassured I proceeded, found the officer, and delivered the order. He was an old friend and inquired what I made so much noise for! My explanation, a laugh, a caution to me not to repeat it, a good-night were given, and I started to our line, shaping my course as well as I could, so as to find my dead man again. Fortune favored me. I found him, took his sword, and then felt in his pockets for what he had! I found a knife, a pipe and a piece of string, and in every pocket, even to the one in his shirt, he had smoking tobacco! I had to take an order to the front again at daybreak, and on my return, looked for my man again and saw that he was a Yankee lieutenant. Soon after this the enemy assailed our position furiously with shot and shell for a short time, and then quiet was restored, lasting in our front the remainder of the day, with now and then a skirmish fire.

On the morning of the 7th the Second Brigade marched by the flank to the extreme left of Gen. Lee's line, and there took a small country road through the woods towards one of the fords at which Grant crossed the Rapidan. After going some distance we halted, formed a line of battle, a few pieces of artillery that accompanied us unlimbered, loaded and were ordered to fire through the woods in the direction of the ford. The firing was fast for a short time. The artillery then limbered up, we returned by the same road, and resumed our place in line with our division. We did not know what this movement was for, until a few days later when we learned that it was a feint on Grant's communications. It is said that it made a great commotion in his army.

The giants had met and Grant was badly worsted in his first encounter! His loss was great. All along Lee's line he had been repulsed! In the little field in our front the ground was literally covered with his dead! Our loss was severe, nearly all of that splendid regiment, the 25th Va. of our brigade, having been captured. F Company had amongst the wounded G. W. Brown, L. M. Couch, N. A. Dowdy, A. C. Legg and H. Smith, and W. D. Cumbia was killed. Among the killed in the division were those splendid soldiers, Brigadier General Stafford of the Louisiana brigade, and Brig. Gen. J. M. Jones of our brigade. Gen. Jones was a strict disciplinarian, and inaugurated several plans for the benefit of his men. According to my information, he was the only officer who made the men take care of themselves as far as they could. He allowed no straggling, even the musicians had to march in their places, and if he saw the men becoming weary or fagged, he ordered every musician to the head of the brigade. One of the regiments had a very good band, the others had small drum corps; all together they were a considerable company of musicians. The general directed the band to play a short time, and then the drum corps would play,—with four or five bass drums and ten to twelve kettle drums and twelve to fifteen fifes, they made a big noise, and always received the hearty approval of the men! It was noticeable that the men began to close up, take step with the music, and march several miles in this way, feeling refreshed.

Always on a march when we reached a stream that must be forded, if the water came below the knee, every man and officer who was walking was required to take off his shoes and socks and roll his pants up above his knees. If the water was deep enough to reach above the knees, all were required to strip; thus when we crossed the stream we had dry clothes. This was a great comfort to the men, but none of them would do it unless compelled. The men of our brigade sometimes tried to evade it. Gen. Jones usually caught them, and woe unto the man who was caught, whether officer or private! He received a severe reprimand, and one of his staff marched him back across the stream, and saw that he stripped and then forded according to orders.

Well do I remember a laughable occurrence at Front Royal. In one of our marches through the town after the bridges over the Shenandoah river had been burned, the citizens desired to see the soldiers ford the river. Our brigade was in the front of the army that day, and when we reached the river the hill around the ford was covered with citizens, mostly women and children. Gen. Jones and staff had ridden into the water to allow their horses to drink; the colonel at the head of the column gave the order to halt, he then looked at the hill and then at Gen. Jones, and then looked at the men; the men did the same thing. The General looked up, and not seeing the men making preparation for fording, he called to the colonel to know why the men did not strip and come along. The colonel looked again at the hill and the men, and then gave the command in a loud voice. "Strip, men, and be ready to ford!" The men hesitated, but the general now hallooed to them to strip at once. This we commenced to do, and several of the men had their pants off before the citizens were aware of what was going on. Then over the hill they went, pell mell, amidst a general yell from the men! They did not see us ford the river that day!

CHAPTER XXIV
SPOTTSYLVANIA C.H.

On THE MORNING of May 8th, 1864, the Second Corps, the Second Brigade in front, marched from the left of Lee's line to the right of his line in the Wilderness. As we passed along the rear of the army, occasional Yankee cannon shot passed over us, and occasionally a musket ball. When on reaching the right of Lee's line we continued our march in the same direction until we came to woods on fire. Several miles our course was through this fire, at times the heat was intense, and the smoke suffocating! The men were very uneasy all the time, fearing an explosion of their cartridges. We finally emerged from the woods into a fair road, which carried us by Todd's tavern and a mill. We had left the mill behind us several miles, and overtook some of our cavalry, who, since it was then two or three o'clock in the afternoon, informed us that they were mighty glad to see us, because they had been all day fighting Yankees, who were not far ahead. We heard the musketry, and the order was given to "close up"; we marched along the road for about half a mile, when we filed to the left and marched in various directions, sometimes at a snail's pace and then in a run! We stood seemingly for hours, and finally at a double quick were thrown into line of battle at Spottsylvania C. H. This was just about sunset. We did not become engaged, but heard the enemy taking position, too. About eight or nine o'clock our line was moved about thirty or forty feet to the front, and as we were in the presence of the enemy it was necessary to use strategy. The markers were taken to the new line and the officers in forming an alignment called out: "John" or "Bob," who answered, "Where are you?" The officer in reply indicated a step or two to his right or left, as the direction and distance he wished the marker to go, when the marker made the necessary change of position, and the line quietly dressed on him. In this way the line was finally formed, and we lay on our arms for the night. Early in the morning of the 9th we moved farther to our right, Johnson's division occupying the right of Lee's line. The Stonewall Brigade was on the left of the division, the Louisiana Brigade next on its right, the Second Brigade next, and the Third Brigade next; they occupying the right of the division and also of the army. The Second Brigade occupied what is known as the "Bloody Angle," my regiment, the 21st Va., being near the toe of the horseshoe, as it is often called. As soon as our line was formed we began to throw up breastworks. After our brigade finished their works, our regiment secured a few axes and commenced to cut down the pine bushes that ran nearly up to our line at this point. While we were thus engaged, the Yankees opened fire on our line from several batteries, and we took refuge at once in our breastworks, which the 21st Va. Regt. found to be no protection, since the angle was so abrupt that the enemy threw their shell in our rear, as well as in our front! As soon as they ceased firing, we went to work and made regular pens large enough to hold eight to ten men each, thus protecting ourselves in all directions. Our regiment, the 21st Va., had just finished the pens and the men were taking places in them, when an order came from the division commander for us to report to Gen. Geo. H. Stewart, who commanded the Third Brigade of our division. All the men and officers of our regiment protested against this order. We had never fired a gun from behind a breastwork and these were made so much better than any we had ever made, we desired to have the honor of defending them! We were compelled to go, nevertheless; we left our pens with many a grumble, and reported to Gen. Stewart, who sent us about three-quarters of a mile to the front. We halted in a large wood, on the south side of a small branch, and formed a skirmish line along this branch. The left of the line ran a short distance along the border of a field, the remainder of the line straight through the wood, and ended along the border of another field. About one-third of the regiment was placed on the line, the remainder took a position about two hundred yards in the rear of the center and was held as a reserve and also a relief. One of F Company was detailed to take orders along the line, and to the regiment. No enemy as yet had been seen, but about half an hour after the line had been formed there came a message along the line, saying, "The Yankees have made their appearance and are moving to the left;" that is our right. Late in the evening their skirmishers advanced within range, in front of our left, and skirmishing continued until night. During the night other companies from our regiment relieved those on the skirmish line; and when morning came, we found that the enemy had moved far enough to their left to come in contact with our right, where skirmishing was kept up all day, with an occasional shot on our left. The enemy had not made their appearance before our center. Heavy fighting occurred along the line of breastworks during the day, to our left. The breastworks occupied by Dole's Brigade and a company of Richmond Howitzers, just to the left of the Stonewall Brigade of our division, were captured by the enemy; but troops near-by were hurried to that point, and as soon as they could be formed in line, the order was given to charge, and drive the Yanks out! This was done quickly and our line was reestablished. In this charge a portion of the Second Brigade participated, and were among the first to plant our standard on our breastworks again. On the 11th an occasional shot was fired from their extreme left, and right of our regiment skirmish line, and we could hear some heavy fighting along the line of battle on our left. Soon after dark the Yankees commenced to move in front of our skirmish line,—we could hear the rumble of wheels and the noise of marching and the command to "close up," and it was far in the night before the sounds ceased. This was the prelude to an attack such as was not witnessed during the war, and, I expect, was the heaviest attack ever made at a single point by any army of the world! It seems that Gen. Hancock, with his corps of 25,000 men, consisting of four divisions, eighty-five regiments of infantry and thirteen batteries of artillery, assisted by Wright's Sixth corps of 15,000 men, was ordered to break our line on the right. During the night of the 11th Gen. Hancock moved this force to the front of the skirmish line of the 21st Va. Regt., and formed a line of attack,—two divisions front, the regiments massed, double columns on center, making ten or twelve lines of battle. They were ordered to move right ahead at the firing of the signal gun at 4:30 A. M.—but the time was changed to 4:35—and not to fire a shot until they were inside of our works. Day broke on the 12th of May with a heavy fog, drops of water were dripping from the trees, as if after a rain. I had started from the reserve of our regiment to the skirmish line with an order, when the stillness was broken by a cannon shot and the screaming of a shell! I put my hands instantly to my head to see if it was on my shoulders; the shell seemed to come so near me that it certainly took off my head! (Such feelings as this often come to a soldier!) Recovering from my dazed condition I proceeded. Before I reached our line I could hear the sound of the marching of 40,000 men, and soon a few shots from our skirmish line on the left put all on the

watch. I saw the line approaching to my left, ran back to
the colonel and reported to him; and he immediately
called the regiment to attention. By this time the enemy
had approached so near that the regiment could see them.
We saw their immense numbers. Some of the skirmish
officers appeared and reported to the colonel that the
enemy had run over some of their men, that they seemed
to pay no attention to our men, and that the body was the
largest they ever saw! I was immediately sent out on the
line to recall all the skirmishers whom I could find; and
as soon as this was done, we faced about and marched to
our line of battle, making a circuit to the left so as to avoid
the enemy, who had now passed between us and our
breastworks. We at once heard heavy fighting in our front.
As soon as we came in sight of a field the regiment halted,
and the colonel sent me forward to make a recognizance.
Running to the field, I saw that the farther end of it was
perfectly blue with Yankees, and saw the smoke of the
terrific fighting that was going on further off! Running
back, I made my report to the colonel. He called the
regiment to attention and made a circuit further to the
left. This was the second and last time during the war that
a feeling of dread came over me that I would be captured,
and I said to myself, "Well, old fellow, you are gone this
time, and I will not give ten cents for your chances of
getting away!" I was sent forward as a pilot, and in a shot
time an old, ragged, dirty Confederate rose up from
behind a bush in my front, and took deliberate aim at me
with his musket. I cried, "Don't shoot! we are friends!" I
saw an expression of doubt on the old fellow's face, he
knowing it was the direction of the enemy, momentarily
expected. I made haste to exclaim again that we were
skirmishers driven in, and were the 21st Va. Regiment!
Men rose up all along the line, and I knew we were in front
of a Confederate skirmish line. How my heart jumped! I
felt so good I could have hugged every one of them! We
passed through their line and soon reached the
breastworks occupied by Davis's Brigade. While our

regiment was at the front, our line of battle was extended
to the right by troops from Hill's corps, and this was a part
of his line. We went to the rear and reported to Gen.
Ewell, who informed us that our division had been
captured and that he thought we had been captured too.
This was a terrible blow to the army, the capture of
Johnson's division!—this was Jackson's old division, and
those were the men who had done so much fighting, and
who had made those wonderful marches for him. They
were now prisoners in the hands of the Yankees. The
number was small it is true for a division, but they were
such trained soldiers that they counted as many in a fight.
Jackson's old division was annihilated, and ceased to be a
division from that date. The Old Stonewall, the Second,
Third, and the Louisiana Brigades lost their organization
also. Hancock struck the breastworks and rushed over
them, his men turning to the right and left after getting
inside, and took our division in the rear. The artillery that
was supporting the line had been withdrawn during the
night, and had just gotten back, when the attack was
made, and only one piece had time to get into position and
fire one shot when the captain said he heard someone in
his rear say, "Don't you fire that piece!" and on looking
around, he was confronted by hundreds of Yankees. They
captured all sixteen pieces! The situation seemed so
critical at this time, that "Marse Robert" came to the front
to look after it; he sent for Brig. Gen. Gordon, who was in
command of the reserves, and gave him directions about
bringing them up, where to place them, etc. Gordon soon
had them in line, when Gen. Lee's presence was noticed
amongst the troops, and it was here that the men showed
the second time their devotion to him. A great cry went
up from them, "Gen. Lee to the rear! Gen. Lee to the rear!
If Gen Lee will go to the rear we promise to drive the
enemy back!" But the old hero did not stir. Gen. Gordon
then rode to him and took his bridle and gently led him
to the rear, saying to him, "Those are Virginians and
Georgians, Gen. Lee. and they will do their duty!" "Yes!

Yes! we will drive the Yankees back, if Gen. Lee will go to the rear!" was the cry from the men, many of whom were in tears! And well did they redeem their word! As soon as the order was given, "Forward!" they went, and it was one of the most terrible battles of the war, in which the slaughter of Hancock's men, who were hemmed in this angle, was so great that it received its name of "The Bloody Angle." The enemy were finally driven back, and sought refuge in a part of our captured breastworks, where they were compelled to stay. The men of the reserve covered themselves with glory. The troops who helped them shared the praise with them! Gordon was made a Major-General at once!

All this had taken place while my regiment was being driven in, and while it was at the rear. We were given fresh ammunition and ordered to the front, a staff officer being sent with us to show to us our position. On arriving at the designated point, we formed a line and advanced through a large wood, and soon we were under fire; but the undergrowth prevented us from seeing the enemy. We advanced until we came to a small bottom and going through that, reached the rise and plainly saw the Yankees about one hundred and fifty yards from us. They were in the pens made by our regiment, they were standing up in those pens as thick as herrings in a barrel, and as far back behind them as the smoke would allow us to see,—such a mass of men I never saw! We found one Confederate soldier, an Alabamian, who was standing behind a large pine tree, loading and firing with as much deliberation as if he were firing at a target. He was keeping the whole of Hancock's force back at this point. He said he was a sharpshooter, and his line was on each side of him! There certainly was no other Confederate in front of our regiment line, nor could we see one either on the right or left. We lay down, taking advantage of everything that offered a protection, and opened on the enemy;—musket balls were fairly raining, great limbs of trees were cut off by bullets, as if by an ax, the men seemed more uneasy about them than about the balls. No cannon were used here. This was the heaviest fire the world ever saw at a single point! The fire from those 40,000 men was so heavy that they literally shot trees to pieces! The enemy used mules to bring ammunition on the field, and some of their men fired over 400 rounds, and there is on exhibition at the War Department in Washington an oak tree about fourteen inches in diameter, that was severed by minie balls at this time. Our colonel and lieutenant-colonel were wounded here early in the action, Seay and Richardson of F Company, and many of the regiment were wounded. After staying here about two or three hours, we were ordered to the rear, and stayed there the remainder of the day, gathering up the stragglers, and those of our division who had escaped capture. That night we lay down on the ground for rest, with truly grateful hearts that our regiment had been ordered out of the breastworks, even against our protest, and sent to the front on special service, escaping capture!

We remained in the rear until the morning of the 15th. We found in the middle of our camp, in the open field, an old hare's bed containing four little ones, the old mammy having run away on our approach! I do not know that I ever saw men more solicitous for the welfare of anything than were those grizzly warriors for those little bunnies. It was raining, and some wanted to make a house over them, others wanted to hold their oilcloths over them, no one was allowed to touch them, one might look as much as one choose, but, hands off! When we left it was a sad parting.

This attack by Hancock that was so formidable and was intended to cut Lee's lines, was one of the most terrible battles of the war, and ended in a miserable failure. Our line was straightened across the bend that night, breastworks were thrown up and we had a much better line than before, both as to direction and position. While we were in the rear, we collected about six hundred men of the division, and marched to the front and took position in this new line. The day was quiet in our front. On the 16th we had some skirmishing. On the 17th Rodes' skirmishers and our regiment made an attack on the enemy. On the 18th, the enemy, having been heavily reinforced, made an attack in our front, and were easily repulsed with heavy loss. On the 19th the enemy disappeared from our front during the night, moving to their left. The Second Corps followed them, and came up with them late in the evening, when we made a fierce attack, lasting until late in the night. During the night we marched back to our old position in the breastworks, and rested there.

About the coolest thing I saw during the war was under that terrific fire from the Yankees who were in our breastworks. It should be remembered that when we took our position in their front, we found one lone Confederate who was keeping up a steady fire on them! This man had captured a Yankee knapsack which he had strapped to his back. Soon after our arrival he stopped firing, and said he wanted to see what it had in it, and that he needed a change of underclothing very badly. Taking off the knapsack, he opened it, and from the remarks he made as he took out each article and inspected it, he seemed to have gotten possession of a big clothing store with a notion store thrown in! He selected a suit of underclothing, laid them aside, then replaced the remainder in the knapsack, fastened that, then deliberately undressed, taking off every piece of his clothing, even his socks, put on the clean ones, donned his old uniform, quietly took his gun, brought it up to his shoulder, took deliberate aim and fired, and loaded and fired as long as we were there!

Brig. Gen. Walker, the commander of the Stonewall Brigade, in writing of this battle says: "The rapid firing of our skirmishers in a heavy wooded ravine in front of the center of Johnson's line, gave notice that the enemy was advancing, and the heavy tramp of a large body of infantry

and the sharp words of command could be distinctly
heard. Our men were all up and ready for them with
muskets cocked, peering through the gloom for the first
glimpse of their foes. The enemy had emerged from the
ravine, and advanced about one-third of the way across the
open plateau before they could be seen, or could
themselves see our works on account of the fog. All at
once the slow lifting fog showed them our heavily fortified
position, some four or five hundred yards in their front. At
this unexpected but unwelcome sight, the advancing
column paused and wavered and hesitated and seemed to
refuse the task before them. Their mounted officers rode
to the front and urged them on, while many officers on
foot and horseback shouted, 'Forward! men, forward'! and
repeated the words again and again. Then the moment for
the Confederate fire had come, and the men rising to full
height, leveled their trusty muskets deliberately at the
halting column, with a practiced aim which would have
carried havoc into their ranks. But the searching damp
had disarmed them, and instead of the leaping line of fire
and the sharp crack of the musket came the pop! pop! pop!
of exploding caps as the hammer fell upon them! A few,
very few pieces fired clear, fresh caps were put on only to
produce another failure; the powder had gotten damp and
would not fire!

"As the enemy received no fire from our line, they took
heart and again moved forward with rapid strides; on they
came unopposed and in a few moments had torn our well
constructed abattis away and were over our works taking
prisoners of our unarmed troops. This statement as to the
failure of the muskets of our men to fire is true, as to that
portion of our line between the Stonewall brigade and the
salient, which was as far as my vision extended; but I have
been told by officers of the Second Brigade that the right
of that brigade had been more careful or more fortunate,
and their muskets were in good order, and that the enemy
was repulsed in front of that portion of our line with great

loss, and that they held their position until the enemy's troops, who had crossed to their left, had swung round in their rear and come up behind them."

Major D. W. Anderson of the 44th Va. Regiment of the Second Brigade was officer of the day on the 11th, and he says: Capt. Clary of Gen. Johnson's staff came to him at 4 A.M. on the 12th, and stated that Gen. Johnson sent him orders to see the regimental commanders, and tell them to wake up their men and have them in the trenches, and see that their guns were in good order. This order was promptly obeyed, and he further says that when the enemy advanced they were repulsed with great slaughter, not one getting to the breastworks until they had crossed to the left and came up in their rear, when they were taken prisoners and marched back some two or more miles to Provost Marshal General Patrick's headquarters, where, he says, one of Gen. Patrick's staff said to him, "They charged us with only 45,000 this morning!"

Among the lost in our division were Major Gen. Johnson and Brig. Gen. Stewart, captured; Brig. Gen. Walker and Col. W. A. Witcher, who commanded the Second Brigade, were wounded. F Company lost W. B. Edmunds and P. S. Richeson, wounded; and W. C. Seay died a few hours after being wounded.

While we were engaged in these battles, Sheridan with his cavalry left Grant's army May 9, 1864, on a raid to cut Lee's communications, and capture Richmond! On the morning of the 12th, he arrived at Brook schoolhouse, about three and a quarter miles from Richmond on the Brook turnpike. At that time my grandmother, the widow of Capt. John Goddin, lived on the west side of that road two and a quarter miles from Richmond, her house fronting south. In front of it, several hundred yards off, was a fort, situated on the turnpike at Laburnam. On the Hermitage road was a similar fort, and they were connected by breastworks.

On the morning of the 12th grandmother got up early to do the churning, preferring to do it herself, taking her position on the front porch. When the butter "had come," she went to the well at the side of the house to cool the churn dasher, and get some cold water to take the butter up. At the same moment a squad of Yankee cavalry came around the other side of the house, and, perceiving the churn, helped themselves to buttermilk, and when the old lady came back she found the Yankees on the porch, one with the churn to his lips, drinking! It made the old lady hot, and she whacked him as hard as she could with the dasher, and said some very plain words to the party. They ran off in a good humor, saying they would see if our breastworks were manned. Going down a dividing fence until they reached the Laburnam fence, they fired a few shots and at once discovered the breastworks were manned! Running back to the house they went to the barnyard, took possession of a mule and cart, filled the cart with corn, and drove off towards the main body, which was at Brook schoolhouse. All at grandmother's home lamented the loss of the fine mule and cart, but about two hours after the mule came back with the empty cart!

That party of Yankees went nearer to Richmond than any during the war. I should say the distance by the Brook turnpike was about two miles and one hundred yards.

CHAPTER XXV

HANOVER JUNCTION,
BETHESDA CHURCH,
COLD HARBOR

O<small>N</small> M<small>AY</small> 19th the Second Corps singularly occupied the left of Lee's line of battle at Spottsylvania C. H. When the line was first formed we were on the right, but Grant made all his movements to our right, and Gen. Lee, in withdrawing men from the left to strengthen his right, had taken all except our corps. On the 21st we were aroused at daybreak, and as soon as we formed ranks, marched out of our breastworks towards the right of our line and as we passed, an occasional cannon shot and minie ball from the enemy passed over us. We marched past our right a short distance and took a road leading in the direction of Richmond, continuing the march in that direction till night, when we stopped to rest.

It will be remembered that Edward Johnson's division were nearly all captured on May 12. This was Jackson's old division and consisted of the Stonewall (the First), the Second, and Third brigades, all Virginians, except two North Carolina regiments in the Third, and the Fourth Brigade, which consisted of Louisianians. After bringing together the Virginia stragglers and such as were not captured, and putting regiments into companies, and brigades into regiments, we found we had about six hundred men. These men were organized and called a brigade, and William Terry, an officer of the Stonewall brigade, was made Brigadier General and appointed its commander. It was known to the end of the war as Terry's Brigade. The Louisiana brigade was consolidated with another from that state in Early's division, and was commanded by Brig. Gen. York. The North Carolinians joined some brigade from that state.

When Terry's brigade marched out into the road the morning of the 21st, we were joined by Evans' brigade and York's brigade and were told that Brig. Gen. Gordon had been made a Major-General and put in command of these three brigades, which were afterwards known as Gordon's division of the Second Corps (Jackson's old Corps), the division taking a prominent part in all its operations until the end came at Appomattox. While the brigade was known officially as Terry's, its members continued to designate the different bodies as the Stonewall brigade, the Second, and Third, and in speaking or writing of them I use these names. Thus the Stonewall brigade consisted in our view of its old members who were present, however few, and we spoke of the members of other brigades in the same way. We did this instead of using regiments to designate portions of this multiform brigade.

Gen. Gordon soon rode by, and we filed into the road and followed him, reaching Hanover Junction in the night and ahead of Grant, who was marching for the same point. The next morning we formed a line of battle in a wood across the road on which he was marching, and when his advance approached, it found Lee in his front again. We remained in our position, momentarily expecting an attack. Grant moved some of his troops across the South Anna river, and made a demonstration in front of our line. We were joined during the day and night by the remainder of Lee's army, who took position to our right and left. The next morning our division was hurried at a double quick to the left of Lee's line, and at once formed a line of battle. The hurry and the firing in our front, caused us to expect to become heavily engaged. We waited several hours and marched to the right of the line, staying there all night. The following morning we took position on the east of the Richmond, Fredericksburg & Potomac railroad, and threw up breastworks; and continued in that position until the morning of the 27th.

Grant, after making a slight attack, left our front during the night of the 26th, swinging around to our right. The Second corps, early on the morning of the 27th, were on the march to oppose him again. We marched to Pole Green Church, the place where Jackson first struck McClellan's outpost in 1862. On the morning of the 29th, we formed a line of battle not far from Bethesda Church and threw up breastworks, and when Grant came along the road that evening, he found our division across the road in his front and again ready for him! After slight skirmishing he drew off without making an attack. On the next morning the Second corps made an attack in our front and drove him about one and a half miles; we then returned to our line, resuming our position in the breastworks.

Tucker Randolph, the gallant boy soldier, an old F, was killed in this fight. He deserves more than a passing notice. Entering the service at seventeen years old, he took an active part in the company from the first, and was one of the first men promoted on getting into the field. A corporal, then a sergeant, wounded at Kernstown, he was soon after promoted to a lieutenancy and appointed an aide on Gen. John Pegram's staff, and was killed while displaying conspicuous gallantry!

We moved to the right on the 31st, and again threw up breastworks. On June 1st the Second corps marched to the front to make an attack on the enemy, but for some reason it was not made; after sharp skirmishing lasting until sunset, we returned to our breastworks. On the next morning we moved out again and made the attack, taking three lines of fortifications and capturing about seven hundred prisoners. We remained in the enemy's line next to them until about midnight of the 3d, when we withdrew, and took our old position in our breastworks. While we were in the enemy's works, they made several slight attacks on us, firing their artillery through the woods and once they fired two rammers of their cannon, the rammers sticking in the ground a little in rear of the 21st Va. Regt. Corporal Anderson of F Company was wounded in those fortifications on the 3d, and Captain Jordan was severely wounded while he was on the skirmish line in front of them.

The enemy left the front of our corps during the night of the 5th. We followed them the next morning, and found them fortified about one and a half miles to our right. On the 7th, the skirmishers were ordered forward, and our division was ordered to support them. We found the enemy strongly fortified. On the 9th, the Second corps moved to the right and rear of Gen. Lee's line, where we stacked arms and went into camp, after being on active duty for thirty-five days and under fire each day.

Because Lieut.-Gen. Ewell was sick, the corps was under the command of Major-Gen. Early during these operations, and Major-Gen. Ramsuer was assigned to command Early's division.

The Second Corps now consisted of Rodes', Gordon's, and Ramsuer's divisions of infantry with the usual artillery. Since the battle of the Wilderness May 5th, our corps had lost heavily in men and officers; Maj.-Gen. Edward Johnson and Brig.-Gen. Stewart were captured, Brig.-Generals Pegram, J. A. Walker, R. D. Johnston and Hays were wounded, and Brig.-Generals Stafford, Doles, Daniel and J. M. Jones were killed. The "hammering" had commenced and was telling, although we did not realize it at that time.

The Army of Northern Virginia had inflicted terrible losses on the enemy. It is said by their historians that Grant lost at this time about as many men as there were

in Gen. Lee's army—the loss he sustained before crossing
James river made the total about ten thousand more than
Lee's whole force.

One of the incidents of this campaign was the visit of
an old up-country man, who came to see his son in our
division. He wore a stovepipe hat, and the men had great
fun over the hat, but he was a jolly old fellow and was not
worried by them;—he was very anxious to see a battle. We
made one of our advances while he was with us; he
accompanied his son, and returned with us unhurt, the
most enthusiastic man I ever saw.

While we were marching through Hanover County, an
old lady came to the fence, which ran along the road, and
wanted to know of us if we belonged to "Mr. Lee's
Company." We told her we belonged to *Gen*. Lee's *army!*
She wanted to know how her son was, and when we
informed her that we did not know him, she was perfectly
astonished to think any man in "Mr. Lee's Company" did
not know all the men in it.

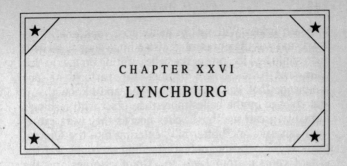

CHAPTER XXVI
LYNCHBURG

O N JUNE 12th the Second Corps received orders to cook rations and be ready to move early the next morning. We were aroused about midnight, formed line, and before day marched out of the woods into a road leading towards Mechanicsville. Arriving there we turned towards Richmond, thinking we were going to head Grant off on the south side of the Chickahominy. Soon after crossing that stream, we turned to the right instead of the left, as we supposed. "What does this mean?" was the question among the men. We marched around Richmond to the Three Chops Road and then turned to the right again—we gave up guessing, except that possibly Jackson's old corps was going back to the valley.

In marching around Richmond, our route was about a mile from the home of relatives of mine, and I went to see them. When I reached the house I found all the ladies of the family and two of Richmond's belles assembled in a large porch. I was welcomed most cordially, and told I was just in time for luncheon. In a few minutes the dining-room servant appeared with a large waiter filled

with ash cakes. Without formality each took one in his
hand, and was then presented with a huge glass filled with
buttermilk and ice, one of the belles waiting on me. In this
plain but wholesouled manner we partook of our
luncheon. That was a rich treat to me, and I know that it
was enjoyed by the belles more than if set with fashion's
formality. I can see those belles now as they were eating
their ash cake and buttermilk, entering into the fun and
mirth of the occasion, notwithstanding we could hear the
distant cannon from Lee's and Grant's armies and the
cheers from my own corps, marching we knew not
whither. We marched until late in the afternoon, and went
into camp near Ground Squirrel bridge, having marched
over twenty-five miles. On the following morning we
marched again. About ten o'clock Gen. Gordon passed us
and told us not to march so fast, or the mules to the
wagons would not be able to keep up with us, and in
consequence we would not have any supper. Gordon
always had something pleasant to say to his men, and I
will bear my testimony that he was the most gallant man
I ever saw on a battlefield. He had a way of putting things
to the men that was irresistible, and he showed the men,
at all times, that he shrank from nothing in battle on
account of himself. Many a time I saw him ride along the
skirmish line in our valley campaign and say to the
skirmishers, "Let's drive those fellows (the enemy) away,
and let our line of battle stay where they are! They are lazy
fellows, anyway!" or some similar remark. The
skirmishers were devoted to him, and would generally do
as he wished.

On the 15th we came in sight of the Central Railroad,
passing Trevillian's depot, where Sheridan's cavalry and
ours, under Hampton, had had a fight two or three days
before. We could see the dead horses, torn-down fences,
etc., as nothing had been touched; and we saw the rail
pens used by Hampton's men that Sheridan made such an
ado about, saying he could not whip Hampton as his men
were behind such strong fortifications! On the evening of

the 16th we went into camp about one mile beyond
Keswich depot. On the 17th my brigade got on the cars a
little north of Keswich and was carried to Lynchburg.
Much to the surprise of the men we found the town in
great excitement, because the enemy, under the command
of Gen. Hunter, had advanced to within two miles of the
place. There was a small force in his front and the citizens
expected immediately to see the enemy march into the
town. Our presence brought an immediate change. We
were cheered to the echo, and the ladies waved their hands
and gave us lunches and cool water as we marched
through the city. All wished that Hunter would stay until
Early could bring all his army. We marched past the fair
grounds and formed a line of battle, were ordered forward
and halted near the schoolhouse, remaining there all
night. We heard skirmishing in our front and heavy
cannonading on our left. We remained in line of battle
until the afternoon of the 18th, when we received orders
to cook rations and be ready to move early in the morning.
This meant that the remainder of our force was up, and we
were going to attack Hunter as soon as it was light enough
to see. Our skirmish line advanced in the morning and
found that Hunter had slipped out of the trap during
the night, and was in full retreat. Immediate pursuit
commenced, and we overtook him going into camp at
Liberty, Bedford County. Our advance attacked him at
once and he retreated further on, we camping in the place
selected by him. We marched twenty-five miles during the
day, and it is seen that we did not let him rest much. We
followed Hunter closely until we came to Salem, Roanoke
County, when Gen. Early gave up the pursuit and turned
towards the valley. Before we reached Salem, he sent
McCausland with his cavalry around to the rear of Hunter.
McCausland succeeded in cutting off part of the enemy's
wagon train, and captured ten pieces of artillery.

During this march, soon after passing Big Lick, in the
afternoon, approaching one of the handsome residences in
that part of the country, we noticed several ladies standing

on the side of the road, and when we came nearer we saw two beautiful young ladies and their maids and near them were two huge wash tubs. The young ladies gave us an invitation to come forward and partake of some ice water and brandy julep. The men needed no second invitation; the head of the column marched up, the young ladies handed each man a drink, which was received eagerly, with many grateful wishes for their future welfare. I was told that the tubs were repeatedly emptied and filled. This was the biggest julep treat of my experience.

We marched a short distance from Salem and encamped, remaining in this camp the next day, taking a much-needed rest. Many men were barefooted,—some for want of shoes, others having sore feet from new shoes and unable to wear them, and to the latter class I belonged. I started from Richmond wearing a new pair of heavy English shoes and when I took them off at the close of the first day's march, nearly all the skin on my feet came off with my socks, and I went through the campaign as far as Washington City and back to Winchester barefooted, and kept my place in the ranks, too. Several days I carried my shoes tied together and thrown over my shoulders, but was troubled so much by questions and requests to buy them, that I finally gave them to a comrade who had none. On the 23d we took up our march, and the next day, at the request of the men, we were marched over the Natural Bridge, and were allowed to stop there an hour or two to rest and view the bridge. Resuming our march, we went into camp about sunset. The next morning as we passed through Lexington, the whole corps marched through the burial ground and past Jackson's grave. What hallowed memories it brought up! and many a tear was seen trickling down the cheeks of his veterans; and how many of them had crossed the river, and were then resting "beneath the shade of the trees" with him! We continued our march, and on the 27th reached Staunton.

Fourteen days had elapsed since we left Lee's line at Richmond. During that time we marched in eleven days,

235 miles, the last day marching only six miles. On our march from Lynchburg, we passed many private places that had been pillaged or destroyed by Hunter's army, and at Lexington we passed the ruins of the Virginia Military Institute which was burned by him while he was on his march to Lynchburg.

On the 28th we resumed our march down the valley and felt perfectly at home, since nearly all the valley from Staunton to the Potomac river was familiar to us, and many of its inhabitants old acquaintances. We stopped regularly at night and continued the march each day. On the afternoon of July 3d we reached Martinsburg, running in on the Yankees who were there, so suddenly, that they did not have time to move any of their stores. They were making big preparations to celebrate the Fourth, and many of the men had received boxes of good things from home and friends. The depot and express office were filled with articles of this kind. A guard was placed around these buildings and their storehouses. The express office was put in charge of a quartermaster who was an old friend of mine. At night I went there and inquired of the guard for him and he let me into the building. He was very glad to see me, as he had only one man to help him get these articles in shape, and asked me to help him; this I consented to do, if he would give me a barrel of cakes. He said "all right." I found one and carried it out and turned it over to my company. Returning, I went to work with a will, but with so many good things in sight, and others we knew were in the boxes, I was compelled to say to my friend that I must have something to eat before I could work any more, and added. "I hadn't "nary' mouthful for three days." I looked over some of the boxes and choosing one, opened it, and found it filled with cakes, oranges, bananas, lemons, etc., and a bottle of wine. I got a chair, as the soldiers said "a sure enough chair," and sat down to my box and ate, and ate, until I could eat no more. Then I went to work again with renewed energy. The quartermaster just then wanted something from one of his associates who was at the depot, and I offered to go for him, which was agreed to, and he gave me his directions. When I reached the depot I found it filled with trunks, boxes, etc. After discharging my errand, I looked around the depot a few minutes, and told the man in charge that he ought to send his friend, the quartermaster, one of the trunks for him to put some of the articles at the express office in to take with him. He said he would be much obliged if I would take one. I shouldered one at once, carried it out, and got a comrade to help carry it to the express office. I made my report and opened the trunk. In it was a magnificent saddle and a lot of clothing, which I gave to the quartermaster, a fine pair of boots, a gold pen, a lot of writing paper, and a plum cake which I "confiscated," the boots fitting me to a T. When my feet were healed so that I could wear them, I wore them until I went home. I joined my company, who were profuse in their thanks for the cakes, and soon fell asleep,—dreaming of little cakes, big cakes, and a mountain made of cakes.

The next morning was the Fourth of July, 1864! Gen. Early did not move us at the usual early hour, but issued to the men the good things captured the evening before. They were divided among the men as fairly as possible, F Company getting a few oranges, lemons, cakes and candy, and a keg of lager beer. We certainly enjoyed the treat, and celebrated the day as well as we could for our hosts, and regretted they did not stay to preside for us. We drank their health with the wish that they would do the like again. This was the biggest Fourth of July picnic celebration we enjoyed during the war. We took up our march and crossed the Potomac river at Shepherdstown. I took off my clothing, made a bundle, secured it around my neck with my belt. I walked into the water and commenced to ford. About one-third of the way the bottom of the river was covered with large round stones, then a smooth and level bed of granite which extended nearly to the opposite bank. I got along very well until I reached the level granite bottom, which was covered with minute shells, adhering to the granite, so very sharp that they stuck into my feet at every step. I walked on them until I thought I could not take another step, stopped, but could not keep my feet still,—thought of sitting down, but the water was just deep enough to cover my mouth and nose if I had sat down. I thought I would turn back, but I saw it was just as far back as to the other side. Tears actually came into my eyes. I was never in as much torture for the same length of time in my life. Finally I got over, with the resolve never to ford there again without shoes.

We went into camp at night on the banks of the Antietam, on the ground occupied by a part of McClellan's army at the battle of Sharpsburg. The next day Gordon's division marched to Harper's Ferry, where we drove the enemy into their fortifications. We remained there the succeeding day, skirmishing, and left during the night, marching to Norristown, where we joined the remainder of our corps. The next morning we crossed South Mountain at Fox Gap, and went into camp near Middletown.

During these operations Gen. Early had been joined by Gen. Breckenridge's command, which we found at Lynchburg. It consisted of two brigades of infantry, some cavalry, and artillery. Gordon's division at this juncture was assigned to Breckenridge, making a corps or wing under his command.

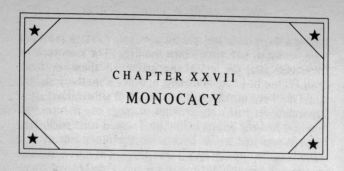

CHAPTER XXVII

MONOCACY

CHAPTER XXVII

MONOCACY

W<small>E LEFT CAMP</small> or rather our bivouac near Middletown early on July 9th. Taking the road to Frederick City, Maryland, we marched around the town and in sight of it. It was a beautiful day in this beautiful country. The sun was bright and hot, a nice breeze was blowing which kept us from being too warm, the air was laden with the perfume of flowers, the birds were singing in bush and tree, all the fields were green with growing crops; the city, with its thriftiness, looked as if it had just been painted and whitened; a few floating clouds adding effect to the landscape. It was a day and hour to impress all. We were quietly marching along, talking about the scene and the day.

In our march we had left the city in our rear and were nearing the Monocacy, a river crossing the road on which we were marching. We soon heard the crack of muskets, and at almost the same moment the roar of cannon! We knew what that meant, that the Yankees were going to dispute our crossing of the river. The two divisions in front of us were hurried forward, our division halted after going a short distance, and we were told to stack arms and rest, as we would not go into the fight. The men took off blankets, oilcloths, etc., and stretched them in fence corners, on muskets and rails, to make a shelter from the sun. We were in the road and on a hill which overlooked the battle that was about to be fought in our front. We made ourselves comfortable and lay down under the shelter provided, to *look* at a battle, something we had never done. We were Jackson's old "foot cavalry." We saw our men take position in line of battle, the skirmishers go forward, become engaged with the enemy on the opposite side of the river, a battery here and there on the other side shelling our men, while the continual *crack* of muskets told that the shelling made no impression on our skirmishers, who were now in the bushes along the river bank. Some of our guns went into position and opened fire, our line of battle moved forward,—all this in plain view of our division. It was very exciting to us old Confederates, and a yell went up along our line every few minutes as we saw our men get into some better place and nearer the enemy. The men of our division were suggesting to each other a line on which the two divisions should cross over. Suddenly our attention was called to a man riding up the road towards us, leaving a streak of dust behind him. He rode up to Gen. Gordon, who was at the head of the division, delivered a message, the general gave an order to his officers in front, and mounted his horse. We were called to attention, the men taking down their blankets and oilcloths, and rolling them up to take with them. The order was given, "Take arms!—no time now for blankets, but get into your places at once." "Right face! forward march!" was the command all down the line, and away we went. "What is the matter?" was the question amongst the men. We thought we were to be spectators, and why just as things had begun to get interesting in front, break in upon us and actually make some of us leave our blankets and oilcloths, articles we had captured in some former battle. The men seemed to dislike to lose

those articles more than miss seeing the battle. We were
hurried along the road a short distance, and filed to the
right, going through fields and over fences until we came
to the river, we suppose a mile or so from our line of
battle. We found a small path on the river bank leading
down to water, and on the opposite bank a similar one,
denoting a ford used by neighbors for crossing the river.
The cracking of muskets on the opposite side of the river
told us that the front of our division, which had crossed,
was engaged. My brigade was the rear one, and, as the
regiments crossed, they marched up the river along the
low bank and formed in line, and were ordered forward to
the attack. As the Second Brigade mounted the hill, we
saw in our front a field of corn about waist high, extending
to a post and rail fence, and behind that fence the Yankee
line of battle. They began to shoot at us as soon as we were
in sight. Our men on our right were heavily engaged, and
we broke into a run with a yell and went toward the fence.
In a moment or two we captured it, and the Yankees were
running to another. An officer came along our line and
said that we were not wanted there, that Gen. Gordon was
waiting for the Second Brigade, that we were wrong and
must fall back through the corn, behind the hill, on the
low bank, and form at once and go to Gen. Gordon. We
had been fighting all the time, but as soon as the men
could be made to understand, they ran to the rear. The
brigade was soon formed and we marched by the flank
further up the river, then the head of the column was
turned to the right, and we marched up on top of the hill.
There was Gordon,—I shall recollect him to my dying
day,—not a man in sight,—he was sitting on his horse as
quietly as if nothing was going on, wearing his old red
shirt, the sleeves pulled up a little, the only indication that
he was ready for the fight. Our division was heavily
engaged on the right, and the troops on the other side of
the river were keeping up their fire, as we could plainly
hear. We were to the left of the corn field, and marching
obliquely from it. The ground had a gentle inclination and

the fields were enclosed with post and rail fences. As we approached Gen. Gordon, he rode forward to meet us and said, "Hurry up, boys," turning his horse and taking the lead. The head of the column was soon near a fence, and high enough up the hill to see some distance. Looking through this fence, we could see another fence parallel to and about two hundred yards from it; just on the other side of the second fence was a line of Yankees marching towards the river. They were going at a double quick step and at a right-shoulder-shift arms, every man seemed to be in place, and the manner of their marching looked more like a drill than a movement in battle. The men at the head of our column seeing this, gave a yell, and sang out, "At them, boys!" Now came Gen. Gordon's part; turning quietly in his saddle he said, "Keep quiet, we'll have our time presently." As we were now near the fence Gen. Gordon said, "Some of you pull down the fence, so that we may go through!" In an instant several panels of the fence were down, the men quietly stepping aside to let the general go through, and as soon as this was done, they hurried through the fence. The first man to follow the general through the fence was one of F Company, and he was barefooted. The general led in the direction in which we had been marching, and tried to allay the excitement of the men; this he was able to do, until about a hundred passed through the fence, when the cry went up from the men, "Charge them! charge them!" It was useless for Gen. Gordon to try to stop it now,—nothing but a shot through each man could have done it,—and with a yell, we were at the fence. A volley from our guns,—and that magnificent body of men who were taking their places in line were flying! The other men of our brigade came up as fast as they could run and delivered their fire at the fleeing enemy. Over the fence we went, the enemy running in all directions. Up went our old yell all along the line of our division, and it was answered by our comrades on the other side of the river. A little way beyond the fence the hill falls abruptly to a small valley, and through this valley ran the road to Washington. Some of the enemy stopped at that road, turned, and fired at us. It was just here that Porter Wren of F Company received his fatal wound. He turned and managed to walk back to the fence, tried to get over it, but fell back—dead! Immediately on the brow of the hill I passed a Yankee colonel, laying on the ground dead.

This was the most exciting time I witnessed during the war. The men were perfectly wild when they came in sight of the enemy's column, knowing as they did, that the first line that fired would have the advantage of the other. It was as much as Gen. Gordon could do to keep the head of the column from making an attack. Our division pursued the enemy a short distance, when the pursuit was taken up by Ramsuer's division, who had crossed the river on the railroad bridge, as soon as we cleared the way. It was about sunset now, and my brigade went into camp in an orchard near the road,—on the same ground over which we chased the enemy a few minutes before. In this orchard were several of the enemy, wounded. One of them asked me for some water, and stated he had had a canteen but one of our men had taken it from him. Poor fellow! I went to a spring, filled a canteen and carried it to him, and as I had two canteens, gave him this one, and told him that in case some of our men wanted it, he must tell them what I had done for him, and I was sure none of our men would take it. I had a full haversack that I had taken from the body of a dead Yankee on the hill, and offered him something to eat, but he said he had his own haversack, and it was full. He seemed to be very grateful for my little attention.

A mill pond was near us, and many of us took a bath, which refreshed us very much. I ate a good supper out of my Yankee haversack, and soon went to bed for the night. F Company had H. C. Fox wounded, and J. Porter Wren killed. Early's loss was not large, and was confined principally to Gordon's division. Among the wounded was

Brig.-Gen. Evans. We captured five or six hundred prisoners, and Gen. Early sent us word to take no more, as he did not know what to do with them. The tables were completely turned on Gordon's division. We thought we would *witness* the battle, but our little army saw our division of 2,300 men whip Wallace's force of 10,000.

The road to Washington was now open, and we hastened the next day as fast as men could travel.

Gen. Breckenridge, who commanded his own and Gordon's division during this campaign, said to Gen. Gordon about this battle, "Gordon, if you had never made a fight before, this ought to immortalize you."

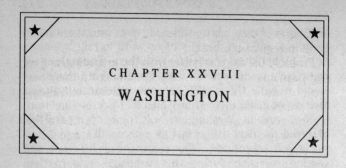

ON THE MORNING of July 10th we marched early, passing through Urbanna, Hyattstown, and Clarksburg, going into camp about sunset, having marched twenty odd miles. The day was a terribly hot one and the men straggled a great deal, although it was reported that the enemy's cavalry we left at Harper's Ferry were following us, and picking up all they could reach from our stragglers.

We were up and moving early the next morning, passing through Rockville, Maryland, and at two or three P.M. the head of Gordon's division passed the toll gate about four or five miles from Washington. We inquired what road we were on, and were informed that it was the Seventh Street pike. The enemy were shelling the road at this point with their big guns. We soon came in sight of the Soldiers' Home, where the enemy had a signal station, and we were really at Washington City. We could see their fortifications and the men marching into them on each side of the road on which we were. Their dress induced us to think they were the town or city forces, some of them looking as if they had on linen dusters, and there being none in regular uniform.

Probably the day was hotter than the preceding, and we had been marching faster too. Consequently there was more straggling. Our division was stretched out almost like skirmishers, and all the men did not get up until night. Rodes' division was in front. He had formed a line of battle and sent forward his skirmishers, who had driven the enemy into their fortifications. Our division stacked arms on the side of the road, the men broke ranks and looked around. A house between the two lines was burning. I went to Silver Springs, the country home of Mr. Blair, one of Lincoln's cabinet, and got water, and examined the place. It was a splendid home. When I came back I went to the front and looked out on the situation. As far as my eye could reach to the right and left there were fortifications, and the most formidable looking I ever saw! In their front the trees had been cut down so that the limbs pointed towards us and they were sharpened. About midway of the clearing was a creek that seemed to run near the fortifications and parallel with them. The enemy had a full sweep of the ground for at least a mile in their front, and if their works were well manned, our force would not be able to take them, since, as I suppose, Gen. Early's entire command did not number 10,000. Night came on and found us occupying the same position. The next morning Gordon's division marched to the front, formed line of battle, advanced to the edge of the wood and lay down, while our skirmish line was sent forward to the creek. We remained in our position all day. The enemy were shelling us at intervals, and in the afternoon they sent forward their skirmishers with a large force following them. They made an attack on Rodes' front. He repulsed them and drove them back into their works. At night we left Washington, and retraced our steps on the road as far as Rockville. There we took a road to the left, marched all night, and stopped about midday for several hours' rest near Darnestown, then resumed the march and continued it all night, passing Poolville and crossing the Potomac the next day at White's Ford, going into camp near Leesburg.

Thirty-one days had passed since we left Lee's army at Richmond. We had marched during that time four hundred and sixty-nine miles, fought several combats, one battle, and threatened Washington, causing the biggest scare they ever had. It was believed by the men that we could have gone into the city on the evening of the 11th, if our men had been up, but straggling prevented it. I can not say that they straggled without excuse, because as I before said, many of them were barefooted and footsore, and we had made a terrible campaign since we left our winter quarters on the 2d of May. I was still barefooted, my feet being too sore to wear my boots. The scars made on that march are on my feet to this day. Many men, like myself, marched right along without shoes, but many of them were physically unable to keep up.

It is said that the enemy concentrated over sixty thousand soldiers at Washington while we were threatening the city; this force pursued us to the Potomac, but did us little injury.

The next day, the 15th, the 21st Va. Regt. was detailed to take charge of a lot of horses that had broken down on the way, others having been captured and put into their places. We immediately converted ourselves into a regiment of mounted infantry, the most motley ever seen. Some of the men secured saddles, some bags and filled them with straw, some used their blankets to ride on; some horses had bridles, some ropes, some grape vines for bridles, and some ridden without any form of bridles. As soon as we were mounted, we took up the march, driving the loose horses. We passed through Union and Upperville, stopping about sunset to let our horses graze, the only food they had. After several hours of rest, we again mounted and continued the march, passing through the Blue Ridge into the valley at Paris, marching all night. We stopped the next morning near Millwood, Clarke County, and turned our horses loose to graze, having marched about thirty-three miles. We were the most completely used up men you ever saw,—foot cavalry could not be converted at once into mounted men, as we found out to our cost,—and when the order to mount was given about midday, we were so sore and disabled that nearly all the men needed assistance in mounting. We left this place and marched to Middletown, on the Valley pike, stopping several times to graze our horses. On the morning of the 19th, we turned our horses over to a quartermaster and marched to Winchester, where we joined our division.

The next day the army marched up the valley. Reaching Middletown, Gordon's division was sent out in the direction of Berryville, it having been reported that the enemy were advancing in that direction, and, after some brisk skirmishing, we drove them back. That night we marched to Hupp's Hill. The next day the army formed a line of battle and awaited an attack from the enemy. They came in sight of us, fired a few cannon and had some skirmishing. Their army was now under the command of Gen. Crook and Gen. Averill was the officer in command of his cavalry.

CHAPTER XXIX

KERNSTOWN THE SECOND, AND THE ENEMY'S CAVALRY AT LEETOWN

T HE ENEMY having left our front at Hupp's Hill, we, on the morning of 24th July, marched down the valley. When we reached Barton's Mill we learned that the enemy had made a stand at Kernstown. Gen. Early immediately made preparations to attack them. The Second Brigade was deployed as skirmishers, and was posted on the left of the Valley pike, its right resting on the pike. The rest of Gordon's division was formed on the right of the pike, with the remainder of Breckenridge's command. The Second Brigade, in skirmish line, was ordered forward. In our front there was an open field almost level up to the enemy's line of battle. There the country became gently rolling and on the hills they had stationed their artillery. The fields were separated by stone fences, several of them running across our front, and were occupied by the enemy. Soon after we began to advance, we came in sight of the hill that was occupied by a battery which fired at our regiment in March, 1862, when we crossed this same field. They sent shell after shell at us, and as soon as we were within range, the Yankees behind the first stone wall

commenced to fire with their muskets. We were ordered
to lie down. From this point we could see a long line of
the enemy on the right of the pike, and on their extreme
left a body of cavalry. We saw also Breckenridge advancing
against their left. The Yankees in front of our brigade were
shooting rapidly at us, who were lying down in the field,
and our men were becoming uneasy, since we had no
opportunity to reply. They, stooping down behind the
wall, loaded, rose, and fired and lay down before we could
locate them. Our men sent a message along the line,
"Let's take the wall!" The answer came back, "All right!"
We were up in a second, and at the wall in a few more
seconds, the enemy retreating to the next wall. This was
not very far from us, and our men were mounting the wall
already taken, some were over, for we were going to take
the next wall. An officer came from Gen. Early with an
order for us to halt, retrace our steps, and lie down in the
field again. Our brigade commander, Col. Dungan of the
48th Va. Regt., told him that he did not give the order to
advance, but he saw no reason to stop it after the men had
started. "Well, you must stop them now," said the officer.
Col. Dungan gave the order to halt, but it was obeyed very
reluctantly, the men standing where they were, the
Yankees shooting at them all the time. Our officer from
Gen. Early, Major Mann Page, an old F, could not stand
this; he was very impetuous and called to the men to
return, but could not induce them to do so. They cried
out, "Let's drive them away from the wall!" and away we
went, leaving the major stamping with rage. We took the
second wall in about the same time it takes to tell it,
driving a line of battle from it. By this time Breckenridge
had struck their left, and their whole line was in rapid
retreat, and as those on their left made for the Valley pike,
nearly all of them passed us; we loaded and fired into their
ranks as fast as we could, some of our men in their
excitement sitting on the stone wall loading and firing
from it. The retreating column of the enemy seemed to be
so intent on getting away, that they gave no attention to

our small line on the wall. As soon as all of them passed us, over the wall we went in close pursuit. They went through the village of Kernstown, keeping the pike until they reached the old stone church and burial ground, turning to the left between them, going direct to the hills around Winchester. The first fire we received from them in their retreat was from a fence just beyond the old church. As we reached the church and turned around it towards the fence through which they went, a few skirmishers of theirs along this fence fired on us. Sergeant Griever of the 48th, who was carrying the flag, was shot dead at my side, and one or two more were wounded. They had no time for a second fire, as we were upon them. The field was filled from this fence to another about a quarter of a mile off with fleeing Yankees, and beyond the second fence, I could see them making their way over the hill. In order to help their men in the field, some of them were firing at us from the farther fence. An officer on a white horse seemed to be directing them; some of us paid our respects to him, the balance shooting into the mass of the enemy in the field. Before we were half way across the field, their fire ceased and they and the officer on the white horse disappeared over the hill. When we reached the hill we were so tired that we could run no longer, but we continued the pursuit, following the trail, and only came in sight of the enemy as they went up the hill just behind Winchester. On that hill they had one piece of artillery, which fired at us once, then limbered up and joined in the retreat. We continued the pursuit until sunset, when we halted, stacked arms, and soon lay down to rest for the night, Rodes' division keeping up the pursuit into the night.

This was the most easily won battle of the war. We had very few casualties. We could trace the line of the enemy's retreat to the hills by their dead and wounded, a loss inflicted on them mostly by the skirmishers of the Second Brigade. We were in the advance until we were stopped, and stacked arms, and we were within one hundred yards of the enemy until they reached the hill.

The next day we followed the retreating enemy, and Gordon's Division went into camp at Bunker Hill. The next day we marched to Martinsburg and remained in the neighborhood until the 31st, tearing up the B. & O. Railroad for miles. This is the fourth time I took part in the ruin of this railroad. We left Martinsburg and marched to Darksville, remaining until August 4th, when we moved to the Potomac and crossed at Shepherdstown on the 5th, marching to Sharpsburg, passing a few miles beyond and into camp for the night.

How soon the scars of war are removed when they are made in a country that is kept in a state of cultivation and improvement! We could see very little of the great battle of Sharpsburg, and when we passed the Tunker or Dunkard church everything looked so nice and clean that one would not know that it was the scene two years before of the most severe fighting of the war! The battle of Jackson's Corps and McClellan's right was at its fiercest around this church. Lines were driven back and forward, around and around the old church, hundreds of musket balls struck it, and several cannon shots went through it. Dead and dying men were lying in sight of it by thousands.

The next day, the 6th, we marched, passing through Tillmantown and crossing the Potomac at Williamsport, and camped at Falling Waters. Thence we marched to Darksville, Bunker Hill, and the Woolen Mill, not far from Winchester, camping for the night at each place. At the latter place we arrived in the afternoon. My brigade had stacked arms, broken ranks, and taken off our accouterments, when the long roll was heard. We were ordered to "fall in," and marched some distance to repel an advance of the enemy's cavalry. On the 11th Gordon's Division was at Newtown skirmishing on the White Post road with the enemy. There W. H. Divers of F Company received a terrible wound through the leg, and died two days afterwards. From Newtown we marched to Strasburg, where our army formed a line of battle and waited an attack from the enemy. Thence we moved to Fisher's Hill, staying there until the 17th, when we marched to Winchester. There we found the enemy in line of battle awaiting us. We made preparation for an immediate attack. Gordon's Division was formed in line of battle on the right of the pike, divided into three sections; our skirmishers were ordered forward, and the right section soon followed. As soon as they advanced their length ahead of the middle section, the middle section advanced, and so with the third, our line advancing in echelon. The Second Brigade was on the left of the line and was the third or last section; we continued to advance in this way for a mile. Our skirmishers encountered the enemy in our front, who gave way at once. Our brigade was shelled heavily from a battery posted on a hill towards our left. We came to a corn field and, as we passed through it, I took a well-filled haversack from one of the dead Yankees, swung it round my neck, and continued my march. Looking in it I found it filled with roasting ears, that had just been boiled, and hot. I commenced to eat at once, giving my comrades some. Passing through the corn field we right-faced and joined the division, which was now marching by the flank. The skirmishers were so far off that we decided the enemy preferred a retreat to a fight. Night soon came on, we stacked arms and bivouacked.

The next day, 18th, Maj.-Gen. Anderson joined us with a division of infantry, his artillery, and cavalry. On the 19th we marched to Bunker Hill, the next day towards Charlestown, encountering the enemy's cavalry in force, and finally coming up with his army well fortified near Charlestown. Skirmishers were thrown forward and were heavily engaged all day. The enemy left during the night, and when morning came and we ascertained they had left, we were off at once in pursuit, Gordon's Division passing through their fortifications. They were the best hurriedly thrown up works I saw during the war. About one hundred yards in their front, rails from the adjacent fences had been placed in the ground about six inches apart, leaning to the front. They were about waist high with their ends sharpened. When we reached them in our march, we found it a heavy task to remove enough of them for the division to pass through. We found the enemy in position at Halltown, and again fortified. It was reported to Gen. Early that a fine lot of hogs were in a field on their right, inside their skirmish line. Gordon's Division was immediately sent for the hogs, which we soon took possession of and that night all had fresh pork for supper. We remained in the enemy's front until the morning of the 25th, when Gordon's Division, with some of the other divisions, marched towards Leetown. Gen. Early accompanied us and left Gen. Anderson in command of the force in front of the enemy. Soon after passing Leetown our division, which was in front, came in contact with the enemy's cavalry. A long line of skirmishers was thrown forward on each side of the road, our division formed in line of battle, and all were ordered forward. Soon the skirmishers became engaged and, as they advanced, fighting became heavy; but they drove the enemy at all points. The enemy's cavalry made a charge on the left of the road in a large field, and succeeded in capturing a few of our men, but they were hurriedly driven back. The line of battle was halted occasionally to allow the skirmishers to clear the way. During one of these halts, we stacked arms and were ordered to lie down near our guns. A Yankee battery on our right occasionally sent a shot at us. One of these, a round shot, struck the ground near my front, ricocheted, and came directly towards us. Every one in the locality was watching it, and it became evident that it would strike a stack of muskets just to my right, in its second descent. Then it was seen that as it was an oblique shot, it might strike two stacks. The guns were loaded, and fearing that some of our line might be injured by the firing of the guns should they be struck, the men who owned both stacks jumped to them to take arms, and get away before the shot struck. In the hurry and confusion they became mixed, the shot fell in their midst,—men, guns, shot, and all went down together. In a few seconds the men were on their feet, hurrahing and laughing, and one man held up the shot, neither men nor guns having been injured,—but it was a close shave. These men laughed and jested at death, as all old soldiers do. Constant exposure to danger hardened the best of them. We resumed the advance for a short distance; the enemy seemed to have had enough and to have withdrawn. Our skirmishers were called in, and my division resumed its march by the flank in the road. We went along quietly, Gen. Early and some other officers riding at the head of the column. Someone now approached Gen. Early, and soon he left the pike by a country road on our right and rode to the top of a hill. Then he turned and beckoned to the officer who was riding in our front, and he turned into this road. We followed a short distance, the column halted, and it was rumored that the enemy were just over the hill in our front. I ran to the top of the hill, and found that it fell on the opposite side about as suddenly as it rode on our side. It was a ridge, at the foot of which on the other side there was a corn field extending to another pike, which ran at nearly right angles to the one on which we had been marching and joined it about a mile away. In this pike there was a Yankee column of cavalry marching along quietly, seeming to be ignorant of the proximity of a Confederate. They were about four hundred yards from us. I do not know how it affected Gen. Early, but it was the most thrilling scene I ever saw, and gave me the "shakes" at once. I was ordered to run down the pike as fast as I could until I met some of the skirmishers, and give the officer in command an order to come to the front as fast as possible. I hastened away and soon met Capt. Hays' command, delivered the order, and described the situation to him. Poor fellow! he and his men were so completely exhausted by skirmishing with the enemy's cavalry for two or three hours, that they could not double quick, but started off at a quick step. When they came to the front, they deployed in the corn field and advanced at once. Our line of battle was formed by regiments as fast as they could enter the corn field, and each regiment was ordered forward. The skirmishers were near the road before they were observed by the enemy, and poured a withering fire into them. The enemy attempted to reply to this, and when some of our regiments came into view, they broke and ran in every direction! We cut their column in two, some of them going towards Shepherdstown and the others returned towards Harper's Ferry, whence they had come. Those who were returning towards Harper's Ferry ran out a battery, that shelled us for a few minutes, then limbered up and followed the crowd;—a part of our division pursuing them, and a part pursuing those going towards Shepherdstown.

When I came out of those two fights, I surely was the best equipped man in our army. I captured a horse with splendid equipments, even the poncho and blanket rolled up behind the saddle. Before the fight was over, I got a Colt's five-shooter, a sixteen-shot Winchester rifle, a saber, a nose bag for my horse and a bag of oats, also a canteen, six extra saddles, and a Yankee haversack filled with rations.

About midnight, the division having come together, we went into camp, and heard that Fitz Lee had captured the party that went towards Shepherdstown. All of us slept well on that news and a heavy day's work. In the morning we learned that the enemy had escaped from Fitz Lee, although he at one time had them in a tight place. August 27th found Gordon's Division at Bunker's Hill.

On the 29th Gordon's Division was ordered to the front. We found the enemy's cavalry at Opequan Creek and attacked them at once, driving them about five miles; and returned to our camp. September 3d found Early's army in camp around Winchester. On the 7th the enemy drove in the pickets of our brigade. Gordon's Division was ordered to their support, and drove the enemy back across the Opequan, which was the dividing line between the two armies.

At this time I received the following communication, which explains itself:

> Hd. Qrs. 21st Va. Infantry,
> Sept. 12th, 1864.
>
> SPECIAL ORDER.
> No.——
>   Sergt. J. H. Worsham Co. "F." is announced as Act. Adjt. of this Regt. from this date.
>   By order Col. Moseley.
>   E. E. ENGLAND, Lt. & Act. Adjt.

This made three adjutants the company has furnished the regiment. It has also furnished the regiment three sergeant-majors.

September 13th found Gordon's Division near Brucetown, where our pickets had again been driven in by the enemy. The Second Brigade was ordered to their support, driving the enemy across the Opequan, the 21st Va. Regt. remaining on picket. On September 14th Gen. Anderson left us, taking his artillery and Kershaw's division of infantry with him, leaving Fitz Lee's cavalry with us. The 17th found Gordon's and Rodes' division at Bunker's Hill.

While in camp at Darksville on August 2, 1864, I made my last morning report of the company as orderly sergeant, and herewith give a copy of it. It was made on a piece of paper torn out of an old account book and the ruling and heading I did with pokeberries, according to the "Form" provided by the adjutant of the regiment.

Morning Report of Company F.

PRESENT

1864	Captains	1st Lieut.	Sergeant	Corporals	Music	Privates	Extra Duty O.	Extra Duty N.C.O.	Extra Duty P.	Sick O.	Sick N.C.O.	Sick P.	In Arrest O.	In Arrest N.C.O.	In Arrest P.	Officers	Enlisted Men
Aug. 2		1	1	1	¹	8		2	1		1					1	14
" 30		1		1		8		3	1		1					1	14

ABSENT

1864	Detached Service O.	Detached Service N.C.O.	Detached Service P.	With Leave O.	With Leave N.C.O.	With Leave P.	Without Leave O.	Without Leave N.C.O.	Without Leave P.	Sick O.	Sick N.C.O.	Sick P.	Missing O.	Missing N.C.O.	Missing P.	Officers	Enlisted Men
Aug. 2		1	11		1	1			10	1	1	11		1	7	1	44
" 30		1	11		1	1			10	1	1	11		1	7	1	44

1864	Officers (Present & Absent)	Enlisted Men	Aggregate	Aggregate Yesterday	In hands of the Enemy	Cooks	Discharged	Transferred	Died	Recruits	Nance, discharged	Peaster, transferred	Cumbia, died	Smith, recruit
Aug. 2	2	58	60	60	1	1								
" 30	2	58	60	60	1									

M. L. Hudgins, 1st Lt.

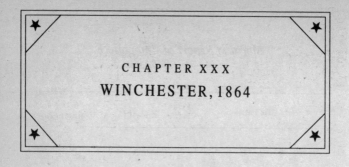

CHAPTER XXX

WINCHESTER, 1864

ON THE 18th of September, 1864, Gordon's Division left Bunker's Hill and marched to Martinsburg. There we encountered some of the enemy's cavalry who skirmished with us and retired, firing at long distance. We stopped at Martinsburg a short time, and marching back to Bunker's Hill, encamped for the night. It had been rumored in our camp a week or two that Gen. Sheridan from Grant's army was in command of the enemy, and that he had been largely reinforced. Their force in the valley had all along been three or four times as large as Early's, and now since Sheridan was receiving more men, it must be five or six times as large. It was believed by us that Sheridan had more men in *his* cavalry alone, than the number of Early's entire army. On the 19th we marched from Bunker Hill in the direction of Winchester, and in a short time we heard the boom of a cannon in our front. Some of our army had been engaged daily with the enemy for the last month, and considering this shot in our front to be a part of the daily attack, we paid little attention to it. We kept quietly on our way until we passed Stevenson's depot, when we saw a

The Battle of Winchester

horseman approaching us hurriedly. When he rode up to
Gen. Gordon in our front we recognized him as Col.
Pendleton, Gen. Early's Adjutant-General. He had a
moment's talk with Gen. Gordon, wheeled his horse and
rode off. We hurried up and our ranks closed. Soon we left
the pike by our left and marched across the fields. The
firing in our front had become heavy and we heard the
musketry. We decided that it was a general attack by
Sheridan, but our men were not disturbed by it, because
we knew we could whip Sheridan easily, notwithstanding
the large odds we believed he had against us. We marched
in the same direction a mile or more, and, coming in sight
of a small body of cavalry, were told it was part of Fitz
Lee's force, and towards our right we saw some of our
artillery firing. We marched towards this artillery but in
front of it. The fight was raging in our front, and in a wood
on our left there was heavy skirmishing. We continued to
march by the flank past this wood, the head of the column
being nearly in front of our artillery. When we came to an
open space between the woods just passed and another a
little farther on, we saw our artillery firing through this
opening at a line of battle of the enemy's, that was
advancing through a field beyond the woods. Our column
continued its march until it reached a line opposite the
second woods, when we halted, were ordered to front face,
and load. Our skirmishers formed along the whole front of
the division, and were ordered forward. We followed them,
our artillery firing over us at the advancing enemy. Terry's
Brigade (ours) was on the right, the Louisianians next,
and Evans on the left. We saw our skirmishers in front
engage the enemy, and from the increased firing in the
woods on the left, we knew that they were at it, too. We
continued to advance and soon met the enemy with a
volley; they turned and ran, we pursuing. We kept up the
pursuit for three-quarters of a mile, when we halted, and
were ordered back. We had made a clean sweep,—not a
Yankee could be seen in our front. Falling back about half
a mile, Terry's Brigade was ordered to form in line with

Rodes' Division,—which arrived a little later than we, and had advanced on the enemy in their front and repulsed them as easily as we did. After we made the connection with his line, we lay down to rest. We had been in action only about an hour, and we thought we had gained an easy victory. Gen. Early said it was a grand sight to see those two divisions numbering a little over 5,000 muskets hurl back in utter disorder the immense body of the attacking force, consisting of the Sixth and Nineteenth Corps!

We heard that Gen. Rodes had been killed, and was lying near Gordon's right. Our men were much grieved, because Rodes had been associated with us so long, and Gordon's men had become very much attached to him. He was a gallant soldier and splendid fighter, and we lost a great man in his fall. The loss in Gordon's division at this time was very small; Brig.-Gen. York, of the Louisiana Brigade, was wounded, and Gen. Terry had his horse killed under him. Through an opening in the woods on our right, we saw Ramsuer on the extreme right of Early's line, still heavily engaged, but gaining ground. Along Gordon's and Rodes' front not a sound was heard and not an enemy was in sight, but the stillness was soon broken by the advance of a brigade of the enemy through a field on our left, towards the woods. Evans' Brigade was in those woods, the same that was occupied by the enemy in our attack on them, from which they were driven by Evans. This body of the enemy advanced in splendid line,—our brigade on their flank could see down their entire line as they advanced on level ground. When they came within firing distance, Evans let them have his fire; they halted at once; we saw the dead and wounded on the ground, and many wounded going to the rear. They advanced again,—their men under Evans' fire falling as they advanced,—they entered the woods, we heard the heavy fighting there, and soon we saw the enemy hurriedly driven out, disappearing behind the hills. This ended the fighting of Gordon's Division at this part of the line.

Far around on our left, on the Valley pike, little fighting had taken place, as only a few of the enemy had made their appearance. Now they came, nearly the whole of Sheridan's cavalry, and it must be recalled that they were as many as Early's entire army. A corps of infantry accompanied them. They advanced up the Valley pike and charged our weak force, consisting of a small cavalry force and a brigade of infantry from Wharton's Division. As stated by a northern writer, "Hell broke loose now!" Our cavalry and the small infantry force was soon driven back, but fought so stubbornly that the Yankees made little progress. Our force was reinforced by Gen. Early as soon as possible. Now the hardest fighting of the day took place. Our men were flanked, new lines were formed to be flanked again, but our men stood to their work fighting every inch of the way.

Orders now came for Gordon's Division to go to the assistance of the left; we retired through some bushes, then through a large open wood, into a field,—this field was immense and surrounded Winchester. We heard the heavy fighting on the left of our line as we went through the woods, and reaching the opening, saw the whole field in the direction of the Valley pike filled with men fighting; saw that our men were being driven, and that parts of the Yankee cavalry had possession of some of the hills which overlooked the surrounding country. When we reached a large white house, the last outside of Winchester, Generals Early, Breckenridge, and Gordon came riding together from our right towards the left, and reaching our division they told the men they desired to make a stand there. The Mayor of the 21st Va. Regt., the only field officer, not being in sight at the time, the Adjutant approached General Gordon and declared to him that our color-bearer would take his colors anywhere he might order them, and desired to know where he wished the line to be formed. His answer was "Right here." "Men, form on the colors of the 21st," was his command. Our color-bearer, Cumbia, halted, faced towards the enemy, stepped out a few paces, stopped, and waved his flag. The 21st Va. Regt. dressed on him, and the line grew each minute from other commands. The sharpshooters of the enemy then made their appearance, and a body of them took possession of the brick house and outbuildings about three or four hundred yards in our front, and opened fire on us at once. We then saw a line of battle of the enemy approaching, appearing to be a brigade. They advanced in splendid order, and when they came within about four hundred yards of us, a colonel who was standing on my right and a short distance from me, gave the order to fire. I ordered the 21st Va. Regt. to hold their fire, and turning to the colonel, asked that the enemy be allowed to come nearer. At this moment a shot wounded me in the knee. It did not hurt much, I had been struck a few minutes before on the shoulder by a spent ball, which hit hard enough to raise a knot, but did not break the skin. As the ball fell, I stooped down, took it up and put it into my pocket, thinking no more of it until I received this second shot which I thought was of the same character; but in a few minutes I became so sick that I was compelled to lie down. One of my comrades ran to me and asked if I was shot. I replied, "I don't think I am; it was a spent ball." By this time I was so sick that I thought my time to die had come, and as I looked at my knee, I saw the blood running freely down my pants. The enemy on the hill had a battery on our flank, enfilading our line. Two of my comrades took me by my arms and carried me off the field. After going a short distance I begged to be allowed to lie down, thinking I would otherwise die. They would not listen to me while the cannons were plowing great gaps in the earth all around us, but they promised that as soon as they reached a large rock, which we were approaching, they would let me lie down under its protection. We soon reached it, and I lay at full length in hopes of getting some relief, but a cannon shot struck the rock, glanced, and

went up out of sight. In an instant I was taken up by my
comrades and carried on, and we reached the first house
in Winchester, a small, one-story brick building at the
corner of an alley. I was allowed to lie down behind this,
and almost instantly a cannon shot went crashing through
it, throwing pieces of brick and mortar on us. They had
me going again at once. I met Richie Green, an old F, who
was sorry he could not do anything for me. Soon after we
met Ira Blunt, our hospital steward and also an old F. He,
running to me, put a canteen to my lips and told me to
take a good pull. I drank some new apple brandy; its effect
was instantaneous. I felt perfectly well. Thanking him, I
went on looking for our surgeon. I was then in
Winchester, and as I turned the corner of the next street,
I saw our surgeon mounting his horse. I called him, he
rode to meet me, and said he had sent all his stores to the
rear, and had just mounted his horse to follow, but that
he would get me away if possible. All the ambulances he
knew anything of had gone. Just at this moment an
ambulance turned the corner into our street, and came
towards us with the mules in a run. The surgeon ordered
the driver to stop. For answer, he whipped his team into
a faster gait. Our surgeon mounted his horse, and putting
him into a run, overtook the ambulance and catching one
of the mules, by main force, stopped it. I went forward and
when I reached it, my two comrades pitched me in behind.
The surgeon let the mules go, and we were off! The
ambulance was filled with medical chests, and I tried to
arrange them so as to make a comfortable seat, but could
not. In the hinder part of the ambulance was a chest, and
at its end was a bucket, the handle of the chest coming
over the bucket in such a manner that the bucket could
not be moved; the other part of the ambulance was filled
with chest piled one on top of the other, leaving only the
chest in the rear for me to sit on. I managed to put the
foot of my wounded leg in the bucket, and let my good leg
hang out. By this time the ambulance caught up with the
wagon train, moving up the Valley pike two abreast. The

enemy on the right of our line now opened on our wagon train with one piece of artillery. The first shot they fired went over the train a little in front of my ambulance, the next shot went through the top of the wagon just in front of us. Amidst cracking of whips, yells, and oaths, the wagon train went in a hurry up the pike! In a few minutes they got behind the woods, and the firing from the Yankee gun ceased. My ambulance driver became demoralized, wheeled his team to the right, and over the stone wall he went! How it was done I shall never know, but he did it, and through the field his flying mules went! It was an old corn field, and the reader may know how comfortable I was! We went over several cross walls, and finally, along in the night, reached the pike again and continued our ride until about 8 o'clock the next morning, when the ambulance was halted by a surgeon on the road side. The driver was told to take his mules out, water and feed them. I was so sore that I could hardly move, and asked the driver to help me down, but he positively refused! I however got out, made my way to a branch near by, got a drink of water, washed my face, came back to the ambulance, and breakfasted on articles in a Yankee haversack, which I took the day before from one of their dead. I will state here that the only rations I had after leaving Winchester until I arrived at Staunton, were out of that haversack, and since it was such a good friend, I carried it home! While I was eating my breakfast, a surgeon came and asked the driver whom he had in his ambulance. I told him who I was and my command, and asked him to look at my wound and say if it needed anything. His inhuman reply was, "As you do not belong to my command, you must get your own surgeon." After an hour or two of rest the team was hitched up, and I, fearing I might be left, took my old place in the ambulance, while the hitching was done. I prevailed on the driver just before we started, to pull off my boot,—it was full of blood and running over the top! Soon after it was pulled off, my wound seemed to stop bleeding, and I proceeded more comfortably. We rode until four o'clock in the afternoon, when we halted at a church in Woodstock. Here the ladies brought to the wounded fruit, flowers, eatables, water and bandages, and made themselves very useful to two or three hundred wounded. A surgeon cut open my pants and drawers, and examined my wound and dressed it,—this was the first time it was seen even by myself. It had hurt me none to speak of. About sunset the wounded were put into wagons on a little straw and started up the pike. Riding all night, stopping a short time during the morning and then continuing until night, when we rested. We traveled thus until we reached Staunton, two days after we left Woodstock, where my wound was dressed the second time after I was shot. From Staunton, we were, the next morning, carried to Charlottesville, where the ball was taken out. I write this lengthy narrative of myself, because it was the experience of hundreds in this battle!

Returning to the account of the battle, our left being driven back, the new line which had been moved back occupied some slight breastworks. Here the enemy were checked, and as night approached Gen. Early's force retired up the valley. On reaching Fisher's Hill he took position, whence he was driven on the 22d, with a considerable loss. Among the killed in that engagement was our old comrade, Col. A. S. Pendleton, Adjutant General of the Second Corps. He was one of the first officers appointed on Jackson's staff and had been with us since the commencement of the war; he was a gallant and splendid officer, beloved by all the old command.

The battle of Winchester was as hotly contested as any of the war, and was a regular stand-up fight; but we were so outnumbered that we could not prevent the flanking by the enemy.

I do not agree with the Northern writer alluded to before, who said: "Early was beaten before that battle commenced from the great disparity in numbers." He also said: "When Early was driven, he left a track of blue killed and wounded in his rear." Our loss in the evening was heavy. Among the wounded was Maj.-Gen. Fitz Lee.

In F Company, N. Dowdy, J. C. English and G. W. Houston were wounded.

Here is an interesting incident about the battle of Winchester taken from Gen. Phil Sheridan's autobiography:

"Gen. Sheridan, wanting to know something as to Early's army, learned of an old colored man, who had a permit from the Confederate commander to go into Winchester and return three times a week for the purpose of selling vegetables to the inhabitants. The scouts sounded the man, and finding him both loyal and shrewd, suggested that he might be made useful to us within the enemy's lines; and the proposal struck me as feasible, provided there could be found in Winchester some reliable person who would be willing to coöperate and correspond with me. I asked Gen. Crook, and he recommended a Miss Rebecca Wright, a young lady whom he had met there before the battle of Kernstown, who he said was a member of the Society of Friends, and he thought she might be willing to render us assistance. I hesitated at first, but finally decided to try it. The negro was brought to his headquarters, given the letter, which was written on tissue paper, wrapped in tin foil so that it could be placed in the man's mouth, and instructed, if searched by the Confederate picket, to swallow it. Early next morning it was delivered to Miss Wright, the negro telling her he would come back in the evening for an answer. The evening before a convalescent Confederate officer had visited her mother's house, and in conversation about the war had disclosed the fact that Kershaw's division of infantry and Cutshaw's battalion of artillery had started to rejoin Gen. Lee. Miss Wright now perceived the value of the intelligence, and determined to send it at once."

Here is a copy of Gen. Sheridan's letter, and Miss
Wright's answer:

"I learned from Major General Crook that you are a loyal
lady, and still love the old flag. Can you inform me of the
position of Early's forces, the number of divisions in his
army, and the strength of any or all of them, and his
probable or reported intentions? Have any more troops
arrived from Richmond, or are any more coming, or reported to be coming?

"I am, very respectfully, your most obedient servant,

"P. H. SHERIDAN, Major General Commanding.

"You can trust the bearer."

"September 16, 1864.

"I have no communication whatever with the rebels,
but will tell you what I know. The division of General
Kershaw, and Cutshaw's artillery, twelve guns and men,
General Anderson commanding, have been sent away, and
no more are expected, as they cannot be spared from Richmond. I do not know how the troops are situated, but the
force is much smaller than reported. I will take pleasure
hereafter in learning all I can of their strength and position, and the bearer may call again.

"Very respectfully yours,

"_____"

The above letter from Miss Wright is not signed in Gen.
Sheridan's book.

I thought while writing this I would see if I could find
the negro, too. So wrote to Major Saml. J. C. Moore of
Berryville, Va., an officer on Gen. Early's staff, asking him
if he could give me the name of the negro who carried the
letter. Here is his answer:

"In 1869 I employed a negro man as gardener, whose
name was Tom Laws. I had heard something about his
being the man who was the bearer of the letter, and I
broached the subject to him. At first he was not inclined
to talk about it, but upon my assuring him that I would

not harm him, I got him to talk freely about it. On the 17th of September, 1864, he went to Winchester, to see some relations he had there. Miss Rebecca Wright, having heard he was in town, sought him and told him to come to her house before he left. He went there, when she asked him when he was going home, he told her he was ready to start at once. She then said she wanted him to carry a letter to Gen. Sheridan, and taking a small piece of thin tissue paper, she wrote upon it, and then enveloped it in a small piece of tin foil, which she gave him, and charged him that he must not let the rebels get it, and if they caught him he must swallow it, and that found it on his person they would kill him, and it might cost her life. She directed him to give it to no one but Gen. Sheridan in person. He found the general and gave the note to him, who read it, and promised him he should be paid fifty dollars in money for bringing it, but he never got the money."

Gen. Sheridan said this information caused him to decide to attack Early the next morning, but having received a telegram from Gen. Grant, who said he was coming to see him that day, he determined to defer it. After his conference with Gen. Grant he decided to attack the next morning, and that letter brought on the battle of Winchester.

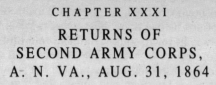

Returns of Second Army Corps, A. N. Va., Aug. 31, 1864, and Organization of Early's Command in the Valley, Aug. 20, 1864. From War Records. They give the number of Early's infantry with the exception of one brigade of Wharton's division, and his artillery, but omit the cavalry and horse artillery.

There was skirmishing daily with Sheridan, in which our cavalry, infantry and artillery participated. Losses were inevitable and reduced these figures by Sept. 19, when the battle of Winchester took place.

Returns of Second Corps A. N. Va., Aug. 31, 1864. Lieut. Gen. Jubal A. Early.	Aggregate Present for Duty.	Aggregate	Aggregate Present & Absent.	Present Effective for the Field.	Present of Artillery.
Rodes' Division, Maj.-Gen. R. E. Rodes					
Battle's Brigade, Brig.-Gen. C. A. Battle.	951	1163	3252	951	
Grimes' Brigade, Brig.-Gen. B. Grimes.	883	1091	3293	832	
Cook's Brigade, Brig.-Gen. P. Cook.	674	883	2421	599	
Cox's Brigade, Brig.-Gen. W. R. Cox.	797	973	4052	679	
Total............................	3305	4110	13,018	3061	
Gordon's Division, Maj.-Gen. J. B. Gordon					
Terry's Brigade, Brig.-Gen. W. Terry.	864	987	6485	783	
York's Brigade, Brig.-Gen. Z. York.	658	813	3507	658	
Evans' Brigade, Col. E. N. Atkinson.	1311	1526	4204	1210	
Total............................	2833	3326	14,196	2651	
Early's Division, Maj.-Gen. S. D. Ramsuer					
Pegram's Brigade, Brig.-Gen. Jno. Pegram.	621	851	2325	599	
Johnston's Brigade, Brig.-Gen. R. D. Johnston.	618	774	2401	598	
Goodwin's Brigade, Brig.-Gen. A. C. Goodwin.	806	935	2270	775	
Total............................	2045	2560	6996	1972	
Artillery—Nelson					
Braxton's Battalion, Lt. Col. C. M. Braxton.	243	284	380	280	11
Nelson's Battalion, Capt. T. J. Kirkpatrick.	275	314	459	275	12
McLaughlin's Battalion, Maj. W. McLaughlin.	262	316	454	247	12
Total............................	780	914	1293	802	35
Grand Total....................	8963	10910	35503	8486	35
Wharton's Division					
Wharton's Brigade.................	638				
Echol's Brigade	503				
Smith's Brigade......................	....	....	....	...	..

It will be seen from the above that the report of Wharton's Division is only partial, and there is no Report of Cavalry. Sheridan's force at same time was 56,958.

ORGANIZATION OF EARLY'S COMMAND IN THE VALLEY AUG. 20, 1864.
RODES' DIVISION
MAJ.-GEN. ROBERT E. RODES

Battle's Brigade
Brig.-Gen. Cullen A. Battle.
Lt. Col. E. LaF. Hobson.
  3d Alabama,——.
  5th Alabama, Lt. Col. E.
    LaF. Hobson.
  6th Alabama,——.
  12th Alabama, Capt. P. D.
    Ross.
  61st Alabama, Maj. E.
    Pinhard.

Grimes' Brigade
Brig.-Gen. Bryan
  Grimes.
32nd North Carolina. } Col. David G. Cowand
53rd North Carolina.

  Battalion.
  2d North Carolina. } Col. J. R. Winston
  42d North Carolina.
  45th North Carolina.

Cook's Brigade
Brig.-Gen. Philip Cook.
  4th Georgia, Lt. Col. Wm.
    H. Willis.
  12th Georgia, Capt. Jas.
    Everett.
  21st Georgia, Capt. Henry T.
    Battle.
  24th Georgia, Lt. Col. Jas.
    W. Beck.

Cox's Brigade
Brig.-Gen. William R. Cox.
  1st North Carolina, Capt.
    Wm. H. Thomson.
  2d North Carolina,——.
  3d North Carolina, Capt.
    Wm. H. Thomson.
  4th North Carolina,——.
  14th North Carolina, Capt.
    Jos. Jones.
  30th North Carolina, Capt.
    Jno. C. McMillan.

RAMSUER'S DIVISION
MAJ.-GEN. STEPHEN D. RAMSUER

Pegram's Brigade
Brig.-Gen. Jno. Pegram.
  13th Virginia, Capt. Felix
    Heishell.
  31st Virginia, Lt. Col. J. S. K.
    McCutchen.
  49th Virginia, Capt. Jno. G.
    Lobban.
  52d Virginia, Capt. Jno. M.
    Humphreys.
  58th Virginia, Capt. Leroy C.
    James.

Johnston's Brigade
Brig.-Gen. Robert D.
  Johnston.
  5th North Carolina,——
  12th North Carolina,——.
  20th North Carolina, Col.
    Thos. F. Toon.
  23d North Carolina,——.
  1st North Carolina Battal-
    ion, Capt. R. E. Wilson.

Goodwin's Brigade
Brig.-Gen., A. C. Goodwin.
6th North Carolina,——.
21st North Carolina,——.
54th North Carolina,——.
57th North Carolina,——.

GORDON'S DIVISION
Maj.-Gen. John B. Gordon

Evans' Brigade
Brig. Gen. Clement A. Evans.
Col. Edmund N. Atkinson.
13th Georgia, Col. J. H. Baker.
26th Georgia, Lt. Col. J. S. Bain.
31st Georgia, Col. Jno. H. Lowe.
38th Georgia, Maj. Thos. H. Bomer.
60th Georgia, Capt. Milton Russell.

61st Georgia, Capt. Eliphalet F. Shaw.
12th Georgia Battalion, Capt. Jas. W. Anderson.

York's Brigade
Brig.-Gen. Zebulon York.
5th Louisiana,——. ⎫
6th Louisiana,——. ⎬ Hay's old
7th Louisiana,——. ⎭ Brigade

1st Louisiana,——. ⎫
14th Louisiana,——. ⎪ Stafford's
2d Louisiana,——. ⎬ old
10th Louisiana,——. ⎪ Brigade.
15th Louisiana,——. ⎭

Terry's Brigade
2d Virginia,——. ⎫
4th Virginia,——. ⎪ Col. John
5th Virginia,——. ⎬ H. S. Funk.
27th Virginia,——. ⎪ Old Stone-
33d Virginia,——. ⎭ wall Brigade.

21st Virginia,——. ⎫
25th Virginia,——. ⎪ Col. Robt.
42d Virginia,——. ⎬ H. Dungan.
44th Virginia,——. ⎪ Old Second
48th Virginia,——. ⎪ Brigade.
50th Virginia,——. ⎭

10th Virginia,——. ⎫ Lt. Col.
23d Virginia,——. ⎬ Samuel H. Saunders
37th Virginia,——. ⎭ Old Third Brigade.

WHARTON'S DIVISION
BRIG.-GEN. GABRIEL C. WHARTON

Wharton's Brigade
45th Virginia,——.
50th Virginia,——.
51st Virginia,——.
30th Virginia Battalion,——.

Echols' Brigade
22d Virginia,——.
23d Virginia Battalion,——.
26th Virginia Battalion,——.

Smith's Brigade
Col. Thomas Smith
36th Virginia,——.
60th Virginia, Capt. Albert A. P. George.
45th Virginia, Battalion, Capt. W. B. Hensly.
Thomas Legion, Col. James R. Love, Jr.

ARTILLERY

Braxton's Battalion
Virginia Battery, Carpenters.
Virginia Battery, Hardwicke.
Virginia Battery, Cooper.
Cutshaw's Battalion
Virginia Battery, Carringtons.
Virginia Battery, Tanner.
Virginia Battery, Garber.

King's Battalion
Virginia Battery, Bryan.
Virginia Battery, Chapman.
Virginia Battery, Lowry.
Nelson's Battalion
Georgia Battery, Milledge.
Virginia Battery, Kirkpatrick.
Virginia Battery, Massie.

CAVALRY
MAJ.-GEN. L. L. LOMAX

Imboden's Brigade
18th Virginia,——.
23d Virginia,——.
62d Virginia,——.
McCausland's Brigade
14th Virginia,——.
16th Virginia,——.
17th Virginia,——.
25th Virginia,——.
37th Virginia Battalion,——.

Bradley T. Johnson's Brigade
8th Virginia,——.
21st Virginia,——.
22d Virginia,——.
34th Virginia,——.
36th Virginia,——.
Jackson's Brigade
2d Maryland,——.
19th Virginia,——.
20th Virginia,——.
46th Virginia,——.
47th Virginia,——.

HORSE ARTILLERY

Maryland Battery, Grippin.   Virginia Battery, Lurty.
Virginia Battery, Jackson.   Virginia Battery, McClanahan.

Lt. Gen. Anderson's forces, consisting of the following, were in Culpeper Co. and joined Early on the 17th Aug., staying with Early until the 14th Sept., when they returned to Culpeper with Kershaw's division and the artillery, leaving Fitz Lee's Cavalry with Early. Kershaw's division and the artillery again joined Early on Sept. 26th, and participated in the battle of Cedar Creek Oct. 19, 1864.

Rosser's Brigade of cavalry joined Early on Oct. 5, '64, coming by way of Lynchburg, and was not with Anderson in Culpeper.

KERSHAW'S DIVISION
Maj.-Gen. Joseph B. Kershaw

Conner's Brigade
Maj. James M. Goggin.
2d South Carolina, Maj.
B. R. Clyburn.
3d South Carolina, Maj.
R. P. Todd.
7th South Carolina,—.
8th South Carolina,—.
15th South Carolina,—.
20th South Carolina, Col.
S. M. Boykin.
3d South Carolina Battalion,
Capt. B. A. Whitenor.
Wofford's Brigade
16th Georgia,—.
18th Georgia,—.
24th Georgia,—.

3d Georgia Battalion,—.
Cobb's Georgia Legion,—.
Phillips Georgia Legion,—.
Humphreys' Brigade
Brig.-Gen. Benjamin G.
Humphreys.
13th Mississippi,—.
17th Mississippi,—.
18th Mississippi,—.
21st Mississippi,—.
Bryan's Brigade
Col. James P. Simms.
10th Georgia, Col. W. C. Holt.
50th Georgia, Col. P.
McGlashan.
51st Georgia, Col. Edward
Ball.
52d Georgia,—.

ARTILLERY
Carter's Battalion

Alabama Battery, Reese.   Virginia Battery, Pendleton.
Virginia Battery, W. P. Carter.   Virginia Battery, Frys.

CAVALRY
Fitz Lee's Division

Wickham's Brigade
1st Virginia,—.
2d Virginia,—.
3d Virginia,—.
4th Virginia,—.

Rosser's Brigade
7th Virginia,—.
11th Virginia,—.
12th Virginia,—.
35th Virginia Battalion,—.

Payne's Brigade
5th Virginia,—.
6th Virginia,—.
15th Virginia,—.

HORSE ARTILLERY
Virginia battery, Johnston.
Virginia battery, Shoemaker.
Virginia battery, Thomson.

CHAPTER XXXII

CEDAR CREEK AND WINTER
1864–5

T HE READER will want to know something of the old command after my leaving it. I can give some facts gathered from members of my company.

After the battle of Fisher's Hill, Early retired up the valley to Mt. Jackson,—Sheridan following him slowly. On the 24th they marched about five miles beyond Tenth Legion, on the road to Port Republic, and the next day to Brown's Gap in the Blue Ridge mountain, where they were joined by Kershaw's division. On the 27th they marched from Brown's Gap towards Harrisonburg, and returned to Port Republic. There Gen. Early learned that Sheridan's cavalry had gone in the direction of Staunton. They marched to Waynesboro and Rockfish Tunnel to intercept the enemy in case they marched to those places. They found that the enemy had occupied Waynesboro a short time before, and they attacked at once and drove them back with some loss. Early camped in the neighborhood until Oct. 1st, when he marched to Mt. Sidney on the Valley pike and was joined by Rosser's brigade of cavalry on Oct. 5th. Early then marched down the valley to Fisher's Hill, which place he reached on the 13th. There he stayed until the night of the 18th, when he put his troops in motion to attack Sheridan, who was in a strongly fortified position along Cedar Creek. To Gordon was assigned the duty of attacking the enemy in their rear on the left of their line. He moved down the Shenandoah river, fording it twice, and was in line at the designated place as the streaks of day appeared, and with a yell dashed upon the enemy! This was the signal for Early's line in front to move forward, which they did, and they swept everything before them, taking the fortifications, guns, and camp of the enemy. Sheridan's army was utterly routed with the exception of the Sixth Corps, which was encamped some distance in the rear. They formed a line and marched back with the fugitives until they reached Middletown, when they formed a line of battle requiring such of the fugitives as they could control to join them. Our line that had been pursuing the enemy was so thin that it was not much more than a line of skirmishers!

The world will never know the extreme poverty of the Confederate soldier at that time! Hundreds of the men who were in the charge and captured the enemy's works were barefooted, every one of them was ragged, many had nothing but what they had on, and *none* had eaten a square meal for weeks! In passing through Sheridan's camp they had a great temptation thrown in their way; many of the tents were open, and in plain sight were rations, shoes, overcoats and blankets! The fighting continued farther and farther, and some of the men stopped, secured well-filled haversacks, and as they investigated their contents, the temptation to stop and eat was too great, as they had had nothing since the evening before, and they yielded. Others tried on shoes, others put on warm pants in place of the tattered ones, others got overcoats and blankets, articles so much needed for the coming cold! They had already experienced several biting frosts to remind them of the winter near at hand. In this

way half of Early's men were straggling, and this accounts
for his thin line in front.

This was an awful hour! Gen. Early then noticed the
thinness of his line and being informed of its cause, sent
officers back to hurry his men up. His advance line by this
time had come up to the enemy in their position at
Middletown. They attacked at once, but so feebly and were
so easily repulsed, that the enemy felt emboldened, made
an advance and drove our men off the field of battle! The
stragglers who arrived were not in sufficient numbers to
check the enemy's advance. The fighting continued until
night put a stop to it. Gen. Early withdrew during the
night to Fisher's Hill, but, owing to the breaking down of
a bridge, most of the captured guns and between fifteen
and twenty of our own were taken by the enemy. We lost
about one thousand men taken prisoners, but brought off
nineteen hundred of the enemy, whom we had captured.
Our loss was heavy, and among the killed was that
splendid soldier, Maj.-Gen. Ramsuer!

F Company lost Sergeant R. M. Tabb, killed; Corporal
W. C. Tyree and L. M. Couch, wounded. That gallant
young officer, Lieut. M. L. Hudgins, had command of a
line of skirmishers and was shot through both legs, but
succeeded in bringing off his command, and took to the
mountains! Here he was captured a few days later and
taken to Winchester, and from there sent to a Northern
prison to stay until Mar. 30, 1865. I was told that old man
Mason of the same company was quietly walking to the
rear, when a Yankee cavalryman rode up to him, and with
uplifted saber, ordered the old man to halt. He looked over
his shoulder, and, seeing who it was, threw up his gun and
shot the Yankee off his horse! The old fellow was, however,
captured not long after!

Gen. Early fell back to New Market, but Sheridan did
not follow him. Here Gen. Early stayed until Nov. 10th.
Learning that Sheridan had fallen back to Winchester, he
advanced to Newtown, and from there he fell back again
to New Market, where in December, Gordon's, Ramsuer's

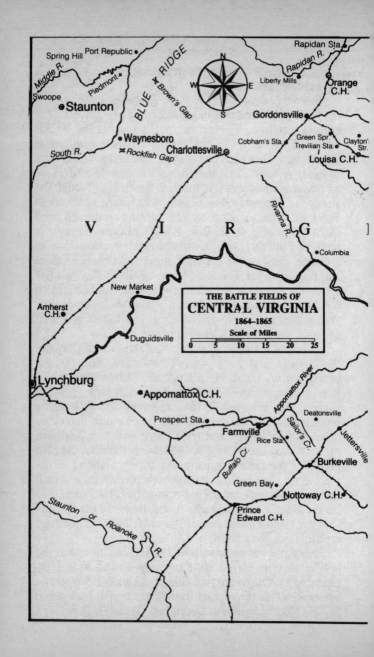

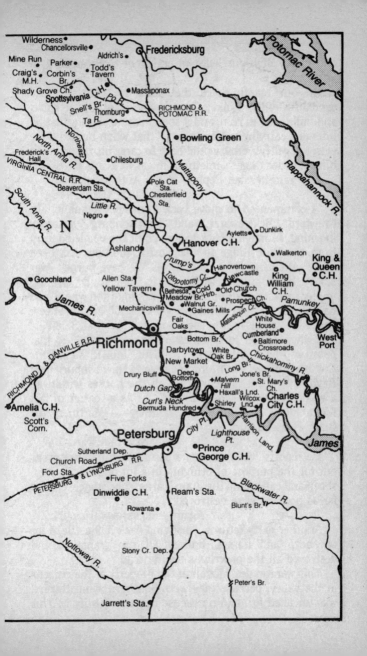

and Rodes' divisions left him and went to Petersburg to join Gen. Lee.

On our march down the valley we witnessed the vandalism of the Yankee General Sheridan! All the barns and mills were in ruin, and it soon became evident that he intended carrying out his boast, "that when he was done with the valley a crow would have to carry his rations with him in order to get something to eat in going across it."

General Sheridan Reports to the Authorities from

"WOODSTOCK, Oct. 7, 1864.

"I commenced to move back from Port Republic, Mt. Crawford, Bridgewater, and Harrisonburg yesterday morning. In moving back to this point the whole country from the Blue Ridge to the North Mountain has been made untenable for a rebel army. We have burned over 2,000 barns filled with wheat, hay and farming implements, over 70 mills filled with flour and wheat, and have driven in front of the army over 4,000 head of sheep; have killed and issued to the troops not less than 3,000 . . . and when we get to Winchester the entire valley to that point will be a Wilderness . . . Lieut. Jno. R. Meigs, my Engineer officer, was murdered beyond Harrisonburg near Dayton. For this atrocious act all the houses within an area of five miles were burned." . . . As a matter of fact Lieut. Meigs was killed in a fight by——Martin of the Black Horse cavalry.

"NEWTOWN, Nov. 10."

He reports "the return of a party which had been sent out for the purpose of bringing in a lot of stock, horses, sheep and cattle, and the grain, barns, subsistence, etc., as far as possible were destroyed" . . .

Again, "KERNSTOWN, Nov. 11."

Another party returns, "bringing back 300 cattle, a lot of sheep and horses, burned all the granaries, and destroyed all the provisions on the road." . . .

This wanton destruction of the property of the citizens of the valley, because they were Southern sympathizers, was uncalled for, and no excuse can ever justify it! This was a favored country, and to burn everything in the way of hay, grain, etc., barns and mills, not excepting agricultural implements; to kill and drive off all the horses, stock, etc., belonging to those people because it would compel the Confederate army in the valley to haul those articles, was a crime without reason or excuse, especially when those citizens were not paid by the United States a cent for their loss.

I think Gen. Early did everything a commander could do in the valley with the number of men he had in his command, and, as an humble member of that army, I would like to ask those who have criticized Gen. Early if they ever thought of the great disparity in numbers in the two armies? It is said that Sheridan's cavalry alone numbered as many if not more than Early's entire force, and I never heard Sheridan's infantry placed at less than thirty thousand. Gen. Early did not have more than twelve thousand men in his entire army at the battle of Winchester,—the first of his disasters. Let me recall the fact that Early was detached from Lee's army at Richmond, and sent to Lynchburg to intercept Hunter, who was marching on that place with a large force. He disposed of Hunter in quick time, driving him beyond the Alleghany mountains. He was then ordered to threaten Washington City, which he promptly did. On his arrival before that place the Yankees concentrated a force over sixty thousand to repel him! A large part of this force was taken from Grant's army at a time that greatly helped Lee at Petersburg. Early, by his activity, kept nearly all this force in his front until late in the year 1864. Gen. Early certainly accomplished all, if not more, than he was sent to the valley for. It is needless for me to say anything about Gen. Early's gallantry and fighting in the field. That is too well known.

Since the opening of the campaign May 2, 1864, the Second Corps had marched over sixteen hundred miles and fought seventy-five battles and skirmishes in the majority of which F Company participated. The loss was heavy in officers and men as well as guns, but they inflicted a loss on the enemy in men and officers twice as large as the Second Corps numbered, and a great loss in stores, etc.

On the arrival in Petersburg of the troops who left Early, Maj.-Gen. Gordon was made commander of the Second Corps, it was ordered to the front, and on the 5th of Feb., 1865, had a hard battle with Grant at Hatcher's Run. It was in this battle that the gallant Capt. Jordan of F Company distinguished himself. While the brigade was marching by the flank, through a dense pine wood, they were suddenly assailed by the enemy's sharpshooters. This threw our men into confusion, and they fell back out of fire to reform the line. Jordan at once turned towards the enemy and succeeded in getting seven men to join him,—two from the 42d Va., two from the 25th Va., and three from the 21st Va. regiments, among the latter W. R. Richeson of F Company. Those men he hurriedly placed along the road to stop the advance of the enemy at that point. They rapidly approached and commanded Jordan and his little band to surrender; but for answer they received bullets, and when the smoke cleared up, one Yankee lay on the ground and the remainder were seeking safety! At this moment Gen. Gordon rode up and learned that the advance of the enemy had been stopped by Jordan and his few men. He complimented them on the spot, in that peculiar way of his, which bound those men to him forever, rode off to the brigade, made a speech and closed by telling them "that Capt. Jordan, by his bravery and coolness, had with only seven men stopped the advance of the enemy." He hurried them forward and the fight became general. After the battle when the troops had returned to camp, Gen. Gordon sent a messenger to Capt. Jordan, asking the names of the seven men, which he desired to be forwarded to his headquarters through the regular channels, as he wished to publish to the army their names as well as that of Captain Jordan for gallant and heroic conduct on the field of battle! This Jordan did, but the end came before the account of this battle was published—hence this incident is not known to the public.

I would like to say a word about W. R. Richeson, an humble man from Caroline County, who joined us in 1863, so infirm that he ought not to have been in the army, but in several battles he showed the mettle he was made of, and well deserved this recognition from Gen. Gordon!

In this battle W. Bates and A. D. Brown were wounded. On Mar. 25th Gordon made an attack on and captured Fort Steadman. There Capt. Jordan was wounded, Geo. Hutchie Rennie, J. A. Kidd and H. C. Fox were killed in the attack, and N. C. Dowdy captured, all of F Company.

Here is what one of the old company says of this battle: "On the night before the battle we were in camp, and quietly sleeping, when about midnight we were awakened and told to 'fall in' as soon as possible. As soon as the line was formed we were marched off hurriedly through the woods and fields, over ditches and fences, and finally formed a line of battle facing east. The streaks of day were just beginning to show themselves, when we were turned loose, and we ran over two lines of the enemy's breastworks almost before I can tell about it, the troops on our right capturing at the same time the fort. We halted a short time after passing the second line of breastworks, reformed lines and then were ordered forward again. Soon I was captured, and that is all I know of the battle."

On the retreat from Petersburg, Gordon's command was the guard, and after leaving Amelia C. H. they were engaged every hour of the day and half of the night in repelling attacks by some body of the enemy. The hardships our men underwent in the retreat to Appomattox were such that it seems impossible for men to go through them and live! They left Petersburg without rations, on roads full of mud from the recent rains, marched all night and nearly all the next day before stopping to rest! Gen. Lee had ordered a train of cars,

loaded with rations to be at Amelia C. H. Depot on the
Richmond and Danville railroad, and led his army there to
get them. When they arrived, they learned that by the
mismanagement of some officials, the train with rations
had gone on to Richmond, where it fell into the hands of
the enemy! The men of his army had been eating parched
corn and anything else they could get their hands on, with
the hope of getting something on reaching Amelia C. H.
When they learned that disappointment awaited them,
they almost gave up,—but the old spirit soon came back
to the army of Northern Virginia, and they dragged
themselves along the road on their way towards
Lynchburg, where they knew rations could be gotten.
Combats nearly every hour with some portion of Grant's
force which were this time in advance of our army as well
as following close on our rear. They marched along this
way until they neared Appomattox C. H., where they found
a train of provisions on the Norfolk & Western railroad,
awaiting them,—the first rations since they left
Petersburg!

The day before reaching Sailor's Creek, Gordon was
ordered to take the front, and when he reached
Appomattox C. H., Gen. Lee gave him an order to advance
on the next morning, and if the enemy be encountered in
numbers he must cut his way through them. When
morning came and Gordon found the enemy in large
numbers in his front, he formed his line, ordered them
forward, and they made the attack with so much spirit
that they succeeded in driving the Yankees and captured
two pieces of artillery; and when Gordon sent Gen. Lee
word that he "had fought his corps to a frazzle," those old
fellows could be seen, and heard from too, in that frazzle!
My brother, who was one of them, told me that at the time
the white flag was raised by Gen. Lee, this same "frazzle"
was driving the enemy in its front!

You would like to know what became of the colors of
the 21st Va. Regt. After it was known positively that Gen.
Lee was going to surrender, the gallant John H. Cumbia,

who had carried the colors for such a long time, tore them
from the staff—which was a short one, as it had been shot
off by a cannon ball some months before—broke the staff
and threw it away! Then he tore the flag into small pieces,
giving to each man a piece. That was a great flag! It had
inscribed upon it the names of all the battles from
Kernstown on, in which Jackson's old division had been.
Three cannon balls had been shot through it, and when I
left it, in September, 1864, over one hundred musket
shots through it could be counted!

CHAPTER XXXIII

THE EVACUATION OF RICHMOND AND LEE'S SURRENDER

I WAS IN RICHMOND confined to my bed with my wound when the city was evacuated. I cannot say that I saw or heard much of what went on outside of our house, as there was not a man on the place at the time except myself, and the women were too much alarmed to go out! We heard many rumors Sunday afternoon. The first definite news was about midnight, when a soldier friend came by to bid us good-by, since he was going away with the soldiers who were then marching through the city. He stated that the President, his cabinet and other officials of the government with the archives, etc., had left the city by the Danville railroad, and as soon as the troops crossed the river, the bridges would be burned! A member of the Legislature called soon after and told us good-by, and said that the members of the Legislature were going to Lynchburg on the packet boat by the James river and Kanawha canal. This created a feeling of great uneasiness in our household. We well knew that the ever long wish of the enemy to get to Richmond would soon be gratified, and what would be the result? I dreaded the coming day, and listened to every noise I heard outside. Occasionally I would hear a report as if something was blown up, an arsenal, steamer, or something of that kind. Not long before daybreak, a flash of light came into my room, brighter than the brightest lightning, accompanied immediately by a loud report with rumbling and shaking of the house, and a crash as if the front had fallen! The ladies were in my room in an instant, and as soon as the outer door could be opened, the servants came in too! I explained to them the best I could, that it was the explosion of a large quantity of powder, probably one of the magazines. After they were quieted, one of them went into the front room to see if anything had been broken. She soon returned and stated that the sash of one of the windows had been blown into the middle of the room, and all the glass was broken! About sunrise on Monday, April 3, 1865, the ladies left my room, going to their rooms to dress for the day, the servants going about their accustomed duties. When the ladies returned, they reported that a great fire was raging down town, and it looked as if the whole city would be burned! Some friend now called and stated that the rear guard of our army had set fire to the Shockoe, the Public, the Myers & Anderson tobacco warehouses, the arsenals, magazines, etc.! From those fires, adjacent buildings caught, and the greater part of the business portion of the city was in flames, with no prospect of checking the fire! He also said that the city council and some of the prominent citizens had held a meeting and decided to destroy all liquor in the government buildings and large warehouses, and that it was taken out of those buldings into the streets and emptied into the nearest culverts; that hundreds of citizens were pillaging the stores which were burning and breaking into others and taking everything; and that the town was in the hands of a mob!

About half-past seven my breakfast was brought me by a little negro boy eight to ten years old; he was devoted to me and a great favorite of mine, as he was very quick and smart. He said to me, "Marse John, let me run down to the corner and see if I can see any of the Yankees." At that time he had a great horror of them. After some little begging on his part, I let him go, he promising to return before his mistress would miss him. Before I finished my breakfast he returned, and on entering the room, he said, "Marse John, they is here,"—he had seen a squad coming up towards the capitol and he ran home.

During the boy's absence one of the negro girls ran down to the capitol square and on her return came into my room and stated that she saw fifteen Yankees on horseback ride up 9th Street to the capitol gate, enter and ride up to the building. Some of them dismounted, went inside and soon came out on the roof, where they hoisted a United States flag on the flagstaff! That was the first flag hoisted by the enemy in Richmond. This party made a deep impression on her, for they were the first body of armed Yankees she had seen; she seemed particularly struck with their uniform and long buck gauntlets.

She went out again soon afterwards, staying two or three hours. She came back with a large blanket filled with articles as numerous and as varied as are in a peddler's pack, gotten, she said, out of stores on Main street; that all were open and everybody was helping himself, and she thought she would do the same!

From the great clouds of smoke hovering over the city, it seemed that all down-town must be burning up! Large chunks of fire were falling on our house and in the yard,—the house had been on fire several times,—one of the negro men servants had come home from fear, and we had stationed him on top of the house to watch! He stayed there all day. A man or boy was on nearly every house, although in some places the women were doing this duty. We were about half a mile from the nearest fire, and the smoke at our house was so dense all day, that the sun could not be seen and the appearance out-doors was like that of a heavy fog in the morning.

About midday we heard the music, cheers, and some

firing by a body of the enemy marching on the next street. In our yard, near my window, was a small peach tree; I was sitting up in bed and looking at the tree when the firing took place. I saw a small twig of the tree fall, and almost at the same moment, heard the quick thud of a ball striking the fence! This I call the last shot of Richmond. We were sure now that the enemy were in Richmond. A friend called and told us that nearly all the business portion of the city had been burned, that the Yankees had quelled the mob, and that they were then engaged in stopping the fire. This they succeeded in doing after severe exertion and blowing up several buildings ahead of the fire. One of our old negro women was heard praying nearly all day; she was in the yard and terribly frightened by the thought that the fire would reach us and burn her up.

Hundreds of the residents of the burned district were bivouacking in the capitol square, having moved to it everything they could. It presented the appearance of a vast camp, filled with household goods, women and children! Many had built fires, and were cooking to feed the hungry children. All the people remained there until the next day and some stayed several days.

In the evening we heard that quiet had been restored and that the Yankee soldiers were patrolling the streets and would place a guard throughout the city in order to preserve order among citizens as well as soldiers; that they had marched outside of the city and would allow no soldier except the guard to go about the streets. This had a very soothing effect, the citizens not knowing what would be done for the city. We saw none of the Yankees except a few now and then passing the house,—heard that all the houses would be searched for contraband goods and Confederate soldiers! The next morning one of my good neighbors sent me a piece of corn bread and herring for breakfast, with the message that it was the last of the Confederacy!

On Wednesday or Thursday our door-bell was rung and

the one answering it met three Yankee officers at the door! They were invited in, and introduced themselves by name and stated they were members of Gen. Canby's staff, who was in command of the city. One of the household came and informed me. Thinking the best thing to do was to be candid with them, I sent them information of my presence in the house and my condition, and asked them to come to my room to see me. This they did at once, and they were very polite and courteous to me. We had articles of value and others we desired to keep, hidden about the house in various places. In my room was a large lounge whose springs were out of order. In this lounge I had placed two sabers, because I thought they would not be detected on account of the bad springs. When I invited the officers to take seats all sat down on this lounge. I noticed that some of them moved about occasionally, but could not tell whether their suspicions were aroused as to anything being in it or not. After talking a little while I told them of the hiding-place. They laughed, and when they left they told me to let them remain there for the present, as well as anything else that was hidden, and if any one molested us or any articles in the house, to let them know at headquarters! The next day a guard was placed on that square in front of our house, which remained on this post for several weeks.

On Sunday, April 9, it was rumored in Richmond that Gen. Lee had surrendered his army. None of the Confederate people believed this. It was confirmed the next day. What a blow! The greatest army the world ever saw, the Army of Northern Virginia, commanded by that great soldier, Gen. Lee, had surrendered! It seemed impossible! However few, they would die fighting!—but the officers thought it best to save those few men and determined to surrender! Gen. Grant, the Commander in Chief of the United States Army, who commanded the army of the Potomac in person, paid the Army of Northern Virginia its greatest tribute, when he said the year before that *that* army could not be beaten, it could only be destroyed, and this he intended to do by mere attrition, knowing full well when he destroyed one man, we had no other to put in his place. He was willing to sacrifice ten of his men to one of ours, if necessary. How well he carried this out his campaign will tell, as the Army of Northern Virginia destroyed for him several times it own number before it was finally destroyed.

A few days after the confirmation of the surrender, the men of Lee's army began to arrive in Richmond, and the old chief himself came riding alone to the city! His old followers immediately recognized him and formed in line and followed him to his home, where with uncovered heads they saw him enter his door, and then they silently dispersed. This was the last of the Confederacy!!

All realized that the last hope was gone, and that the great struggle for secession was at an end. Thus ended the war, and at that time the inhabitants of the South were a ruined people.

> Furl that banner—true 'tis gory,
> Yet 'tis wreathed around with glory,
> And 'twill live in song and story,
>   Though its folds are in the dust;
> For its fame on brightest pages,
> Penned by poet and by sages,
> Shall go sounding down the ages,
>   Furl its folds though now we must.
>
> Furl that banner—softly, slowly;
> Treat it gently—it is holy,
>   For it droops above the dead;
> Touch it not—unfold it never,
> Let it droop there, furled forever,
>   For its people's hopes are dead.

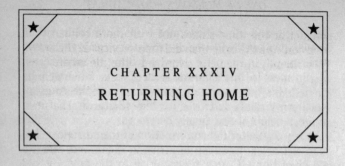

CHAPTER XXXIV

RETURNING HOME

WHEN THE CONFEDERATE soldiers returned from the army after the war the majority of them literally had nothing but the ragged clothing on their backs, not even a change! What a sight met them on their arrival at home! Desolation everywhere. Many found their families scattered all over the state, different members having taken up their abode with relatives or friends in such sections as had not been over-run by the enemy. Many found dwellings, barns, stables, outbuildings, fences and literally everything except the land gone; some found a few outbuildings remaining, no fences, while others found the fences remaining but everything else gone. One could travel along the roads in certain sections of the country for miles and see neither fence nor house nor a single living thing, unless a fox or other wild animal should cross his path!

While some of the soldiers had their land, that was all they had,—no stock, no farming utensils or provisions. If one had these he was an exception. The world will never know the poverty these men were reduced to, and their conduct at this time shines out with more brilliancy, if such could be the case, than did their services in the army! They literally turned the sword into the plowshare, and went to work with a determination to make a living, and, if possible, to recuperate their fortunes! Poverty is a great leveler, and all were on the same footing now. The men accepted any honorable work, and there were actually seen in the streets of Richmond, in the burnt district, men cleaning brick who a short time ago were worth thousands!

It was not uncommon to see a private and a colonel in their old uniforms, working side by side! The men in the country went to work with the same determination—a family who had been raised in affluence and luxury, living in a log cabin, the lady of the house doing the cooking and the landed proprietor following a plow drawn by the only horse on the place!

All the money made by the men for several months was spent in meeting actual needs, and generally it took all they made to feed the family. In consequence, the old soldiers were still wearing their old uniforms. This became a great annoyance to the Yankee army that was stationed in the South. The sight of the old Confederate soldier going about daily in his old uniform reminded them too forcibly of the hard times they had undergone during the last four years. In order to remove these uniforms out of sight as much as possible, the military authorities issued an order that the brass buttons on the coats and jackets of the late Confederate soldier must come off by a certain day. They allowed them the choice of covering the buttons with some material that would hide the shining brass or cut them off,—but the brass buttons must be off or hidden from sight by that date. If the brass buttons were found on their clothing after that date, the United States soldiers had orders to arrest the offender and cut the buttons off. It the man submitted to this or made no resistance he was allowed to go free, if he was caught the second time he would be imprisoned.

Some of our men thought this such a foolish order for the great United States government to issue, that they paid no attention to it; and many were stopped in the streets of Richmond and their buttons were cut off! This accounts for many of the old uniforms that are seen at this day with buttons covered or without brass or military buttons.

A few years after the war I met an old comrade—it was a happy meeting as each had so much to tell the other—when we finally said good-by, he turned to me and said:

> I can't take up my musket
>   And fight 'em now no more,
> But I ain't a-going to love 'em,
>   Now that is sartin sure;
> For I don't want no pardon,
>   For what I was and am,
> I won't be reconstructed,
>   And I don't care a damn.

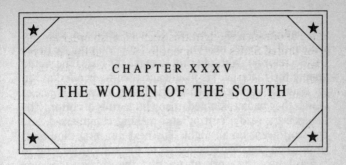

CHAPTER XXXV
THE WOMEN OF THE SOUTH

WHAT HAD THE WOMEN of the South been doing all this time? Would that I had a gifted pen to tell of the noble deeds done by them! They had not been idle. Wherever woman could work or administer comfort, there she was found.

As soon as Virginia seceded, they organized societies throughout the State for work. In Richmond they met daily at certain houses and in the basement of nearly every church, where they made bandages by the mile, lint by the hundred pounds,—using all the old cotton and linen clothing they had for this purpose,—making haversacks, and clothing of all kinds. To show with what energy they could work when it was necessary, I will narrate a circumstance told me soon after it occurred: During the retreat of Johnston from Yorktown, Richmond was thought to be deficient in fortifications, and it was suggested that if the government had bags they might be filled with sand and earth and placed in position, thus forming a wall, and then with earth thrown against this on the outside, earthworks of great strength could be made very quickly,—but how to get enough bags was the trouble! The ladies hearing of this, sent a committee to see the Secretary of War, offering to make the bags if he would supply the material. He gladly accepted their offer and in an hour he had delivered to the ladies, at various places which they had designated, many huge rolls of cotton. The ladies were ready; cutting and making commenced, and the work went on all night. The next morning thousands of finished bags were delivered to the authorities, and in a few hours the work of erecting the fortifications was begun!

The hospital committee were ever present, administering to the sick and wounded. I have heard numerous soldiers say they were glad they were wounded, as the careful attention received from those women more than repaid them for the suffering they endured! Here is a little incident told me after the war, by one of the fashionable young ladies, who lived on one of the fashionable streets of Richmond during the war. She was one of the young ladies who composed one of the hospital committees. In one of the hospitals which she attended, there was a soldier from one of the southern states who was desperately wounded, whom devoted nursing saved. He appreciated it and showed his obligation as well as a man could by thanks. When he was well and was ordered to his command in the field, he asked this young lady if he might call on her at her home. She told him she would be glad to see him at any time, and gave him the number of her residence. A day or two afterwards he called, and after conversing a short while, he told her he knew that the care given him by the ladies had saved his life, and he had asked to call in order that he might thank her and at the same time he wished to make her a little present. This had given him a great deal of thought, as his means were very limited, but he had bought her what he considered the best thing in the world, and he presented her with a small package of "goobers" (peanuts), saying he wished he were able to give her a bushel! She said to me that she considered that the most valuable present she ever received, and prized it as such, because it came from the man's heart; and she thinks it took every cent of money he had to purchase it!

There were committees to look after the poor who had a hard time, as all were poor! They did their duty as nobly and faithfully as the others.

Many households had no male person in them. This entailed much work and anxiety on the women at the head of them, and especially was this true in the country, where it was necessary to attend to the business of the farm, as well as that of the house. Many farms, and some large ones, were operated very successfully by women.

After the war they shared every hardship cheerfully, and, with an abiding faith in the men, they upheld them in all honorable work, and welcomed their old acquaintances to their homes with great cordiality, regardless of their rough hands and ragged clothing.

God bless the Southern women of those days! Would that I were able to build a monument to them. I would have it as high as the steeple of St. Paul's Church, and in its base a room, the walls of which I would adorn with paintings, telling the story of their lives during those trying times. In the center of this room, I would have a statue of a Southern mother, dressed in plain Confederate clothes, holding in one hand a pocket Bible, which she is handing to her boy who is not old enough to wear a coat, her other hand pointing to the open door, and, with tears streaming down her cheeks, telling him his country's needs are more than hers—to go and join the army! Among the paintings, I would have the wife and daughters of Gen. Robert E. Lee, knitting socks for the private soldiers of his army! and Mrs. Gen. John B. Gordon, administering to a sick or wounded soldier on the roadside in the field. She accompanied the General in the field during the war. I would fill the room with such scenes as these.

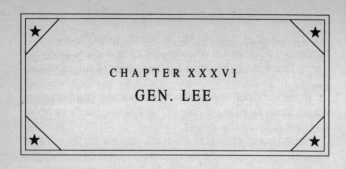

CHAPTER XXXVI
GEN. LEE

I WAS STANDING in the door of our headquarters in Richmond about the middle of April, 1861, when my attention was attracted by a man approaching; he wore a uniform. It was not the uniform that attracted my attention but the man himself. He was tall and straight, and I thought the handsomest specimen of manhood I had ever seen, both in face and figure. He made such an impression that as he came opposite me I could not keep from looking at him, and when he had passed my eyes still followed him, until I actually stepped outside of the door in order to keep him in sight. About an hour later he returned up the street and went into the Spottswood Hotel. I followed and asked some friend if he could tell me who that splendid looking man was. He informed me that it was Colonel Robert E. Lee.

The next time I saw him was on Valley Mountain in Pocahontas Co., Va. (now West Va.). He was a general in the Confederate army and in command of our department. I saw him daily before he was ordered to another command. In our advance to attack McClellan at Cold

Harbor in 1862, after passing through the woods and reaching a field, the first man we saw was our beloved old general on his gray horse, and although he was at some distance, we recognized him at once. He was then in command of the army of Northern Virginia, and we joined him to remain till the end came at Appomattox. I saw him several times after this around Richmond. The next time I saw him he was sitting on a stump on the battlefield of Second Manassas observing Longstreet's men taking position in line of battle, as they came on the field to join Jackson. I saw him often from that time till Grant's campaign of 1864. The last time I saw him he was at Spottsylvania C. H., the day our corps left to head Grant off at Hanover Junction. He appeared to me the same ideal man, except that his hair had become almost white and the dark mustache of my first acquaintance was exchanged for a full beard of gray. As our column approached him, an old private stepped out of ranks and advanced to Gen. Lee. They shook hands like acquaintances and entered into a lively conversation. As I moved on I looked back and the old man had his gun in one hand and the other hand on Traveler's neck, still talking.

It was such scenes as that, that made Gen. Lee so popular. He believed in his men and thought they could do anything that mortals could do. His men worshiped him, and I think the greatest man the world ever saw was Robert E. Lee.

> As troubles gathered round him
>   Thick as waves that beat the shore
> Aetra Cura, rode behind him,
>   Famine's shadow filled his door;
> Still he wrought deeds no mortal men
>   Had ever wrought before.

CHAPTER XXXVII

RECORD OF F COMPANY, 21ST VIRGINIA REGIMENT OF INFANTRY

ROSTER

Captains. R. Milton Cary, enlisted Apl. 21, 1861; promoted colonel of 30th Va. Regt. of Infantry June 15, 1861; and was ordered in 1862 to Belona Arsenal to supervise the making of cannon for the army and navy. In 1865 he was ordered to Goldsboro, N. C., and surrendered with Johnston's army. *Richard H. Cunningham*, Jr., enlisted Apl. 21, 1861; as second lieutenant; first lieutenant May 1, 1861; captain May 16, 1861; elected lieutenant colonel of the 21st Va. Regt. Apl. 1862; killed at Cedar Run, Aug. 9, 1862.

William H. Morgan, enlisted June 1861, as adjutant of the 21st Va. Regt; elected captain of F Company Apl. 1862; killed at Cedar Run Aug. 9, 1862.

William A. Pegram, enlisted Apl. 21, 1861; promoted captain in 1863; killed at Williamsport, Md., July 6, 1863.

Reuben J. Jordan, enlisted Apl. 21, 1861; promoted second lieutenant 1863; and captain in 1864; wounded at Cold Harbor, June 3, 1864; and at Fort Steadman Mch. 25, 1865.

First Lieutenant. James R. Crenshaw, enlisted Apl. 21, 1861; promoted lieutenant colonel 26th Va. Regt. of Inft., 1862.

Jr. Second Lieutenant. Philip A. Welford, enlisted Apl. 21, 1861; second lieutenant May 1, 1861; first lieutenant Dec. 1861; promoted major and commissary of subsistence in 1863.

First Sergeant. Edward Mayo, enlisted Apl. 21, 1861; promoted junior second lieutenant May 1, 1861; first lieutenant June 6, 1861; and resigned Dec. 1861.

Second Sergeant. Henry T. Miller, enlisted Apr. 21, 1861; first sergeant May 1, 1861; promoted junior second lieutenant June 6, 1861; and adjutant of 26th Va. Regt. Nov. 1861; and captain 25th Va. battalion of Inft., Mar. 16, 1864.

Third Sergeant. John A. Pizzini, enlisted April 21, 1861; first sergeant June 6, 1861; promoted lieutenant of infantry in 1862; wounded on Romney expedition winter 1861–2.

Fourth Sergeant. Edward G. Rawlings, enlisted Apl. 21, 1861; second sergeant June 6, 1861; elected second lieutenant Apl. 1862; killed at Second Manassas, Aug. 30, 1862.

First Corporal. John Tyler, enlisted Apl. 21, 1861; sergeant June 6, 1861; promoted first lieutenant Letcher Battery Feb. 1862; transferred to staff duty with Gen. J. L. Kemper.

Second Corporal. Thomas Ellett, enlisted Apl. 21, 1861; sergeant June 6, 1861; promoted lieutenant Crenshaw Battery May, 1862; and captain 1864.

Third Corporal. Edward T. Robinson, enlisted Apl. 21, 1861; transferred 1861 to medical department.

Fourth Corporal. Shirley King, enlisted Apl. 21, 1861; detailed by Secretary of War, 1861.

Anderson, Archer, enlisted Apl. 21, 1861, promoted captain and A. A. G. Gen. Trimbles' staff 1861; major on Gen. Holmes' staff Feb., 1862; lieutenant colonel on

Gen. D. H. Hills' staff July, 1863; and in 1865 as A. A. Gen., Gen J. E. Johnston's army.

Anderson, Junius H., enlisted Apl. 21, 1861; promoted acting master C. S. Navy in 1862.

Anderson, Joseph H., enlisted 1863; promoted corporal 1863; wounded at Cold Harbor June 3, 1864.

Anderson, Henry V., enlisted April 21, 1861; killed at Cedar Run Aug. 9, 1862.

Archer, William S., Jr., enlisted April 21, 1861; promoted first sergeant April, 1863; first lieutenant company K, 48th Va. Regt. of Inft. 1863; wounded near Cold Harbor June, 1864; captured in the Valley of Va., 1864, and carried to Fort Delaware, where he remained until the close of the war.

Ayers, Edward S., enlisted April 21, 1861; transferred in 1861.

Barber, N., enlisted 1863.

Barker, William C., enlisted April 21, 1861; transferred to Second company of Howitzers April 10, 1862; promoted lieutenant in Letcher's battery, 1862.

Bates, E., enlisted 1863; died from effects of campaign March 10, 1864.

Bates, W., enlisted 1863; wounded at Hatcher's Run Feb. 5–7, 1865.

Baughman, Charles C., enlisted April 21, 1861; transferred to Otey battery Nov. 1861.

Baughman, George C., enlisted April 21, 1861; promoted first lieutenant, Caskie battery in 1861.

Baughman, Greer H., enlisted April 21, 1861; transferred to Caskie battery as sergeant July, 1861; wounded at Cold Harbor June 3, 1864.

Beers, Henry H., enlisted April 21, 1861; transferred to Caskie battery 1862.

Binford, James M., enlisted April 21, 1861; transferred to signal corps 1862.

Binford, Robert E., enlisted April 21, 1861; promoted first lieutenant heavy artillery, 1862.

Blunt, Ira W., enlisted April 21, 1861; promoted hospital steward 21st Va. Regt., Jan. 24, 1862.

Boyd, James N., age 15 years. Joined us at Namozine Creek April 1865. Captured a few days after at Sailor's Creek.

Bowe, H. C., enlisted 1863, discharged June, 1864.

Bridgers, David B., Jr. enlisted April 21, 1861; transferred to Richmond Howitzers, 1862.

Bridgers, Richard M., enlisted April 21, 1861; promoted captain of infantry March 18, 1862.

Brock, R. Alonzo, enlisted April 21, 1861; promoted corporal April 22, 1863; detailed by Gen. Lee June 12, 1862, for special service; promoted captain of infantry in 1862.

Brown, A. D., enlisted 1863; wounded at Hatcher's Run Feb. 5–7, 1865.

Brown, A. H., enlisted 1863.

Brown, George W., enlisted 1863; wounded (lost a leg) at Wilderness May 5, 1864.

Brown, Henry, enlisted 1863.

Brown, James R., enlisted 1863.

Bullington, Henry N., enlisted April 21, 1861; detailed by Secretary of War in 1861, for clerical service with Gen A. P. Hill.

Cabell, J. Caskie, enlisted April 21, 1861; promoted first lieutenant company F, 60th Va. Regt. 1861.

Callis, G., enlisted 1863.

Child, Jesse, enlisted April 21, 1861; promoted corporal June 6, 1861; and sergeant 1861; first lieutenant Company A, 42d Va. Regt., 1862; captured at Spottsylvania C. H., May 12, 1864; sent to Morris Island and placed under fire of the Confederate guns of Charleston in order to keep them from firing on certain points occupied by the Yankee army, afterwards taken to prison and kept there until the close of the war.

Chamberlayne, J. Hampden, enlisted April 21, 1861; promoted lieutenant Provisional Army, Va., May 1862;

and assigned as adjutant of artillery battalion, A. P. Hill's division; assigned to Crenshaw battery Jan., 1862; captured near Gettysburg, Pa., July, 1863; promoted captain July, 1864, and assigned to the command of a battery near the Crater; promoted major March, 1865, and assignment not made until just before the Appomattox retreat; commander of rear guard of artillery at Appomattox C. H., April 9, 1865.

Chapman, Isaac W., enlisted April 21, 1861; discharged by the Secretary of War Jan. 1862.

Clarke, Maxwell T., enlisted April 21, 1861; transferred to C. S. Navy June, 1861; commissioned master in charge of navy yard at Richmond, May, 1863; and placed in command of gunboat in James River Squadron.

Clopton, Dr. John, enlisted April 21, 1861; promoted assistant surgeon and transferred in 1861.

Cocke, Lorenzo, G., enlisted April 21, 1861; died in camp at Milboro, Dec. 1, 1861.

Cole, Addison C., enlisted April 21, 1861; discharged by the Secretary of War, Jan. 1862.

Coleman, N., enlisted 1863.

Couch, L. M., enlisted 1863; wounded at Payne's Farm Nov. 27, 1863; and at the Wilderness May 5, 1864; and at Cedar Creek Oct. 19, 1864.

Cowardin, John L., enlisted April 21, 1861; promoted first lieutenant and adjutant of ——Va. Regt., in Floyd's command, 1861.

Craig, John A., enlisted April 21, 1861; appointed hospital steward, Feb., 1864.

Cumbie, W. S., enlisted 1863.

Cumbia, W. E., transferred from 24th Va. battalion of infantry 1863; killed at Wilderness, May 5, 1864.

Danforth, Henry D., enlisted April 21, 1861; promoted lieutenant of ordnance April, 1862; and captain and A. A. General on Gen. Hunton's staff.

Dill, Adolph, Jr., enlisted April 21, 1861; detailed by order of the Secretary of War, 1863.

Dillard, R. H., enlisted 1863; wounded at the Wilderness, May 5, 1864.

Divers, W. H., enlisted 1863; wounded at Newtown Aug. 11, 1864; and died two days afterwards.

Doggett, Francis W., enlisted April 21, 1861; transferred to Dabney's battery in 1861; promoted captain of artillery.

Dowdy, Nathaniel A., enlisted 1863; promoted corporal 1864; wounded at the Wilderness, May 5, 1864; and at Winchester Sept. 19, 1864; captured at Fort Steadman March 25, 1865, and was kept in prison until the close of the war.

Edmonds, W. B., enlisted 1863; captured at Spottsylvania C. H., May 19, 1864, and kept in prison until close of war.

Ellerson, Jock H., enlisted April 21, 1861; transferred to C. S. Navy, June, 1861.

Ellett, Robert, enlisted April 21, 1861; promoted lieutenant in Letcher's battery Sept. 23, 1861; killed in front of Petersburg, April 2, 1865.

English, J. C., enlisted 1863; wounded at Winchester Sept. 19, 1864; captured and sent to Elmira, N. Y., where he died.

Etting, Samuel, enlisted April 21, 1861; transferred to Caskie battery 1861; promoted sergeant 1861.

Exall, Charles H., enlisted April 21, 1861; promoted sergeant in Letcher's battery, May, 1862.

Exall, William, enlisted April 21, 1861; killed at Bath Jan. 3, 1862.

Field, William G., enlisted April 21, 1861; transferred to cavalry in 1861; killed at Malvern Hill, July I, 1862.

Floyd, George C., enlisted 1863.

Fontaine, R. Morris, enlisted April 21, 1861; discharged by the Secretary of War, July, 1861.

Fox, Henry, C., enlisted 1863; wounded at Monocacy, Md., July 9, 1864; killed at Fort Steadman March 25, 1865.

Gentry, John W., enlisted April 21, 1861; promoted corporal 1862; transferred to Assistant A. Genl's department, June, 1862.

Gentry, M. G., enlisted 1863; detailed by Gen. Lee and ordered to report to Gen. Winder at Richmond, in 1864.

Gibson, William T., enlisted April 21, 1861; discharged by the Secretary of War, Dec. 1862.

Gillian, Robert H., enlisted April 21, 1861; wounded at Cedar Run Aug. 9, 1862; promoted second lieutenant 25th Va. battalion of infantry, Feb. 1864; acting adjutant of the battalion when captured at Sailor's Creek, April 6, 1865.

Gouldman, E., enlisted 1863; promoted corporal 1863, and sergeant 1864.

Gray, W. Granville, enlisted April 21, 1861; promoted second lieutenant Dec. 6, 1861; elected first lieutenant April 19, 1862; resigned March 25, 1864.

Gray, Summerville, enlisted April 21, 1861; transferred to Howitzers in 1861.

Green, John W., enlisted April 21, 1861; transferred to artillery 1861; assigned to ordnance department: entered cavalry service in 1863; killed near Liberty Mills Sept. 22, 1863.

Green, T. Richie, enlisted April 21, 1861; transferred and promoted lieutenant of artillery, 1861.

Griffin, J., enlisted 1863; captured at Spottsylvania C. H., May 19, 1864.

Harrison, Thomas R., enlisted April 21, 1861; transferred to Second Richmond Howitzers; promoted lieutenant and A. D. C. on Gen. Garnett's staff, 1862; wounded and captured at Gettysburg, Pa., and kept in prison until close of the war.

Harvie, William O., enlisted April 21, 1861; transferred to quartermaster's department 1861; promoted Major A. Q. M.

Hawkins, L. A., enlisted 1863; discharged by the Secretary of War, April 9, 1864.

Haynes, George A., enlisted April 21, 1861; promoted ordnance sergeant 21st Va. Regt. Oct., 1862.

Henry, Dr. Patrick, enlisted May 16, 1861; promoted assistant surgeon in the army, 1861.

Hobson, Deane, enlisted April 21, 1861; transferred to artillery 1861.

Houston, G. W., enlisted 1863; wounded at Winchester Sept. 19, 1864.

Hudgins, Malcolm L., enlisted May 16, 1861; promoted junior second lieutenant 1863; and first lieutenant April, 1864; wounded and captured at Cedar Creek, Oct. 19, 1864, and kept in prison until March 30, 1864, when he was exchanged.

Hull, Irving, enlisted May, 1861; transferred 1861.

Jenkins, William S., enlisted April 21, 1861.

Jones, David B., enlisted April 21, 1861; promoted quartermaster sergeant of 21st Va. Regt., 1862, and acting Q. M. of the regiment, 1864.

Jones, Philip B., Jr., enlisted April 21, 1861; promoted captain and A. Q. M., Oct. 26, 1861.

Johnston, J. W., enlisted 1863; captured at Wilderness May 5, 1864; kept in prison until close of war.

Kayton, P. W., enlisted 1863; captured on skirmish line at Spottsylvania C. H. May 12, 1864; kept in prison until close of war.

Kellogg, Timothy H., enlisted April 21, 1861; promoted second lieutenant company H, 21st Va. Regt. April 22, 1862; promoted Major and A. C. S. Nov., 1862.

Kidd, J. A., enlisted 1863; wounded at Payne's Farm, Nov. 27, 1863; killed at Fort Steadman March 25, 1865.

Legg, A. C., enlisted 1863; wounded at the Wilderness, May 5, 1864; died from its effects June 26, 1864.

Lindsay, Roswell S., enlisted April 21, 1861; promoted corporal April, 1862; killed at Cedar Run, Aug. 9, 1862.

Lorentz, A., enlisted April 21, 1861; transferred 1861.

Macmurdo, Richard C., enlisted May 18, 1861; promoted captain and A. C. S. March 30, 1862.

Maddox, R. G., enlisted May, 1861; transferred 1861.

Mason, J. M., enlisted 1863, captured at Cedar Creek, Oct. 19, 1864; kept in prison until close of war.

Mayo, Joseph E., enlisted May 10, 1861; transferred to signal corps 1863.

McEvoy, Charles A., enlisted April 21, 1861; resigned June 27, 1861, by order of Gov. Letcher.

Meade, Everard B., enlisted April 21, 1861; promoted lieutenant regiment of engineer troops; and A. D. C. to Brig.-Gen. James H. Lane.

Mebane, James A., enlisted April 21, 1861; promoted hospital steward in 1861.

Meredith, J. French, enlisted April 21, 1861; transferred 1861.

Merryman, J. T., enlisted 1863; captured on skirmish line at Spottsylvania C. H., May 12, 1864.

Mitchell, Samuel D., enlisted April 21, 1861; promoted lieutenant A. D. C. to Gen. C. S. Winder May 9, 1862; killed at Gaines Mill, June 27, 1862.

Mittledorfer, Charles, enlisted April 21, 1861; transferred 1861.

Morris, Walter H. P., enlisted April 21, 1861; transferred to Marye battery 1861; promoted lieutenant and A. D. C.

Mountcastle, John R., enlisted April 21, 1861; promoted lieutenant of cavalry June, 1862.

Munt, Henry F., enlisted 1863; promoted corporal 1863; captured at Wilderness, May 5, 1864, and kept in prison until close of war.

Nance, J. L., enlisted 1863; discharged by the Secretary of War in 1864.

Norwood, William, Jr., enlisted April 21, 1861; promoted lieutenant and A. D. C., Sept. 11, 1861, and captain and A. A. Gen. 1862. Wounded at Cedar Run, Aug. 9, 1862.

Nunnally, Joseph L., enlisted April 21, 1861; wounded at Kernstown, March 23, 1862; killed at Cedar Run, Aug. 9, 1862. Run, Aug. 9, 1862.

Pace, George R., enlisted April 21, 1861; promoted corporal June, 1861, discharged by the Secretary of War, June, 1862.

Pace, Theodore A., enlisted May 6, 1861; discharged by the Secretary of War, June, 1862.

Page, Mann, enlisted April 21, 1861; promoted sergeant major of 21st Va. Regt. in 1861; first lieutenant and adjutant 1862; captain and A. A. Gen. in 1862; Major on Gen. Early's staff, 1864.

Pardigon, C. F., enlisted April 21, 1861; promoted lieutenant in Provisional Army C. S., and Captain on Gen. Kershaw's staff.

Payne, James B., enlisted April 21, 1861; promoted junior second lieutenant Dec. 28, 1861; wounded at Bath, Jan. 3, 1862.

Peaster, Henry, enlisted April 21, 1861; wounded at Payne's Farm Nov. 27, 1863; transferred to Maryland line, 1864.

Peagram, William R. J., enlisted April 21, 1861; promoted lieutenant Purcell battery May, 1861; promoted captain, lieutenant, colonel and colonel of artillery; killed at Five Forks, April 1, 1865.

Peterkin, George W., enlisted April 21, 1861; promoted sergeant 1861; and elected junior lieutenant April 19, 1862; promoted first lieutenant and A. D. C. on Gen. W. N. Pendleton's staff, June, 1862.

Picot, Henry V., enlisted April 21, 1861; wounded at Kernstown, March 23, 1862; and died from its effects.

Piet, William A., enlisted April 21, 1861; transferred to Third company Howitzers, June, 1862.

Pilcher, Samuel F., enlisted April 21, 1861; when F Company went to Fredericksburg he was made a sergeant, and left in Richmond to recruit a second company. Ill health soon compelled him to discontinue, his health gradually declined and he died in 1863.

Pollard, William G., enlisted April 21, 1861; promoted sergeant April 19, 1862; killed at Cedar Run, Aug, 9, 1862.

Powell, John G., enlisted May 10, 1861; killed at Cedar Run, Aug. 9, 1862.

Powell, John W., enlisted April 21, 1861; transferred 1861.

Price, Channing R., enlisted May, 1861; promoted lieutenant, captain and major on Gen. J. E. B. Stuart's staff; killed at Chancellorsville, May, 1863.

Randolph, J. Tucker, enlisted April 21, 1861; promoted

corporal June 5, 1861; sergeant 1861; wounded at Kernstown, March 23, 1862; promoted lieutenant on Gen. John Pegram's staff, June, 1862; killed at Bethesda Church, May 30, 1864.

Randolph, M. Lewis, enlisted April 21, 1861; promoted corporal May, 1861; lieutenant in First Va. battalion of infantry 1861; and captain in signal corps, 1862.

Redd, Clarence M., enlisted April 21, 1861; wounded at Cedar Run, Aug. 9, 1862; transferred to Hanover artillery in 1862.

Reeve, David I. B., enlisted April 21, 1861; promoted first lieutenant and adjutant of cavalry in 1862.

Reeve, John J., enlisted May 10, 1861; promoted captain and A. A. General on Gen. Loring's staff April 7, 1862; major and A. A. G. on Gen. Stevenson's staff, 1862.

Rennie, G. Hutcheson, enlisted May 18, 1861; killed at Fort Steadman, March 25, 1865.

Richeson, P. S., enlisted 1863; wounded at Spottsylvania C. H. May 12, 1864.

Richeson, William R., enlisted 1863; and served with his company to Appomattox. Complimented on the battlefield at Hatcher's Run, Feb. 5–7, 1865, by General Gordon.

Rison, John W., enlisted April 21, 1861; transferred to Laboratory department 1861.

Robertson, William S., enlisted May 18, 1861; promoted sergeant 1864; captured at Waynesboro, Mar. 2, 1865, sent to Fort Delaware, and kept there until close of the war.

Robinson, Christopher A., enlisted April 21, 1861; detailed in engineer corps, 1862.

Robinson, Richard F., enlisted April 21, 1861; discharged by the Secretary of War, April, 1862.

Rutledge, W., enlisted 1863; served with his company to Appomattox.

Searles, S., enlisted 1863; sent to hospital Aug. 16, 1864.

Seay, M., enlisted 1863; sent to hospital May 2, 1864.

Seay, W. C., enlisted 1863; wounded at Spottsylvania C.

H., May 12, 1864, and died from its effects May 14, 1864.

Singleton, A. Jackson, enlisted April 21, 1861; discharged by the Secretary of War Feb., 1862.

Simpson, F. J., enlisted 1863; captured at Spottsylvania C. H., May 19, 1864.

Sizer, Milton D., enlisted April 21, 1861; discharged by the Secretary of War Feb., 1862.

Skinker, Charles R., enlisted April 21, 1861; wounded at Kernstown March 23, 1862; transferred to second company of Howitzers in 1862; wounded at Fredericksburg, 1862; promoted first lieutenant Company K, 48th Va. Regt. of infantry 1863; captain 1863; wounded at Chancellorsville, May 2, 1863; captured at Spottsylvania C. H. May 12, 1864; sent to Fort Delaware and rejoined his command in about seven months; wounded at Hatcher's Run Feb. 12, 1865 and permanently disabled.

Smith, Edward H., enlisted April 21, 1861; transferred to Howitzers in 1861.

Smith, Henry, enlisted 1863; wounded at Wilderness May 5, 1864.

Smith, J. T., enlisted 1863; served with his company to Appomattox.

Smith, Thomas, enlisted 1863; captured at the Wilderness May 5, 1864; kept in prison until close of war.

Soles, Peter D., enlisted 1863.

Sublett, Peter A., enlisted April 21, 1861; transferred to Third company of Richmond Howitzers Aug., 1862.

Tabb, Robert M., enlisted April 21, 1861; promoted sergeant 1863; sergeant-major 21st Va. Regt. Sept., 1864; killed at Cedar Creek, Oct. 19, 1864.

Talley, Daniel D., enlisted April 21, 1861; promoted paymaster C. S. Navy, 1862.

Tatum, A. Randolph, enlisted April 21, 1861; detailed and assigned to duty with Gen. J. H. Winder, Feb., 1862.

Tatum, Vivion H., enlisted April 21, 1861; detailed in commissary department in Richmond 1862.

Taylor, Charles E., enlisted April 21, 1861; wounded at

Kernstown, March 23, 1862; transferred to signal corps, 1862.

Taylor, Clarence E., enlisted April 21, 1861; wounded at Cedar Run Aug. 9, 1862; detailed to Quartermaster's department in Richmond, 1862.

Taylor, Edward B., enlisted April 21, 1861; wounded at Kernstown, Mar. 23, 1862; transferred to ordnance department 1862; promoted quartermaster-sergeant with Maj. Turner, 1864.

Taylor, Robert T., enlisted April 21, 1861; promoted Major and A. Q. M., April 15, 1862.

Tiney, W. C., enlisted 1863; promoted corporal May, 1863; killed at Williamsport, Md., July 6, 1863.

Tompkins, Edward G., enlisted April 21, 1861; wounded at Cedar Run, Aug. 9, 1862; permanently disabled.

Trainum, Charles, enlisted 1863; discharged by the Secretary of War, April 11, 1864.

Tyler, James E., enlisted April 21, 1861; promoted sergeant Letcher battery March, 1862; wounded at Harper's Ferry 1862; wounded at Chancellorsville, May 3, 1863; promoted second lieutenant, July, 1864; and commanded battery at close of war.

Tyler, R. Emmet, enlisted April 21, 1861; promoted corporal April, 1862; transferred to ordnance department, 1862.

Tyree, W. C., enlisted 1863; promoted corporal 1864; wounded at Cedar Creek, Oct. 19, 1864.

Van Buren, Benjamin B., enlisted April 21, 1861; discharged by the Secretary of War, 1862.

Waldrop, Richard W., enlisted April 21, 1861; promoted commissary sergeant 21st Va. Regt., 1863.

Walker, T., enlisted 1863; promoted sergeant May, 1863; killed at Williamsport, Md., July 6, 1863.

Wallace, R. H., enlisted 1863; transferred to 24th Va. battalion of Infantry, 1863.

Watkins, A. Salle, enlisted April 21, 1861; promoted second lieutenant company C, 3d battalion Va. Infantry

May 17, 1864; first lieutenant, and captain, March, 1865.

Watkins, H. Harrison, enlisted April 21, 1861; promoted sergeant-major 21st Va. Regt. 1862; wounded at Cedar Run, Aug. 9, 1862; and permanently disabled.

White, Robert C., enlisted April 21, 1861; transferred to Crenshaw battery, Aug. 13, 1862.

Wilkins, J. M., enlisted 1863.

Willis, Joseph N., enlisted April 21, 1861; promoted hospital steward, Nov., 1863.

Wood, S. E., enlisted 1863.

Worsham, John H., enlisted April 21, 1861; promoted second sergeant April, 1863; first sergeant Dec. 1863; adjutant of 21st Va. Regt., Sept. 12, 1864; wounded at Winchester Sept. 19, 1864; permanently disabled.

Worsham, Thomas R., enlisted April 21, 1861; promoted sergeant Letcher battery, second lieutenant in 1862; wounded at Spottsylvania C. H. May, 1864.

Wren, J. Porter, enlisted April 21, 1861; promoted third sergeant April, 1863; second sergeant Dec., 1863; wounded at Cedar Run, Aug. 9, 1862; at Payne's Farm Nov. 27, 1863; killed at Monocacy, Md., July 9, 1864.

Wright, Philip A., enlisted April 21, 1861; transferred 1861.

Zimmer, Louis, enlisted April 21, 1861; promoted captain in ordnance department, 1861.

Dr. Frank B. Cunningham, enlisted April 21, 1861; as surgeon of the company; promoted assistant-surgeon in the army in 1861, and surgeon of Division 1862.

Dr. Peter Lyons, enlisted April 21, 1861; as assistant surgeon of the company; promoted assistant surgeon in the army in 1861, and surgeon, 1862.

This makes a total of one hundred and ninety-two who belonged to the company during the war; below is a list of changes that took place—casualties, transfers, promotions, etc.:

Died, 3; killed, 31; wounded, 49; captured by the

enemy, 19; transferred, 38; promoted to other commands, 57; discharged, 16; resigned, 2.

Promoted to Navy 5
Promoted Hospital Stewards......................... 4
Promoted Assistant Surgeons 4
Promoted Surgeons................................... 2
Promoted Corporals.................................. 14
Promoted Sergeants..................................25
Promoted Jr. Second lieutenants 7
Promoted Second lieutenants...........................16
Promoted First lieutenants 28
Promoted Captains...................................24
Promoted Majors 10
Promoted Lieutenant Colonels 4
Promoted Colonels.................................... 3

I also give a list of casualties, promotions, etc., that took place in F Company while the men were serving with that company; these are included in list above:
Killed, 20; wounded, 27; captured by the enemy, 11; died, 3; discharged, 16; resigned, 2.

Promoted Corporals...................................12
Promoted Sergeants...................................15
Promoted Jr. Second lieutenant 5
Promoted Second lieutenant........................... 4
Promoted First lieutenant............................. 4
Promoted Captains.................................... 4

F. Company participated in the following battles:
1861, Acquia Creek, May 29, June 7–8; Crouch's, Aug. 15.
1862, Bath, Jan. 4; Sir John's Run, Jan. 6; Hancock; Jan.
   7; Romney, Jan. 17; Kernstown, Mch. 23; McDowell,
   May 8; Franklin, May 11; Front Royal, May 23;
   Midletown, May 24; Winchester, May 25; Cross Keys,
   June 7; Port Republic, June 9; Cold Harbor, June 28;
   White Oak Swamp, June 30; Malvern Hill, July 1; Cedar
   Run, Aug. 9; Second Manassas, Aug. 28, 29, 30;
   Chantilly, Sept. 2; Harper's Ferry, Sept. 13, 14, 15;
   Sharpsburg, 16, 17; Fredericksburg, Dec. 13.

1863, Williamsport, Md., July 6; Hagerstown, Md., July 8; Payne's Farm, Nov. 27; Mine Run, Dec. 1, 2, 3.

1864, Wilderness, May 5–8; Spottsylvania C. H., May 9 to 20; Hanover Junction, May 22; Bethesda Church, May 30; Cold Harbor, 2 to 7; Lynchburg, June 18; Monocacy, Md., July 9; Washington, D. C., July 11, 12; Kernstown, July 24; Newtown, Aug. 11; Winchester, Aug. 17, and Sept. 19; Fisher's Hill, Sept. 22; Cedar Creek, Oct. 19.

1865, Hatcher's Run, Feb. 5–7; Fort Steadman, Mch. 25; near Petersburg, Apr. 2; Appomattox C. H., Apr. 9.

Our Regiment, the 21st Va., was in the battles of Chancellorsville, May 2–3, 1863; Winchester, June, 1863, and Gettysburg, July 2, 3, 4, while F Company was absent recruiting. And F Company fought the battle of Williamsport, July 6, 1863, while the regiment was on its way from Gettysburg.

The following members of F Company surrendered at Appomattox C. H., Apr. 9, 1865:

Corporal H. C. Tyree,

William R. Richeson,

William Rutledge,

Joseph T. Smith.

The following old members of F Company belonging to other commands surrendered at Appomattox C. H.:

Ira W. Blunt, Hospital Steward, 21st Va. Regt.

George A. Haynes, Ordnance Sergeant, 21st Va. Regt.

Richard W. Waldrop, Commissary Sergeant, 21st Va. Regt.

John A. Craig, Hospital Steward, 2d Corps.

Henry C. Bullington, Clerk, 3d Corps.

William O. Harvie, Major, A. Q. M., Army N. Va.

Philip B. Jones, Captain, A. Q. M.

Walter H. P. Morris, Lieutenant and A. D. C.

William A. Piet, Second Co. Howitzers.

Peter A. Sublett, Second Co. Howitzers.

George W. Peterkin, First Lieutenant and A. D. C.

D. I. B. Reeve.

E. B. Taylor, Sergeant Quarter-Master's Department.

Robert T. Taylor, Major A. Q. M.

Robert C. White.

Louis Zimmer, Captain Ordnance Department.

Peter Lyons, Surgeon.

H. D. Danforth, Captain and A. D. C.

The following were at Appomattox C. H., but made their escape and were not included in the surrender:

Thomas Ellett, Captain Artillery.

James E. Tyler, First Lieutenant Artillery.

William C. Barker, Second Lieutenant Artillery.

They destroyed their guns, etc., before leaving.

J. Hamden Chamberlayne, Major of Artillery, made his escape and joined Gen. J. E. Johnston's Army.

C. C. Baughman, Artillery, and Greer H. Baughman, Sergeant Artillery, made their escape and went to Gen. J. E. Johnston's army, and thence to Gen. Kirby Smith's army.

Lt.-Col. Archer Anderson, Adjutant-General of Gen. J. E. Johnston's army, surrendered with that army.

Major John J. Reeve, Adjutant-General, also served with that army.

Marches of F Company from the commencement to the close of the war:

1861.		MILES
Apr. 21.	Marched to Wilton. Henrico Co.	12
Apr. 22.	Returned to Richmond on barges by James River.	
Apr. 24.	Took the cars to Fredericksburg. May. Left Fredericksburg on the cars to Game Point. Stafford Co.	
June 14.	Took cars for Richmond.	
July 18.	Marched to Central R. R. depot and took cars for Staunton	4
July 20.	Marched to Buffalo Gap. Augusta Co.	10
July 21.	To Ryans	11
July 22.	To McDowell. Highland Co.	18
July 23.	To Monterey	13

July 24.	To Forks of Road	15
July 25.	To Napp's Creek. Pocahontas Co.	13
July 26.	To Huntersville	8
Aug. 3.	To Edray	11
Aug. 5.	To Big Spring	17
Aug. 6.	To Valley Mountain.	4
Sept. 9.	To Marshall's Store. Randolph Co.	4
Sept. 10.	To Conrad's Store	5
Sept. 11.	The 21st Va. Regt. went on picket to the front	4
Sept. 12.	To Crouch's	2
Sept. 15.	Back to Conrad's Mill	6
Sept. 16.	To Marshall's Store	5
Sept. 17.	To Valley Mountain. Pocahontas Co.	4
Sept. 24.	To Middle Mountain	2
Sept. 25.	To foot Middle Mountain	2
Sept. 28.	To Hogshead's	5
Sept. 30.	To Elk Mountain	5
Oct. 1.	To top of Elk Mountain	3
Oct. 9.	To Edray	5
Oct. 14.	To Greenbrier Bridge	4
Nov. 11.	To Harrold's farm	11
Nov. 13.	To Warm Springs. Bath Co.	22
Nov. 14.	To Bath Alum Springs	5
Nov. 30.	To Milboro	10
Dec. 4.	Took cars at Milboro and went to Staunton. Augusta Co.	
Dec. 18.	Marched from Staunton to Mt. Sidney	13
Dec. 19.	To Harrisonburg. Rockingham Co.	16
Dec. 20.	To Cowan's farm	13
Dec. 21.	To Mt. Jackson. Shenandoah Co.	12
Dec. 22.	To Strasburg	24
Dec. 25.	To Newtown. Frederick Co.	11
Dec. 26.	To through Winchester and camped on Romney Road	16

1862.

Jan. 1.	To Pughtown	12

Jan. 2.	To Ungers X Roads. Morgan Co.	13
Jan. 3.	To near Bath	12
Jan. 4.	To Sir John's Run	5
Jan. 5.	Marched towards Hancock and Capon Bridge	11
Jan. 8.	Back to Ungers X Roads	18
Jan. 9.	To camp on side road	4
Jan. 13.	Marched about 200 yards; the head of the column marched about 4 miles.	
Jan. 14.	To Bloomery Furnace. Hampshire Co.	8
Jan. 15.	To Capon Bridge	5
Jan. 16.	To Camp Meeting grounds	7
Jan. 17.	To near Romney	12
Jan. 24.	To Romney	3
Feb. 3.	To Deep Creek	10
Feb. 4.	To Hanging Rock	8
Feb. 5.	To Back Creek Valley. Frederick Co.	12
Feb. 6.	To near Winchester	9
Feb. 27.	To Berryville Road	5
Mch. 7.	To Strasburg Road	5
Mch. 11.	To Springdale	4
Mch. 12.	To Cedar Creek	11
Mch. 15.	To Woodstock. Shenandoah Co.	15
Mch. 19.	To Mt. Jackson	11
Mch. 20.	To Rude's Hill	5
Mch. 22.	To Fisher's Hill	27
Mch. 23.	To Kernstown, where we fought the battle and back to Newtown. Frederick Co.	26
Mch. 24.	To Woodstock. Shenandoah Co.	23
Mch. 25.	To Mt. Jackson	13
Mch. 26.	Back to Woodstock	11
Mch. 28.	Back to Mt. Jackson	11
Apr. 3.	To Edenburg and back to Mt. Jackson	18
Apr. 5.	To Camp on Valley Pike	2
Apr. 7.	To below Mt. Jackson	7
Apr. 10.	Back to old camp	7
Apr. 13.	To Luray Road	4
Apr. 17.	To Lacy's Spring. Rockingham Co.	10

Apr. 18.	To Gordonsville Road	13
Apr. 19.	To near Swift Run Gap	12
Apr. 23.	To Swift Run Gap	3
Apr. 30.	Marched across the Shenandoah River and recrossed, then marched up the road towards Port Republic	12
May 1.	To Clear Creek	6
May 2.	To Port Republic	8
May 3.	To White Hall, Albemarle Co., crossing the Blue Ridge at Brown's Gap	17
May 4.	To Meechums Depot; there took cars for Staunton, Augusta Co., and marched through and beyond the town	14
May 6.	To Buffalo Gap	10
May 7.	To and across the Shenandoah Mountain	12
May 8.	To McDowell, Highland Co., where we fought the battle	11
May 9.	To Shenandoah Mt. and back to McDowell	13
May 10.	To Hilly Camp. Pendleton Co.	15
May 11.	To near Franklin	10
May 12.	Back to camp on McDowell road	5
May 13.	To Pine Hill. Highland Co.	12
May 14.	To McDowell	8
May 15.	To Lebanon Springs. Augusta Co.	15
May 17.	To Mossy Creek. Rockingham Co.	12
May 19.	To Dayton	12
May 20.	To near New Market. Shenandoah Co.	15
May 21.	To camp on roadside, Page Co., crossing Massanutta Mt.	13
May 22.	To Luray	14
May 23.	To Front Royal, Page Co., where we had a battle	27
May 24–5.	To Middletown, Frederick Co., where we had a battle, marching all night to near Winchester, where we had another battle, and pursuing the enemy beyond that town	26

May 28.	My regiment marched into Winchester and took charge of the prisoners.	4
May 31.	To Cedar Creek, with prisoners	13
June 1.	To Woodstock. Shenandoah Co.	14
June 2.	To Mt. Jackson	14
June 3.	To New Market	9
June 4.	To Harrisonburg. Rockingham Co	14
June 5.	To New Hope. Augusta Co.	17
June 6.	To Waynesboro	12
June 8.	To and across the Blue Ridge at Rockfish Gap. Albemarle Co.	6
June 9.	To North Garden Depot, O. & A. R.R.	12
June 11.	We took the cars here and carried our prisoners to Lynchburg Fair Ground. Campbell Co.	2
June 18.	Left Lynchburg and rode on cars to near Charlottesville. Albemarle Co.	2
June 21.	Marched to Charlottesville and joined our brigade as they marched through on their way to Richmond	9
June 22.	To Gordonsville. Orange Co.	13
June 23.	To Louisa C. H. Louisa Co.	13
June 24.	Left Louisa C. H. and rode on cars to Bumpass Depot, and marched to camp	20
June 25.	To Ashland. Hanover Co.	11
June 26.	To near Pole Green Church	15
June 27.	To near Cold Harbor, where we had the battle	11
June 28.	Marched to Bridge and back	3
June 30.	Crossed the Chickahominy River and marched to White Oak Swamp, where we fought the enemy. Henrico Co.	11
July 1.	To Malvern Hill, where we had the battle	6
July 2.	To Willis Church. Charles City Co.	2
July 4.	To Forks of Road	2
July 5.	To Westover.	7
July 8.	To Creek	2
July 9.	To White Oak Swamp. Henrico Co.	10

July 10.   To Seven Pines 8
July 11.   To Morris Farm on Mechanicsville
           Turnpike 10
July 16.   Marched to Richmond, there took cars on
           R. F. & P. R. R. and went to Louisa C. H.,
           which we reached on the 18th, having
           been detained by damage to the bridge
           across South Anna River by high water ... 10
July 20.   To Gordonsville. Orange Co. 13
July 22.   To Liberty Mills. Madison Co. 8
July 26.   Marched on road to meet the enemy,
           who were reported advancing; not
           finding them, returned.................. 10
July 29.   To Mechanicsville. Louisa Co............ 11
Aug. 4.   Back to Liberty Mills Madison Co. 11
Aug. 7.   To Orange C. H. Orange Co............. 13
Aug. 8.   To camp in Culpeper Co................ 7
Aug. 9.   To Cedar Run, where we had the battle ... 12
Aug. 10.   To camp near battlefield 3
Aug. 13.   To camp across the Rapidan river in Orange
           Co. 16
Aug. 14.   To Terrell's Farm 16
Aug. 16.   To camp near Clark's Mountain 21
Aug. 20.   To Stevensburg. Culpeper Co............ 12
Aug. 21.   To camp on road side.................. 7
Aug. 21.   To Hazel River 11
Aug. 23.   To near Fauquier Springs. Fauquier Co. . . 13
Aug. 24.   To Jeffersonton........................ 1
Aug. 25.   To Salem 26
Aug. 26.   To Gainsville. Prince William Co......... 26
Aug. 27.   To Manassas Junction.................. 5
Aug. 28.   To Groveton, where we fought the
           Second battle of Manassas 10
Sept. 1.   To Bull Run.......................... 3
Sept. 2.   To Chantilly, Fairfax Co., where we had the
           battle 12
Sept. 3.   To camp on road side.................. 2
Sept. 4.   To camp on road side. Loudoun Co....... 12

Sept. 5.   To Leesburg........................... 11
Sept. 6.   To Three Springs, Montgomery Co., Md.,
            crossing the Potomac at White Ford...... 15
Sept. 7.   To Frederick City. Frederick Co., Md...... 13
Sept. 10.   To Boonsboro. Washington Co., Md........ 14
Sept. 11.   To North Mountain Depot, Berkeley
            Co., Va., crossing the Potomac at
            Williamsport 22
Sept. 12.   To Martinsburg........................ 14
Sept. 13.   To Harper's Ferry, Jefferson Co., where
            we captured garrison, arms, etc.......... 18
Sept. 16.   To Sharpsburg, Washington Co., Md.,
            where we fought the battle, crossing
            the Potomac at Boteler's Ford........... 12
Sept. 19.   To camp in Jefferson Co., Va., crossing
            Potomac at Boteler's Ford 8
Sept. 20.   To Martinsburg. Berkeley Co. 20
Sept. 21.   To Bunker Hill 12
Oct. 18.   To Martinsburg, from there to the B. & O.
            R. R., tearing that up as we went 16
Oct. 21.   To Opequan Creek, on road leading to
            Harper's Ferry........................ 4
Oct. 23.   To Bunker Hill 10
Oct. 28.   To Summit Point 16
Nov. 1.   To Opequan Creek, near Berryville.
            Clark Co............................. 10
Nov. 5.   To near White Post.................... 10
Nov. 10.   Through Winchester to Romney Road.
            Frederick Co.......................... 13
Nov. 21.   To Middletown 12
Nov. 22.   To Woodstock. Shenandoah Co. 18
Nov. 23.   To Mt. Jackson 13
Nov. 24.   To camp in Luray Valley, Page Co.,
            crossing Massanutta Mt. at New Market... 23
Nov. 25.   To camp in Madison Co., crossing the
            Blue Ridge at Fisher's Gap.............. 23
Nov. 26.   To Madison C. H. 14

Nov. 28.	To Orange C. H. Orange Co.	14
Nov. 29.	To Union Church. Spottsylvania Co.	12
Nov. 30.	To Wilderness	14
Dec. 1.	To Dorgett's.	15
Dec. 2.	To near Guinea's Station. Caroline Co. . . .	13
Dec. 11.	To Hamilton's Crossing, where we had the battle of Fredericksburg	7
Dec. 17.	To Moss Neck, where we went into winter quarters	12
	To picket on the Rappahannock river, twice and back again	28

1863.

Jan.—	F Company were ordered from this camp to Richmond to recruit. Marched to Guinea's, R. F. & P. R. R.; there took cars for Richmond	10
June 22.	We marched from Camp Lee to Central R. R. and took cars for Staunton; marched.	4
June 24.	To Switcher's. Augusta Co.	14
June 25.	To Harrisonburg. Rockingham Co.	11
June 26.	To Williams	15
June 27.	To Edenburg. Shenandoah Co.	17
June 28.	To Strasburg	18
June 29.	To Winchester. Frederick Co.	18
July 1.	To Bunker Hill. Berkeley Co.	12
July 2.	To Falling Waters	18
July 3.	To Potomac River, opposite Williamsport. .	5
July 5.	Crossed the Potomac and marched east of Williamsport, Md	1
July 6.	Battle of Williamsport	1
July 8.	To Hagerstown	7
July 9.	Marched and met our regiment, and marched back through Hagerstown, with the Second Corps	7
July 10.	Formed line of battle near Hagerstown	1
July 13.	The Second Corps left the line of battle	

during the night and forded the Potomac above Williamsport the morning of 14th and camped in Berkeley Co., Va.......... 14

July 15. To Darksville 10

July 16. Back to and beyond Martinsburg 15

July 17. To B. & O. R. R., where we went to work destroying it 6

July 18. To camp near B. & O. R. R 4

July 19. To camp on the Opequan............... 3

July 20. To mill on Romney Road............... 7

July 21. To Bunker Hill 8

July 22. To Winchester. Frederick Co. 13

July 23. To Manassas Gap, where we had some brisk skirmishing with the enemy. Warren Co. 26

July 24. To camp on Luray Road. Page Co. 16

July 25. To camp near Luray.................... 15

July 27. To Sperryville, Madison Co., crossing the Blue Ridge at Thornton's Gap........ 15

July 28. To camp on road side................... 13

July 29. To Robinson River 10

July 31. To camp beyond Madison C. H............ 6

Aug. 1. To Montpelier. Orange Co............... 15

Aug. 14. To Liberty Mills. Madison Co. 4

Aug. 16. To Montpelier. Orange Co............... 4

Sept. 4. To Review field east of Orange C. H. and back again to camp 12

Sept. 19. To Morton's Ford 16

Sept. 25. To Willis Ford........................ 8

Oct. 8. To Mt. Pisgah Church 20

Oct. 9. To Madison Co. poorhouse.............. 23

Oct. 10. To camp on road side. Culpeper Co....... 17

Oct. 11. To Culpeper C. H...................... 10

Oct. 12. To Warrenton Springs. Fauquier Co. 20

Oct. 13. To Warrenton 7

Oct. 14. To near Bristow Station, Prince William Co., where we formed line of battle on O. & A. R. R.......................... 15

Oct. 16.	To Bristow Station	4
Oct. 18.	To near Bealton Station. Fauquier Co.	20
Oct. 19.	To camp in Culpeper Co.	8
Oct. 21.	To camp near Brandy Station	4
Oct. 26.	To near Bealton Station. Fauquier Co.	8
Oct. 28.	Back to camp in Culpeper Co.	8
Nov. 7.	To Kelly's Ford and then to near Culpeper C. H.	18
Nov. 8.	To camp in Orange Co.	15
Nov. 9.	To Morton's Ford	4
Nov. 12.	To Mt. Pisgah Church	8
Nov. 18.	To Willis Ford	12
Nov. 26.	To Bartley Mill	8
Nov. 27.	To Payne's Farm, where we fought the battle	7
Nov. 28.	To Mine Run, and formed line of battle to meet Meade	3
Dec. 2.	To Morton's Ford	5
Dec. 3.	To Raccoon Ford and back to Morton's Ford	5
Dec. 19.	To Orange C. H.	14
Dec. 22.	To Mt. Pisgah Church	6
Dec. 24.	To Crenshaw's farm near Mt. Pisgah Church, where we went into winter quarters	1

1864.

Jan. 5.	To Morton's Ford	8
Jan. 10.	To camp, Crenshaw farm	8
Jan. 27.	To Morton's Ford	8
Feb. 2.	To camp, Crenshaw farm	8
Mch. 2.	To Mine Run	8
Mch. 3.	To Chancellorsville and back to X Roads. Spottsylvania Co.	16
Mch. 4.	To Chancellorsville	4
Mch. 5.	To camp, Crenshaw farm. Orange Co.	20
Mch. 17.	To Morton's Ford	10
Apr. 26.	To camp, Crenshaw farm	10

May 2.	Broke up Winter Quarters and marched to Bartley's Mill.	10
May 4.	To Locust Grove	10
May 5.	To Wilderness, where we fought the battle. Spottsylvania Co.	5
May 7.	The Second Brigade moved to the extreme left of our line and back to its position on Stone Road.	7
May 8.	To Spottsylvania C. H. by way of Todd's Tavern and the mill, and formed line of battle	15
May 19.	Marched in pursuit of the enemy and attacked him, and returned to our old position in breastworks	10
May 21.	The enemy having left the front of the Second Corps, we marched to Telegraph Road. Caroline Co.	15
May 22.	To Hanover Junction, Hanover Co., where we formed line of battle to meet Grant	12
May 24.	Marched to left of our line of battle and then to the right.	6
May 27.	The enemy having left the front of Second Corps, we marched to Atlee's Station, Central R. R., crossing the South Anna River on the bridge of that company	12
May 28.	To Pole Green Church, where we formed line of battle to meet Grant	16
May 30.	We marched to meet the enemy and attacked them near Bethesda Church	4
May 31.	Moved to the right	2
June 1.	Moved to Dickerson house	2
June 6.	Marched after the enemy and returned	3
June 7.	Marched after the enemy	3
June 9.	Marched to right and rear of our line	2
June 13.	The Second Corps left Lee's line and marched around Richmond to Three Chop	

Road, camping near Ground Squirrel
Bridge. Louisa Co. 26
June 14. To Gardner's X Roads.................. 25
June 15. To Mechanicsville. Louisa Co. 22
June 16. To Keswick Depot. Albemarle Co......... 21
June 17. The Second Brigade marched north of
          Keswick Depot and took the cars for
          Lynchburg. On reaching Lynchburg we
          marched beyond the Fair Grounds and
          formed line of battle. Campbell Co. 5
June 19. To Liberty. Bedford Co. 24
June 20. To Buford's Gap 15
June 21. To Salem. Roanoke Co. 20
June 23. To near Buchanan. Botetourt Co......... 18
June 24. To camp on road side in Rockbridge Co.,
          marching over the Natural Bridge 20
June 25. To near Fairfield, marching past the
          grave of Stonewall Jackson, in the
          Cemetery at Lexington.................. 20
June 26. To camp on road side. Augusta Co........ 19
June 27. To near Staunton 6
June 28. To Mt. Crawford. Rockingham Co. 20
June 29. To Lacey's Springs 16
June 30. To Mt. Jackson. Shenandoah Co.......... 17
July 1.   To camp on road side................... 20
July 2.   To Middletown Mills. Frederick Co. 20
July 3.   To Martinsburg, Berkeley Co., where we
          captured many stores from the enemy.... 25
July 4.   To X Roads 10
July 5.   To Antietam, Washington Co., Md.,
          crossing the Potomac at Boteler's Ford ... 12
July 6.   Towards Harper's Ferry 4
July 7.   Drove the enemy into his fortifications
          and at night marched to Norristown 8
July 8.   To Middletown, Md., Frederick Co.,
          crossing the mountain at Fox Gap 10
July 9.   To Monacacy River, where we had the
          battle 15

July 10.	To camp beyond Clarksburg, Montgomery Co., Md.................................	20
July 11.	To Washington, D.C., city, where we have some fighting.....................	15
July 12.	We left Washington during the night, marched to Darnestown, where we stopped about noon, and rested a few hours; marched all night of the 13th, and crossed the Potomac at White's Ford and camped near Leesburg, Loudoun Co., Va., on the 14th	40
July 15.	21st Va. Regt. marched into Leesburg and took charge of loose horses.	1
July 16.	We left Leesburg with the horses, marched and rode horseback to Millwood, Clarke Co., crossing the Blue Ridge at Paris	35
July 17.	Marched and rode horseback to Middletown, Frederick Co................	20
July 19.	Marched to Winchester and joined our brigade..............................	12
July 20.	To Middletown and then on picket	18
July 21.	To Hupp's Hill, Shenandoah Co., where we formed line of battle................	8
July 24.	To Kernstown, Frederick Co., where we had the battle, pursuing the enemy beyond Winchester. Frederick Co.........	20
July 25.	To Bunker Hill. Berkeley Co.............	10
July 26.	To Martinsburg.........................	12
July 31.	To Darksville...........................	8
Aug. 4.	To Shepherdstown. Jefferson Co.	12
Aug. 5.	To Sharpsburg, Md., crossing the Potomac at Boteler's Ford......................	8
Aug. 6.	To Falling Waters, Berkeley Co., Va., crossing the Potomac at Williamsport.....	20
Aug. 7.	To Darksville..........................	15
Aug. 9.	To Bunker Hill	6
Aug. 10.	To Woolen Mills. Frederick Co...........	11

Aug. 11.	To Newtown, where we skirmished with the enemy	12
Aug. 12.	To Strasburg, where we formed line of battle and then marched to Fisher's Hill. Shenandoah Co.	15
Aug. 17.	To Winchester, encountering the enemy and driving them beyond the town	20
Aug. 19.	To Bunker Hill	15
Aug. 21.	To Charlestown, where we found the enemy strongly fortified	12
Aug. 22.	The enemy left our front during the night and we followed	6
Aug. 23.	My brigade sent on picket	2
Aug. 24.	My brigade made a reconnoissance	5
Aug. 25.	To near Shepherdstown, driving the enemy's cavalry	15
Aug. 26.	To Leetown	8
Aug. 27.	To Bunker Hill	13
Aug. 29.	To near Smithfield, driving the enemy about five miles, then returned to Bunker Hill	18
Sept. 2.	To Charlestown Pike and back to Valley Pike	15
Sept. 3.	To Winchester	8
Sept. 7.	The enemy drove in our pickets; we went to their support and drove the enemy beyond the Opequan	8
Sept. 9.	To Near Brucetown	8
Sept. 13.	The enemy drove in our pickets; we went to their support and drove the enemy beyond the Opequan	5
Sept. 14.	To camp on side road. Frederick Co.	5
Sept. 17.	To Bunker Hill	5
Sept. 18.	To Martinsburg and back to Bunker Hill	24
Sept. 19.	To Winchester, where we had the battle	15
Sept. 20.	To Fisher's Hill	22

Sept. 23.	To Mt. Jackson	25
Sept. 24.	To Tenth Legion, where we took the road to Port Republic	17
Sept. 25.	To Brown's Gap.	20
Sept. 27.	To beyond the Shenandoah River, then back and to Port Republic	16
Sept. 28.	To Rockfish Gap, passing through New Hope and Waynesboro, driving the enemy's cavalry from the latter place	20
Oct. 1.	To Mt. Sidney	15
Oct. 6.	To camp on road side. Rockingham Co.	15
Oct. 7.	To New Market	20
Oct. 12.	To camp near Woodstock.	12
Oct. 13.	To Cedar Creek and back to Fisher's Hill.	17
Oct. 17.	To Hupp's Hill and back to Fisher's Hill.	8
Oct. 19.	To Cedar Creek, where we had the battle, and back to Fisher's Hill	15
Oct. 20.	To near New Market	25
Nov. 10.	To Woodstock	15
Nov. 11.	To Newton	21
Nov. 12.	To Fisher's Hill	11
Nov. 13.	To Woodstock	12
Nov. 14.	To New Market	15
Nov. 22.	To Rude's Hill to meet the enemy and back	25
Dec. 6.	Gordon's division marched to Waynesboro, reaching there on the 7th, where they took the cars for Petersburg, where they were in all the marches and engagements of the Second Corps at Petersburg and on the retreat to Appomattox C. H.	

Marching in the Following Counties:

VIRGINIA

Albemarle
Amelia
Appomattox
Augusta
Bath
Bedford
Berkeley
Botetourt
Campbell
Caroline
Charles City
Chesterfield
Clarke
Culpeper
Cumberland
Dinwiddie

Fairfax
Fauquier
Frederick
Green
Goochland
Hampshire
Hanover
Henrico
Highland
Jefferson
Loudoun
Louisa
Madison
Morgan
Nelson
Orange

Page
Pendleton
Pocahontas
Prince Edward
Prince George
Prince William
Rappahannock
Randolph
Roanoke
Rockbridge
Rockingham
Shenandoah
Spottsylvania
Stafford
Warren

MARYLAND

Frederick   Montgomery
and
District of Columbia   Washington

John H. Worsham

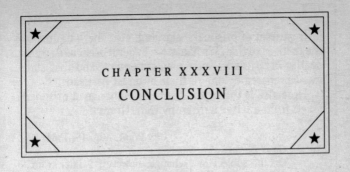

CHAPTER XXXVIII

CONCLUSION

I T IS STATED that the American Civil War was one of the bloodiest of which we have any authentic record; the carnage on both sides was fearful. On the Federal side: 4,142 officers were killed in battle; 2,223 died of wounds; 248 met death by accident. Of the men 62,916 were killed in battle, 40,789 died of wounds, 8,810 met death by accident (most of them by drowning). The deaths from disease were 2,712 officers and 197,008 men. On the Confederate side: 2,086 officers were killed and 1,246 died of wounds; 50,868 men were killed and 20,324 died of wounds. The war lasted about four years. The Federal army had enrolled 2,778,304 men, and the Confederates 600,000.

Secretary Stanton made a report to Congress in which it appears that of all the prisoners in the hands of the Confederates during the four years, there died in all Confederate prisons 22,246; while of the Confederate prisoners held by the United States there died 26,576. The whole number of prisoners captured and held by the United States numbered 220,000, while the number held by the Confederate States numbered 270,000. We are accused of

ill-treatment of prisoners, starving, etc.; these figures tell
the truth as to that. We had more Federal prisoners and the
deaths were less by their own statement, and that statement prepared by one of their bitterest partisans!

Here also is the truth about the exchange of prisoners,
taken from a letter written by Gen. Grant:

"City Point, Aug. 18, 1864.

"To Gen'l Butler:—

"On the subject of exchange, however, I differ from
Gen. Hitchcock. It is hard on our men held in Southern
prisons not to exchange them, but it is humanity to those
left in the ranks to fight our battles. Every man released on
parole, or otherwise, becomes an active soldier against us
at once, either directly or indirectly. If we commence a
system of exchange which liberates all prisoners taken, we
will have to fight on until the whole South is exterminated.
If we hold those caught, they amount to no more than dead
men. At this particular time, to release all Rebel prisoners
North would insure Sherman's defeat, and would compromise our safety here."

I agree with Gen. William T. Sherman, who said, "War
is Hell!" and the private soldier of Lee's army, who did not
see it, walked very close to the burning pit, and caught
glimpses of the fiery furnace.

In closing, I would like to add my little meed of praise.
Where in all pages of history can you find greater deeds of
heroism than those exhibited in the Southern army?

Here is what Lt.-Gen. Early says in his "Memoirs of the
Last Year of the War for Independence in the Confederate
States of America":

"I believe the world has never produced a body of men
superior, in courage, patrotism, and endurance, to the
private soldiers of the Confederate armies. I have repeatedly seen those soldiers submit with cheerfulness, to priva-
tions and hardships which would appear to be almost incredible; and the wild cheers of our brave men (which were
so different from the studied hurrahs of the Yankees) when

their lines sent back the opposing host of Federal troops, staggering, reeling, and flying, have often thrilled every fibre in my heart. I have seen, with my own eyes, ragged, barefooted, and hungry Confederate soldiers perform deeds, which, if performed in days of yore, by mailed warriors in glittering armor, would have inspired the harp of the minstrel and the pen of the poet."

"A King once said of a Prince struck down,
'Taller he seems in death!'
And this speech holds truth, for now, as then,
'Tis after death that we measure men;
And as mists of the past are rolled away,
Our heroes who died in their tattered gray
Grow 'taller' and greater in all their parts;
Till they fill our minds, as they fill our hearts;
And for those who lament them there's this relief,
That glory sits by the side of grief.
Yes, they grow 'taller' as the years go by,
And the world learns how they could do and die."

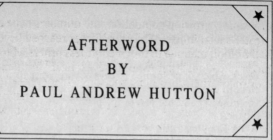

AFTERWORD
BY
PAUL ANDREW HUTTON

FUTURE YEARS will never know the seething hell and the black infernal background of countless minor scenes and interiors (not the official surface-courteousness of the Generals, not the few great battles) of the Secession war," wrote Walt Whitman, "and it is best that they should not—the real war will never get in the books." Perhaps not. How could the pen ever hope to recreate fittingly the pathos and the romance, the sheer horror and the soaring heroism, the folly and the gallantry of that titanic struggle that recreated the United States and gave, as Lincoln so perfectly put it, "a new birth of freedom?"

Grim statistics give one facet of Whitman's "real war." For the North, just short of 360,000 died while another 275,000 were wounded. For the South, at least 260,000 perished with another 194,000 maimed. [Well over 620,000 of the nearly three million Americans who fought the Civil War were consumed by it.] (Union casualties alone exceed American losses in World War II, while deaths North and South are more than the losses in all of America's other wars combined.) While this was but two percent of a rapidly growing population, the numbers belie an even greater social impact. The scars of war reached beyond the half million maimed to touch countless others who carried hidden wounds that would never heal. Millions more mourned fathers, brothers, and sons who never returned— futures unrealized, dreams aborted, songs unsung. What might have been is a part of Whitman's real war that writers can only hint at.

Whitman's admonition notwithstanding, it is not for want of effort that the real war remains elusive. Countless works of fiction and history, poetry and painting, film, stage, and television drama have addressed the great conflict. Civil War statuary, and even one carved mountain, can be found throughout the nation. Clearly the Civil War is America's *Iliad*, yet no Homer has emerged as its chronicler. The most sublime literary works inspired by the war came from the pen of Abraham Lincoln while the conflict still raged.

Most of our greatest fiction writers have ignored the war, or dealt with it only tangentially. Whitman's poetry is magnificent, but narrowly focused. Herman Melville, despite critical interpretations of *Moby Dick* as a metaphor for the coming war, dealt with the real conflict only in passing. The same can be said of that wise deserter Mark Twain. F. Scott Fitzgerald, William Faulkner, and Robert Penn Warren all wrote on the war, but only in relatively minor works. Ambrose Bierce produced a classic short story, Stephen Crane a classic novel, and Stephen Vincent Benét a classic poem, but all fell short of becoming America's Tolstoy.

Popular writers have always found a ready audience for Civil War fiction, but their work has generally been far from epic. Winston Churchill's fine *The Crisis*, John Fox's sentimental *The Little Shepherd of Kingdom Come,* and Thomas Dixon's vicious *The Clansman* were early popular triumphs, but all paled in comparison with the wild success of Margaret Mitchell's lost-cause homily, *Gone With the Wind*. While later novelists never came close to the commercial triumph of Mitchell's novel (twenty eight million copies sold to date), they nevertheless came far nearer to an approximation of the real war; MacKinlay Kantor's grim *Andersonville,* Shelby Foote's gritty *Shiloh,* Richard Slotkin's remarkable *The Crater,* and Michael Shaara's magnificent *The Killer Angels* ranking as the most notable.

Despite this prodigious output, the fact remains that this central moment of American history has inspired but a handful of literary works of a truly high order. Harvard professor Daniel Aaron titled his 1973 book on American writers and the Civil War *The Unwritten War*. Novelist and historian Shelby Foote, in his 1957 literary anthology *The Night Before Chancellorsville,* bluntly stated: "In this country, historical fiction in general has been left to second raters and hired brains, and this is particularly true of those who have chosen the Civil War as a subject. With the exception of Stephen Crane, our best writers have given it either mere incidental attention or none at all."

In this century the new medium of motion pictures has paralleled high literature in its hesitancy to deal with the Civil War. While hundreds of historical films have dealt with westward expansion or World War II, there has been no similar output on the Civil War. While nearly fifty films have dealt with General George A. Custer's last stand at the Little Big Horn, only two have concerned his important role in the Civil War (and both of those were westerns with Civil War components). Lincoln has proven a popular figure with Hollywood, but only one film, D. W. Griffith's *Abraham Lincoln* in 1930, dealt with the Great Emancipator's entire life. The two best Lincoln films, *Young Mr. Lincoln* in 1939 and *Abe Lincoln in Illinois* the following year, covered Lincoln's career before his election as president. Usually Lincoln appeared as a cameo (often played by stage actor Frank McGlynn, Sr.) in films as diverse as *The Littlest Rebel* with Shirley Temple, John Ford's *The Prisoner of Shark Island* with Warner Baxter as the unfortunate Dr. Samuel Mudd (who set John Wilkes Booth's broken leg, was imprisoned for it, and thus gave to the

American language the phrase "your name is mud"), and Cecil B. DeMille's overblown western epic *The Plainsman.* Yet, to put this into perspective, it should be noted that Lincoln has been portrayed in far fewer films than has the young outlaw Billy the Kid. Nor have any films of a truly remarkable artistic order, with the notable exception of D. W. Griffith's 1915 *The Birth of a Nation,* dealt with the Civil War. The Griffith film's unrelenting racism, however, has lost it a modern audience beyond students of the cinema.

As with literature, some fine Civil War films have been made—Buster Keaton's *The General,* John Huston's *The Red Badge of Courage,* William Wyler's *Friendly Persuasion,* John Ford's *The Horse Soldiers,* and Edward Zwick's *Glory.* And, of course, as with popular literature, one of Hollywood's greatest commercial triumphs was David Selznick's adaptation of Mitchell's *Gone With the Wind* (which, despite the fact that its racial sensibilities are only slightly advanced beyond *The Birth of a Nation,* still remains an immensely popular film). Despite the box-office success and enduring appeal of *Gone With the Wind,* Hollywood has generally found Civil War films to be poor commercial performers. It is, after all, a rather dangerous topic, replete with opportunities to offend some major regional or racial segment of American society. For the same reasons television, despite the spectacular but isolated triumphs of the miniseries "Roots" and the more recent multipart documentary on PBS, has only hesitatingly treated the war. It has remained, then, for historians to be the major interpreters of the Civil War. They are the keepers of the flame.

No other topic of American history has proven more popular, or more controversial, than the Civil War. It has attracted some of the best minds and most skilled pens of all American historiography. The turn-of-the-century multivolume history by James Ford Rhodes and the eight post–World War II volumes by Allan Nevins on the war era still stand as unrivaled examples of the historian's art. Similarly, the 1988 one-volume synthesis by James M. McPherson, *Battle Cry of Freedom,* has been rightly acclaimed as a masterpiece.

Much of the best scholarship has focused on the institution of slavery and its central role in bringing on the war. From the valuable if dated *American Negro Slavery* by U. B. Phillips, through the powerful revisionist works of Kenneth Stampp, Stanley Elkins, Eugene Genovese, Willie Lee Rose, Herbert Gutman, and John Blassingame, the "peculiar institution" has emerged as perhaps the most lively, challenging, and compelling historical topic of this century. In the last two decades a new historical consensus has formed, harkening back to the words of James Ford Rhodes at the turn of the century that "of the American Civil War it may safely be asserted there was a single cause, slavery." Even those who remain troubled by "mono-causation" in history agree that without slavery there would have been no war.

Of course, other divisions mixed into the witch's brew of mutual misunderstanding and shared contempt that drove North and South apart. Constitutional differences, economic differences, moral differences, class differences, and social differences all contributed to a breakdown of the political process. Historians have argued incessantly over these differences—Charles Beard seeing a primacy in economic conflict, Frank Owsley romanticizing the South as the defenders of an agrarian ideal against a vicious industrial onslaught, and Avery Craven emphasizing the merging of moral with political issues. James G. Randall felt all wars, and the Civil War in particular, to be irrational acts and laid the blame on fanaticism both North and South. Arthur M. Schlesinger, Jr., and Oscar Handlin were the two most noted historians who were puzzled by Randall's logic, or lack there of, and generally disdainful of those who would downplay the intensity of morality in bringing on the war. "There is surely a difference," Handlin dryly noted, "between being a fanatic for freedom and being a fanatic for slavery."

Several fine historians have dealt with the rise of the moral ideology of the 1850s and of the resultant breakdown of the political process. The works of David M. Potter, and most notably his 1976 *The Impending Crisis*, are crucial to an understanding of the sectional crisis. Eric Foner's *Free Soil, Free Labor, Free Men* remains indispensable to comprehending the rise of the Republican party, while Robert Johannsen's biography of Stephen Douglas details the fatal flaws of the Democratic party.

While academic historians have focused on causation and consequence, other historical writers have dealt with campaigns, battles, and personalities. The fruit of their labor ranks among some of the finest narrative history ever produced. Of course, not all academics have disdained military history or grand narrative, as the writings of James McPherson, T. Harry Williams, and Frank Vandiver prove, but most of our epic narratives on the war come from those outside the academy. It is from the incredibly talented pens of the likes of Bruce Catton and Shelby Foote that Whitman's "real war" comes closest to realization.

The careers of Civil War officers have provided a rich field for biographers. Douglas Southall Freeman's multivolume work on Lee remains a classic, although his effusiveness has been tempered by the more recent works of Thomas L. Connelly and Alan Nolan. Stonewall Jackson has been treated kindly in two classic biographies by British soldier G. F. R. Henderson and American historian Frank Vandiver. J. E. B. Stuart is a natural subject for colorful biography and has received his fair due in books by both Emory Thomas and Burke Davis. James I. Robertson's recent biography of that solid war-horse A. P. Hill was instantly recognized as a standard. Falling into the same category of modern classics are biographies of P. G. T. Beauregard by T. Harry Williams and John S. Mosby by Virgil Carrington Jones.

Bruce Catton's two volumes on Grant at war have never been equaled, despite William S. McFeely's more critical 1981 biography. Those with a taste for soaring prose will

enjoy Lloyd Lewis on Sherman, while others more inter-
ested in keen analysis will discover rewards in B. H. Liddell
Hart's *Sherman*. Stephen Sears's recent biography of
George McClellan has garnered great acclaim, while older
works by Freeman Cleaves on Generals Meade and Thomas
and Jay Monaghan on Custer remain modest standards.

Two classic collective biographies have fleshed out the
varied problems of high command both North and South:
T. Harry Williams's *Lincoln and His Generals* and Douglas
Southall Freeman's *Lee's Lieutenants*. Readers in search of
careers of lesser-known officers can find brief biographies
of all Civil War generals in Ezra Warner's two valuable
guides, *Generals in Blue* and *Generals in Gray*. Nor have
the lives of the men in the ranks been ignored, thanks to
the exceptional volumes *The Life of Johnny Reb* and *The
Life of Billy Yank* by Bell Irvin Wiley.

To do full justice to the rich and varied historiography
of the Civil War era requires far more space than is available here. Detailed accounts of nearly every campaign and
battle of the war are available, as are biographies of all the
major, and many of the minor, military and political leaders of the conflict. Library shelves are bowed with the
weight of generations of remarkable productivity in this
field, with no end in sight.

Yet for all the magnificent narratives, keen analyses,
and illuminating biographies that fill our libraries, those in
search of Whitman's "real war" will find it best represented
in the memoirs and autobiographies of the participants
themselves. No conflict in our history has produced such
a remarkable body of autobiographical writing. The remarkably literate generation that fought the Civil War
grasped the importance of the conflict, and many wished to
record their role in the republic's greatest drama. Some
were talented with the pen, others not so, but all had a
story to tell. Some of their narratives, especially those of
the generals, are defensive in tone; there were actions to
justify, scores to settle, places in history to secure. Other
narratives are remarkably myopic, cloyingly nostalgic, or

frustratingly wrongheaded. The years often clouded memories, and sometimes the haze of battle obscured events for even the most truthful observer.

Still, it is from these eyewitnesses to the Civil War that the most dramatic, personal, and telling accounts of that great struggle emerge. They bring the real war vividly to life, recording flashes of personal history more incredible than any fiction: Phil Sheridan, cursing and cajoling his stricken army to turn around and fight on to victory at Cedar Creek; George Custer, a freshly minted brigadier at twenty-three, leading his wolverines in charge after charge to block Stuart at Gettysburg; Luis Emilio, junior captain of the 54th Massachusetts Volunteer Infantry, assuming command of his shattered regiment after all officers senior to him fall dead or wounded in the assault on Fort Wagner; John Mosby boldly penetrating a Union camp to take General Edwin Stoughton prisoner; John Worsham stunned as four men beside him are mowed down by a single cannonball at Second Manassas; Stonewall Jackson sternly admonishing General Dick Taylor for cursing in the heat of battle at Bowers Hill; Colonel Joshua Chamberlain ordering the 20th Maine, its ammunition expended, to fix bayonets and charge down Little Round Top; Frank Haskell standing transfixed in awe as Pickett's gray host, red flags fluttering above a forest of gleaming steel, advances in the climactic hour of Gettysburg; Horace Porter recording the quiet dignity of Lee and Grant at Appomattox as a nation is reborn.

These proud warriors of the North and South express surprisingly little bitterness. They had played their part as best they could and now looked back without rancor to do honor to themselves and to those they had served with. Most could clearly see that out of the turmoil, chaos, and sacrifice of war something grand had emerged: a better, stronger, more just nation.

Now they spoke no longer of the United States as a plural, but rather as a singular. The great evil and singular hypocrisy of slavery was no more. Four million Americans, and their descendants, were forever free. The Thirteenth, Fourteenth, and Fifteenth Amendments to the U.S. Constitution wrought a radical legal transformation that generations yet unborn would seize upon to ensure a truer equality between the races.

The South found comfort in the myth of the lost cause. So compelling was that story that soon all Americans, North and South, came to embrace Confederate soldiers like Lee, Jackson, and Stuart as preeminent national heroes. Within a decade home rule was established throughout the South, with black rights sacrificed on the altar of regional reconciliation and economic development. Some complained that the South had lost the war but won the peace, but that was hardly true. The war had not only swept away slavery, but also the class-based, agricultural, and rural society that it supported. The United States now turned from that past to heartily embrace a new national vision.

Mark Twain tagged it the Gilded Age. With the triumph of free-labor industrial capitalism in the war came an orgy of speculation, growth, and greed undreamed of before 1861. Technology thrived in this atmosphere, making astonishing leaps forward. Northern industry, fueled by the sweat of millions of new immigrants from Europe and Asia, expanded beyond the wildest expectations. The cities swelled. Railroads spanned the continent. The West was conquered. Fabulous fortunes were made, some of them even by the new immigrants or their children, but mostly the rich got richer and the poor poorer.

Finally the children of the veterans of the Civil War wrought their own social and political revolution, bringing order out of chaotic growth and establishing a semblance of fair play and genuine opportunity to a previously unbridled capitalism. Then they turned their eyes to new opportunities abroad. Before the last veterans of the Civil War passed from the scene, the nation they had witnessed torn asunder by the Civil War stood as the world's preeminent economic and military power, and as a beacon of freedom to a troubled world. National greatness, those grizzled veterans surely could see, had come out of the terrible travail of Civil War.

The cost had been high. Many questioned if the results were worth the price. Others said the war had been avoidable. Others claimed that the same results could have been achieved without bloodshed. Others cast blame. But Lincoln, martyred before he could taste the sweet fruits of his labors, saw the causes and consequences of the Civil War with a clarity of vision lost on many of his own generation and those that followed. His words, spoken at the second inauguration, reach down to us through the ages:

> The Almighty has his own purposes. "Woe unto the world because of offenses! for it must needs be that offenses come; but woe to that man by whom the offense cometh." If we shall suppose that American slavery is one of those offenses which, in the providence of God, must needs come, but which having continued through his appointed time, he now wills to remove, and that he gives to both the North and South this terrible war, as the woe due to those by whom the offense came, shall we discern therein any departure from those divine attributes which the believers in a living God always ascribe to him? Fondly do we hope— fervently do we pray—that this mighty scourge of war may speedily pass away. Yet if God wills that it continue until all the wealth piled by the bondsman's two hundred and fifty years of unrequited toil shall be sunk, and until every drop of blood drawn with the lash shall be paid by another drawn with the sword, as was said, "The judgements of the Lord are true and righteous altogether."
>
> With malice toward none; with charity for all; with firmness in the right, as God gives us to see the right, let us strive on to finish the work we are in; to bind up the nation's wounds; to care for him who shall have borne the battle, and for his widow, and his orphan—to do all which may achieve and cherish a just and lasting peace among ourselves, and with all nations.

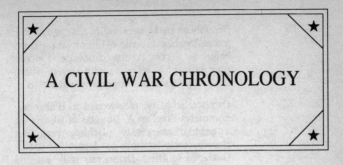

A CIVIL WAR CHRONOLOGY

1859

October 16 — John Brown, with sixteen whites and five blacks, captures the arsenal at Harpers Ferry in anticipation of fomenting a slave rebellion in Virginia. U.S. troops led by Lt. Col. Robert E. Lee storm the arsenal and capture Brown, on the morning of October 18th.

December 2 — John Brown is hanged for treason. Among his final words: "I, John Brown, am now quite certain that the crimes of this guilty land will never be purged away but with blood."

1860

May 3 — Democratic party, meeting in Charleston, South Carolina, adjourns unable to agree upon a candidate following the withdrawal of delegates from eight southern states.

May 9 — Constitutional Union party, meeting in Baltimore, nominates John Bell of Tennessee for president.

May 16 —   Republican party, meeting in Chicago, nominates Abraham Lincoln of Illinois on the third ballot as a compromise candidate. Lincoln promises not to interfere with slavery where it already exists, but opposes its extension.

June 23 —   Democratic party, reconvened in Baltimore, nominates Stephen A. Douglas of Illinois on a popular-sovereignty platform regarding slavery (each territory to decide for itself). Outraged southern Democrats walk out and later nominate John C. Breckinridge of Kentucky.

November 6 —   Lincoln wins the election. Though he has but 40 percent of the popular vote, his Electoral College count is 180, versus 72 for Breckinridge, 39 for Bell, and 12 for Douglas.

November 9 —   The state of South Carolina calls a secession convention.

December 20 —   South Carolina secedes from the Union.

December 26 —   Major Robert Anderson withdraws federal forces in Charleston to Fort Sumter. He has but eighty men.

1861

January 9—   South Carolina shore batteries open fire on the *Star of the West*, carrying supplies and reinforcements to Fort Sumter. The ship is forced out of Charleston Harbor. On the same day Mississippi secedes from the Union.

January 10 —   Florida secedes from the Union.

January 11 —   Alabama secedes from the Union.

January 19 —   Georgia secedes from the Union.

January 26 —   Louisiana secedes from the Union.

February 1 —   Texas secedes from the Union. Governor Sam Houston is removed from office for opposing secession.

February 4 —   A convention meets in Montgomery, Alabama to create a new government for the seceded states. It passes a constitution on the eighth and elects Jefferson Davis of Mississippi provisional president and Alexander Stephens of Georgia provisional vice-president on the ninth.

February 11 —   Lincoln departs from Springfield for Washington. "I now leave, not knowing when, or whether ever, I may return, with a task before me greater than that which rested upon Washington," he tells his friends and neighbors.

February 18 —   Davis is inaugurated at Montgomery, declaring that obstacles "can not long prevent the progress of a movement sanctified by its justice and sustained by a virtuous people."

February 23 —   Lincoln reaches Washington, entering the city secretly for fear of assassins.

March 4 —   Lincoln is inaugurated, declaring that "In your hands, my dissatisfied countrymen, and not in mine is the momentous issue of Civil War."

March 6 —   The Confederate States of America calls for 100,000 volunteers for its army.

April 4 —   Lincoln orders an expedition to relieve besieged Fort Sumter, and it departs from New York four days later.

April 12 —   At 4:30 A.M. General P.G.T. Beauregard orders his men to open fire on Fort Sumter. The commander of the fort had been his artillery instructor at West Point.

April 13 —	Major Anderson surrenders after 34 hours of bombardment.
April 15 —	Lincoln calls upon the states for 75,000 militia to suppress the insurrection in South Carolina.
April 17 —	Virginia secedes from the Union.
April 19 —	Lincoln orders a blockade of Confederate ports.
April 20 —	Col. Robert E. Lee resigns from the U.S. Army. "Whatever may be the result of the contest," he writes a friend, "I foresee that the country will have to pass through a terrible ordeal, a necessary expiation for our national sins."
May 6 —	Arkansas secedes from the Union.
May 6 —	Tennessee secedes from the Union.
May 13 —	Great Britain declares neutrality, in effect recognizing the Confederacy as a belligerent.
May 20 —	North Carolina secedes from the Union.
May 21 —	The Confederacy decides to move its capital to Richmond, Virginia.
May 23 —	Virginia voters endorse secession.
June 3 —	Union troops under Gen. George B. McClellan defeat Confederates at Philippi in western Virginia.
June 10 —	France declares neutrality.
June 11 —	Pro-Union counties in western Virginia disavow secession and are recognized by Lincoln as the loyal Virginia government. This soon evolves into the new state of West Virginia.

July 16 —   Gen. Irvin McDowell, with 30,000 Union troops, advances toward Manassas Junction, Virginia.

July 21 —   Battle of Bull Run ends in the defeat of Union forces, although the Rebels are too disorganized to follow up their victory. A strong stand by Thomas J. Jackson's Virginia brigade earns him the nickname "Stonewall." Each side suffers about 625 killed.

July 27 —   McDowell is replaced by McClellan as commander of the troops around Washington.

August 6 —   A Confiscation Act is passed which allows the seizure of all property used for insurrectionary purposes. This includes slaves.

August 10 —   Confederates under Sterling Price and Ben McCulloch defeat a Union force under Gen. Nathaniel Lyon at Wilson's Creek, Missouri. Lyon is killed in action, and each side suffers about 1,300 casualties.

August 30 —   Gen. John C. Fremont, in command of Union forces in the West, orders the confiscation of all property, including slaves, belonging to Missouri Confederates.

September 10 —   Gen. Albert Sidney Johnston of Texas assumes command of Confederate forces in the West.

November 1 —   McClellan replaces Gen. Winfield Scott as Union general in chief.

November 2 —   Fremont is relieved of his command in the West, and is soon replaced by Gen. Henry W. Halleck.

November 8 —   Capt. Charles Wilkes of the U.S. Navy stops the British mail steamer *Trent* and arrests Confederate envoys James Mason and John Slidell, setting off an international incident. They will be released on December 27 after British saber rattling.

1862

January 19 —
Union Gen. George Thomas, a Virginian loyal to the Old Flag, defeats Rebel forces at Mill Springs, Kentucky, securing federal control of the eastern section of that state.

February 6 —
Gen. Ulysses S. Grant, with 15,000 troops and several naval gunboats under Flag Officer Andrew Foote, attacks Fort Henry on the Tennessee River. The fort quickly falls to Foote's naval forces, but most of its defenders escape to Fort Donelson, a dozen miles away on the Cumberland River.

February 7 —
Gen. Johnston orders his forces to retreat from southwestern Kentucky.

February 13 —
Grant, with 40,000 troops, attacks Fort Donelson, defended by 18,000 Confederates.

February 16 —
Gen. Simon Bolivar Buckner surrenders Fort Donelson. Grant's terms, unconditional surrender, win him a nickname.

February 21 —
Confederate troops under Gen. Henry H. Sibley defeat Union forces under Gen. Edward Canby and Col. Kit Carson at Valverde, New Mexico. Sibley is then able to occupy Albuquerque and Santa Fe.

February 25 —
The Confederates are forced to abandon Nashville.

March 3 —
Andrew Johnson is named military governor of Tennessee by Lincoln.

March 8 —
Gen. Samuel Curtis defeats Gen. Earl Van Dorn at Pea Ridge and Union control of Missouri is secured.

March 8 —
The *Virginia*, a Rebel ironclad converted from the captured Union warship the *Merrimac*, destroys the Union wooden warships the *Congress* and the *Cumberland* and drives the *Minnesota* aground at Hampton Roads, Virginia.

March 9 —
: The *Monitor*, a Union iron-plated raft with a revolving gun turret built by John Ericsson, engages the *Virginia* (*Merrimac*) at Hampton Roads. They battle inconclusively all morning, but the *Virginia* withdraws and does not again threaten the Union blockade. A revolution in naval warfare has been wrought. The *Virginia* is burned to prevent its capture a month later. The *Monitor* sinks in a storm off Cape Hatteras on December 31, 1862.

March 11 —
: Lincoln reorganizes the Union high command: Halleck takes charge of all troops west of the Appalachians while McClellan is reduced from general in chief to commander of the Army of the Potomac.

March 17 —
: McClellan begins moving his forces by sea to Fort Monroe in anticipation of the Peninsular Campaign against Richmond.

March 23 —
: Stonewall Jackson is defeated at Kernstown, Virginia, by a much stronger Union force. The battle raises fears in Washington of a Confederate attack, and troops are withheld from McClellan to defend the capital.

March 28 —
: Union forces defeat the Confederate invaders at Glorieta Pass, New Mexico.

April 4 —
: McClellan's forces on the peninsula advance toward Richmond.

April 6 —
: Grant's 37,000 men at Shiloh Church and Pittsburg Landing, Tennessee, are surprised by A. S. Johnston's 42,000 Confederates and almost defeated. Johnston is killed and Beauregard assumes command.

April 7 —
: Grant, reinforced by 25,000 fresh troops under Don Carlos Buell and Lew Wallace, attacks at Shiloh, recapturing all lost ground. Each side suffers 10,000 casualties. Beauregard retreats to Corinth, Mississippi.

April 8 —   Gen. John Pope captures Island No. 10 in the
                   Mississippi River, taking 5,000 Confederate
                   prisoners.

April 12 —   James J. Andrews leads fifteen men on a bold
                   raid to seize a Western and Atlantic Railroad
                   locomotive at Big Shanty, Georgia, and then
                   race north in it burning all bridges on the
                   line between Atlanta and Chattanooga. The
                   raid fails after a wild eight-hour railway chase,
                   and Andrews and seven of his men are even-
                   tually hanged.

April 16 —   The Confederate Congress passes a conscrip-
                   tion bill.

April 16 —   Slavery is abolished in the District of Colum-
                   bia.

April 25 —   New Orleans is captured by Union naval forces
                   under Flag Officer David C. Farragut.

May 1 —   Union troops under Gen. Benjamin Butler be-
                   gin the occupation of New Orleans.

May 3 —   McClellan's army forces Gen. Joseph E. John-
                   ston to retreat from Yorktown, Virginia.

May 8 —   Stonewall Jackson's 10,000 men in the Shen-
                   andoah Valley defeat attacking Federals under
                   Gen. Robert Schenk at McDowell, Virginia.

May 9 —   Gen. David Hunter at Hilton Head, South Car-
                   olina, declares slaves in South Carolina, Geor-
                   gia, and Florida to be free. His act is later
                   repudiated by Lincoln.

May 9 —   Confederate forces retreat from Norfolk.

May 10 —   Union forces occupy Pensacola, Florida.

May 12 —   Baton Rouge, Louisiana, is occupied by Union
                   forces.

May 25 —   Jackson crushes Gen. Nathaniel Banks's
                   8,000-man force at Winchester, Virginia.

June 1 —

Robert E. Lee assumes command of Confederate forces defending Richmond after Joseph E. Johnston is wounded at the Battle of Fair Oaks.

June 8 —

At the Battle of Cross Keys, Virginia, Union forces under Gen. John C. Frémont are defeated by Jackson's men.

June 9 —

Jackson again defeats Union forces under Frémont and Gen. James Shields at Port Royal.

June 12 —

Gen. James E. "Jeb" Stuart leads his Rebel cavalrymen on a bold four-day reconnaissance completely around McClellan's forces on the peninsula.

June 17 —

Jackson's victorious army departs the Shenandoah to reinforce Lee.

June 19 —

Slavery is abolished in all federal territories.

June 25 —

The Seven Days' Battles begin as the forces of McClellan and Lee contend inconclusively.

July 1 —

Lee's forces are defeated in their assault on the Army of the Potomac at Malvern Hill. He has lost 20,000 men. Nevertheless, the Seven Days' Battles conclude with the nervous McClellan retreating and Richmond secure.

July 4 —

Confederate Col. John Hunt Morgan begins a daring raid into Kentucky.

July 11 —

Halleck is named general in chief of Union forces.

July 17 —

A second Confiscation Act is passed by Congress, freeing the slaves of those who are in rebellion against the government.

July 29 —

The Rebel cruiser *Alabama* departs Liverpool, England, under the command of Captain Raphael Semmes. In the next two years it will capture or destroy sixty four merchant ships.

August 9 — Jackson defeats Union forces under Banks at Cedar Mountain, Virginia.

August 16 — McClellan moves north to unite with the Northern Army of Virginia under Gen. John Pope at Alexandria.

August 26 — Jackson captures the railroad line at Manassas Junction.

August 28 — Gen. Braxton Bragg leads his Rebel forces from Chattanooga to unite with Gen. Kirby Smith in Kentucky.

August 29 — The Second Battle of Bull Run begins as Pope attacks Jackson. The overly confident Pope sends a victory telegram to Washington.

August 30 — Confederate reinforcements under Gen. James Longstreet turn the tide at Second Bull Run and Pope's army is routed.

September 2 — McClellan is given command of Pope's army and the forces defending Washington.

September 5 — Lee leads 55,000 men into Maryland.

September 9 — Lee sends Jackson to capture the 12,000 Union troops at Harpers Ferry. Jackson is then to rejoin Lee for a movement against Harrisburg, Pennsylvania.

September 13 — Near Frederick, Maryland, two Union soldiers discover a copy of Lee's plans wrapped around three cigars lost by a Confederate officer.

September 14 — McClellan, who has 80,000 men and his opponent's plans, still waits eighteen hours before moving. This delay proves crucial in allowing Lee to regroup his army.

September 15 — Jackson captures Harpers Ferry.

September 16 — Jackson hurriedly rejoins Lee at Sharpsburg, Maryland. McClellan masses his forces a mile east across Antietam Creek.

September 17 — The Battle of Antietam becomes the single bloodiest day of the war as the two sides fight to a grisly standstill. 6,000 are killed and 17,000 are wounded.

September 18 — Lee escapes into Virginia.

September 22 — Lincoln decides to issue the Emancipation Proclamation freeing all slaves in states in rebellion as of January 1.

October 8 — Don Carlos Buell's Union forces defeat Gen. Bragg's Confederates at Perryville, Kentucky, repelling the Rebel invasion of Kentucky.

October 30 — Gen. William Rosecrans replaces Buell in command of the redesignated Army of the Cumberland.

November 2 — Grant moves against Vicksburg, Mississippi.

November 7 — McClellan is replaced as commander of the Army of the Potomac by Gen. Ambrose Burnside.

December 13 — Burnside is defeated by Lee at Fredericksburg, Virginia.

December 15 — The Army of the Potomac retreats.

December 31 — Bragg attacks Rosecrans at Stones River near Murfreesboro, Tennessee.

1863
January 1 — Lincoln signs the Emancipation Proclamation.

January 2 — Rosecrans wins the second day of heavy fighting at Stones River. Bragg retreats on January 3.

January 26 — Gen. Joseph Hooker replaces Burnside as commander of the Army of the Potomac.

March 3 —   The U.S. Congress passes a conscription act that provides for a draft of all men between twenty and forty-five.

March 9 —   Confederate partisan ranger John S. Mosby makes a daring raid behind Union lines and captures Brig. Gen. Edwin H. Stoughton. Lincoln, upon being informed that Mosby has taken Stoughton, thirty-two soldiers, and fifty-eight horses, responds: "Well, I'm sorry for that. I can make new brigadier generals, but I can't make horses."

April 16 —   Admiral David Porter's Union gunboats make a daring run past the shore batteries at Vicksburg.

April 17 —   Col. Benjamin Grierson leads 1,700 cavalrymen out of La Grange, Tennessee, and heads south. His goal is to disrupt Confederate communications and divert attention from Vicksburg.

April 30 —   The Army of the Potomac, 115,000 strong, begins to concentrate at Chancellorsville. Lee faces them with but 60,000 men.

May 1 —   Gen. Hooker's 70,000 infantry inconclusively engage Gen. Lee's forces at Chancellorsville. Hooker inexplicably pulls back after fighting in a forest called the Wilderness. That night Lee and Jackson plan a daring flanking attack on Hooker.

May 2 —   Lee faces Hooker with but 15,000 men while Jackson leads 30,000 infantry on a flank march across the Union front. Jackson attacks at 5:15 P.M. and rolls up the Union right, but is mistakenly wounded by his own pickets that night while scouting.

May 2 —   Grierson's cavalry reach Union lines at Baton Rouge after a daring 600-mile raid.

May 3 —

Gen. Stuart assumes command of Jackson's corps at Chancellorsville and continues to pound the faltering Federals.

May 4 —

Gen. John Sedgwick has no success against Lee's rear and retires to Fredericksburg.

May 6 —

Hooker retreats, and Lee achieves his greatest victory. Confederate forces suffer 13,000 casualties while Union losses are over 17,000.

May 10 —

Stonewall Jackson dies at Guiney's Station. "Let us cross over the river and rest under the shade of the trees," are his last words.

May 16 —

Grant, advancing on Vicksburg, defeats Gen. John C. Pemberton's forces at Champion's Hill.

May 18 —

Pemberton pulls his forces into the Vicksburg defenses.

May 19 —

Governor John Andrew of Massachusetts presents four flags to Col. Robert Gould Shaw and the 54th Massachusetts Regiment, the first black regiment raised in the Northeast. The regiment is ordered to join Gen. David Hunter at Hilton Head, South Carolina. Already with Hunter is Col. Thomas Wentworth Higginson's First Regiment of South Carolina Volunteers, made up of contrabands (liberated slaves).

May 19 —

Grant's forces assault Vicksburg but fail to breach the defenses.

May 22 —

Grant's second assault on Vicksburg is repulsed with heavy losses. He begins a siege.

May 27 —

Gen. Banks fails in his assaults on Port Hudson, Louisiana, and lays siege.

June 3 —

Lee departs Fredericksburg for a second invasion of the North. He has three infantry corps and six cavalry brigades—75,000 men.

June 9 —   Gen. Alfred Pleasonton's 11,000 Union cavalry surprise Stuart's 10,000 horsemen at Brandy Station, and the greatest cavalry engagement of the war follows. Stuart holds his ground but Lee's advance is revealed.

June 15 —   Gen. Richard S. Ewell captures Winchester in the Shenandoah.

June 20 —   West Virginia is admitted to the Union.

June 25 —   Stuart leads three cavalry brigades on a ride around Hooker's army. The raid causes great alarm in Washington, but Stuart's separation from the Army of Northern Virginia will prove costly.

June 28 —   Gen. Jubal Early captures York, Pennsylvania.

June 28 —   Gen. George Gordon Meade assumes command of the Army of the Potomac, replacing Hooker.

June 29 —   Lee orders his forces to reunite near Gettysburg, Pennsylvania.

July 1 —   Gen. A. P. Hill's infantry, in search of shoes in Gettysburg, clash with two brigades of Union cavalry under Gen. John Buford. Soldiers from both armies rush to the sound of the guns, and the Rebels soon sweep the Yankees in disorder through the town. Union forces dig in on Cemetery Ridge while the Confederates take up positions on Seminary Ridge.

July 2 —   Lee sends Gen. James Longstreet against the Union left while Gen. Richard Ewell assaults the Union right. Both assaults fail. Stuart finally rejoins the army.

July 3 —   After a terrific artillery barrage, Lee sends 14,000 men against the Union center in Pickett's Charge. Scarcely half return.

July 4 —   Gen. Pemberton surrenders his 30,000 men, and Vicksburg, to Grant.

July 8 —   Gen. John Hunt Morgan leads 2,500 men across the Ohio River into Indiana and toward Ohio.

July 9 —   Port Hudson surrenders to Gen. Banks. The Mississippi is again a Union river and the Confederacy is split.

July 13 —   Four days of antidraft rioting begins in New York City. Much of the violence is directed at blacks before troops suppress a mob estimated at 50,000.

July 18 —   Battery Wagner, defending the entrance to Charleston harbor, is assaulted by Union troops. Spearheading the attack are 600 men of the 54th Massachusetts. The position is impregnable, although the black soldiers of the 54th gain Wagner's parapets and hold them for an hour before falling back. Col. Robert Shaw is killed and the regiment suffers casualties of over 40 percent.

July 19 —   Over 800 of Morgan's raiders are killed or captured at Buffington, Ohio.

July 26 —   Gen. Morgan is captured at New Lisbon, Ohio.

August 21 —   Col. William Clarke Quantrill's Confederate guerrillas sack Lawrence, Kansas.

September 9 —   Gen. Rosecrans's Federal troops enter Chattanooga as Gen. Bragg's forces retire into northern Georgia.

September 19 — Gen. Bragg, reinforced by Longstreet's corps, attacks Gen. George Thomas's corps on the left of Rosecrans's army at Chickamauga Creek, Georgia.

September 20 — Longstreet routs the Union right, and the army is only saved by Thomas's bold stand; Thomas earns the nickname of "Rock of Chickamauga." Rosecrans's army retreats to Chattanooga, where it is besieged. Bragg occupies high ground at Lookout Mountain, south of the city, and along Missionary Ridge to the east. In the fighting each side has suffered 28-percent casualties.

October 15 — The Confederate submarine *Hunley* sinks during a practice run in Charleston harbor, drowning its inventor and seven crewmen.

October 17 — Grant is named commander of all Union forces west of the Appalachians.

October 19 — Thomas replaces Rosecrans as commander of the 35,000-man Army of the Cumberland in Chattanooga.

October 23 — Grant arrives in Chattanooga.

November 4 — Bragg sends Longstreet and 15,000 men to attack Knoxville, thus weakening his forces at Chattanooga.

November 19 — Lincoln, at Gettysburg, gives an immortal speech.

November 20 — Gen. William T. Sherman reaches Chattanooga with 17,000 men from the Army of the Tennessee. Hooker has already arrived on September 24 with 20,000 reinforcements from the Army of the Potomac. Bragg faces them with just over 64,000 troops.

November 24 — Hooker's men take Lookout Mountain at Chattanooga.

November 25 — Sherman's attacks on Bragg's right fail, but Thomas's Army of the Cumberland makes an incredible charge up Missionary Ridge and defeats the Confederates. Bragg, barely escaping capture, retreats into Georgia.

November 27 — Gen. Morgan escapes from the Ohio State Penitentiary.

November 29 — Longstreet's attack on Knoxville fails, and he soon retreats toward Virginia.

December 16 — Gen. Joseph E. Johnston takes command of the Army of Tennessee. Bragg is named an adviser to President Davis.

1864

February 9 — Col. Thomas Rose leads 109 Union prisoners in a daring escape from Libby Prison in Richmond. Rose and forty-seven others are recaptured.

February 14 — Gen. Sherman occupies Meridian, Mississippi, and his troops begin to dismantle the city.

February 17 — The Confederate submarine *Hunley* sinks the *Housatonic* in Charleston harbor, but goes down with the Union sloop.

February 22 — Gen. Nathan Bedford Forrest's cavalry defeat Union cavalry under Gen. William Sooy Smith at Okolona, Mississippi.

March 3 — Gen. Judson Kilpatrick's cavalry raid on Richmond ends in disaster with Col. Ulrich Dahlgren killed. Papers are found on Dahlgren's body insinuating that his mission was to kill Jefferson Davis.

March 17 — Grant is named general in chief and promoted to lieutenant general.

March 18 — Sherman is named commander of Union forces in the West.

April 8 — Gen. Richard Taylor's Confederates stop Gen. Banks's advance on Shreveport at Sabine Crossroads to end the Union's Red River campaign.

April 12 —   Gen. Forrest captures Fort Pillow, Tennessee, where surrendering black soldiers are murdered by his troops.

April 17 —   Grant halts the practice of exchanging prisoners.

May 4 —   Grant advances across the Rapidan with 122,000 men. Lee faces him with under 70,000. Grant also orders troops under Gen. Benjamin Butler to move up the James River against Richmond. In Chattanooga, Sherman prepares to move south against Atlanta.

May 6 —   Longstreet reinforces Lee, and Grant is defeated in the Wilderness. Longstreet is seriously wounded.

May 9 —   Lee's forces entrench at Spotsylvania and repel Union assaults. Union Gen. John Sedgwick is killed.

May 9 —   Grant sends Gen. Phil Sheridan's 10,000 cavalrymen on a raid against Richmond.

May 11 —   Sheridan's cavalry defeat Stuart's horsemen at Yellow Tavern. Stuart, mortally wounded, dies the next day.

May 12 —   Bitter fighting at the "Bloody Angle" at Spotsylvania does not break Lee's lines.

May 15 —   In the Shenandoah, Gen. John Breckenridge's 5,000-man force, including V.M.I. cadets, defeats Gen. Franz Sigel's 6,500-man Union force at New Market.

May 16 —   Gen. Butler is defeated at Drewry's Bluff, eight miles south of Richmond, by Gen. Beauregard.

May 20 —   Grant abandons his Spotsylvania positions in an attempt to flank Lee.

May 24 — Lee takes up new positions on the North Anna River.

May 24 — Sheridan's victorious cavalrymen rejoin Grant.

May 25 — The Battle of New Hope Church, Georgia, begins between the forces of Sherman and Johnston.

May 31 — Sheridan's cavalry battles Rebel horsemen under Gen. Fitzhugh Lee and seizes the junction at Cold Harbor.

June 1 — Union forces, 109,000 strong, and Confederate forces, numbering 59,000, entrench for seven miles around Cold Harbor. In four weeks of constant fighting, the Federals have suffered 44,000 casualties and the Confederates 25,000.

June 3 — Grant launches futile frontal assaults against Lee's lines at Cold Harbor at a cost of 7,000 more casualties.

June 8 — Abraham Lincoln and Andrew Johnson are nominated for president and vice-president by the Republican (National Union) Convention in Baltimore.

June 12 — Wade Hampton's Rebel cavalry blocks Sheridan's cavalry at Trevilian Station from raiding westward to unite with Gen. David Hunter's forces in the Shenandoah. Both sides suffer 20-percent casualties in the bloodiest cavalry battle of the war.

June 14 — Grant begins to move his army across the James River to attack Petersburg.

June 18 — Grant's assaults on Petersburg fail and he begins a siege.

June 18 — Gen. Jubal Early defeats Gen. Hunter at Lynchburg. Hunter retreats into West Virginia, leaving the Shenandoah to Early.

June 19 — The *Kearsage* sinks the Rebel cruiser *Alabama* in a duel off Cherbourg, France.

June 27 — Johnston repulses Sherman's attacks at Kennesaw Mountain, Georgia.

July 6 — Early invades Maryland.

July 11 — Having swept aside Federal defenders at Monocacy River, Early reaches the defenses of Washington. The Sixth Corps, detached from Grant's forces, arrives on the same day.

July 12 — Early pulls back from Washington, heading for the Shenandoah.

July 17 — Gen. John Bell Hood replaces Johnston as commander of the Army of Tennessee.

July 20 — Hood attacks Thomas's forces at Peachtree Creek, Georgia, and is defeated.

July 22 — Hood attacks Gen. James B. McPherson's Army of the Tennessee and is again defeated. McPherson is killed in action.

July 28 — Hood again attacks the Army of the Tennessee, now commanded by Gen. Oliver Otis Howard, at Ezra Church and is again defeated.

July 30 — A 511-foot tunnel has been dug beneath the Rebel lines at Petersburg and four tons of gunpowder placed at the end. The explosion creates a 170-foot-long, 30-foot-deep crater, but the Federal assault that follows is disorganized and halfhearted. 4,000 casualties and a big hole in the ground is all Grant has by nightfall.

July 31 —   Gen. George Stoneman, raiding south from Sherman's army to liberate the prisoners at Andersonville, is captured along with 500 of his men.

August 1 —   Sheridan is given command of Union forces in the Shenandoah.

August 5 —   Admiral Farragut defeats the defending Confederate ships in Mobile Bay. "Damn the torpedoes, full speed ahead," Farragut reportedly exclaims during the action.

August 22 —   Gen. Judson Kilpatrick's cavalry raid against Hood's Atlanta supply lines fails.

August 23 —   Fort Morgan, in Mobile Bay, falls to Union forces.

August 29 —   George B. McClellan is nominated for president by the Democrats.

August 31 —   Howard defeats Hood at Jonesboro while Gen. John Schofield's forces cut the last railroad line into Atlanta.

September 1 —   Hood evacuates Atlanta.

September 2 —   Sherman enters Atlanta.

September 4 —   John Hunt Morgan is killed at Greeneville, Tennessee.

September 17 —   John C. Frémont, nominated for president by Radical Republicans unhappy with Lincoln, announces that he will withdraw from the race for fear of splitting the Republican vote.

September 19 —   Sheridan defeats Early at Winchester.

September 22 —   Sheridan crushes Early's army at Fisher's Hill.

September 27 —   Confederate guerrillas under Bloody Bill Anderson loot Centralia, Missouri, and murder twenty-two captured Union soldiers. They then slaughter over 100 pursuing Federals under Maj. A. V. E. Johnston. Young Jesse James kills Maj. Johnston.

September 28 —   Sherman orders Gen. Thomas to Nashville to
                  defend that city from Hood's army.

September 29 —   In the fighting around Petersburg, Grant
                  takes Fort Harrison but is repulsed from Fort
                  Gilmore.

October 2 —   A Federal raid into southwest Virginia is de-
                  feated near Saltville, and over 100 Union pris-
                  oners, mostly black soldiers, are murdered by
                  their captors.

October 6 —   Sheridan begins the systematic destruction of
                  the Shenandoah Valley.

October 13 —   Confederate partisans under Mosby capture a
                  train near Kearneyville and escape with nearly
                  $2 million from Union paymasters on board.

October 16 —   Sheridan leaves his army for a meeting with
                  Stanton and Halleck on the Valley Campaign.

October 19 —   Lt. Bennett Young leads Rebel raiders across
                  the Canadian border to St. Albans, Vermont.
                  They rob three banks and escape back over
                  the border.

October 19 —   Sheridan's army is taken by surprise when
                  Early's army strikes at dawn. The left flank of
                  the Union army, under Gen. George Crook,
                  is routed, but the sudden arrival of Sheridan
                  on the field (he gallops in from Winchester)
                  rallies the men. The Union counterattack de-
                  stroys the Confederate army. The Battle of
                  Cedar Creek ends the Rebel threat in the
                  Shenandoah. The North is captivated by
                  "Sheridan's Ride," soon immortalized in a
                  popular poem.

October 23 —   Gen. Curtis defeats Gen. Sterling Price at the
                  Battle of Westport, ending the Confederate
                  threat to Missouri.

October 26 — Bloody Bill Anderson is killed in a Union ambush near Richmond, Missouri.

October 27 — Lt. William P. Cushing destroys the Confederate ram *Albemarle* in the Roanoke River, North Carolina.

October 30 — Sherman sends Schofield to reinforce Thomas at Nashville.

November 8 — Lincoln is reelected.

November 16 — Sherman's army, 62,000 strong, departs Atlanta to begin the March to the Sea to Savannah. Atlanta burns behind the Federals as they advance.

November 25 — Confederate raiders fail in their attempt to burn New York City.

November 30 — Schofield repulses Hood's assaults at Franklin and retreats under cover of darkness toward Nashville.

December 1 — Schofield unites with Thomas at Nashville.

December 13 — Fort McAllister, guarding Savannah, is captured by Sherman's troops.

December 15 — Thomas attacks Hood before Nashville.

December 16 — Hood's army is routed at Nashville.

December 21 — Sherman's army enters Savannah.

1865

January 7 — Gen. Benjamin Butler is relieved as commander of the Army of the James.

January 15 — Gen. Alfred H. Terry captures Fort Fisher, closing the last major Confederate port at Wilmington, North Carolina.

January 23 — Gen. Richard Taylor is given command of what is left of the Army of Tennessee.

January 31 —   The Thirteenth Amendment to the Constitution, abolishing slavery, is passed by the House of Representatives and sent to the states for ratification.

February 6 —   Lee is named commander of all Confederate forces.

February 17 —   Sherman occupies the South Carolina capital, and that night the city burns. Sherman blames fleeing Rebels, but on the eighteenth his troops begin the destruction of what is left of Columbia.

February 17 —   The Confederates abandon Charleston, and Fort Sumter again comes under Union control.

February 18 —   Lee speaks out in favor of arming blacks for service in the Confederate army in exchange for their freedom.

February 22 —   Schofield's Union troops occupy Wilmington.

March 2 —   Sheridan's cavalry, under Gen. George A. Custer, destroys the last remnant of Early's army at the Battle of Waynesboro.

March 4 —   Lincoln's second inaugural address calls for reconciliation: "With malice toward none; with charity for all; with firmness in the right as God gives us to see the right, let us strive on to finish the work we are in; to bind up the nation's wounds; to care for him who shall have borne the battle and for his widow, and his orphan—to do all which may achieve and cherish a just and lasting peace among ourselves, and with all nations."

March 13 —   President Davis signs a bill, narrowly passed by the Confederate Congress after heated debate, that calls for the use of black slaves as soldiers. The question of emancipation in exchange for service is left to the individual states.

March 17 —   Gen. Edward Canby opens the assault on Mobile, Alabama.

March 22 —   Gen. James Wilson begins a cavalry raid through Alabama to capture Selma.

March 26 —   Sheridan rejoins Grant before Petersburg.

April 1 —   Sheridan defeats Gen. George Pickett at Five Forks, capturing that vital crossroads and large numbers of Rebel prisoners.

April 2 —   Grant assaults Lee's weakened lines at Petersburg with great success. Gen A. P. Hill is killed in action. Lee retreats toward Amelia Courthouse.

April 3 —   Petersburg is occupied. Richmond surrenders. Jefferson Davis and his cabinet flee to Danville, Virginia.

April 4 —   President Lincoln tours Richmond.

April 5 —   Sheridan blocks Lee's route southward, forcing the Confederates westward.

April 6 —   6,000 Confederates are captured at Sayler's Creek, including Gen. Richard Ewell, as Lee's retreat continues.

April 8 —   Custer blocks Lee's retreat route at Appomattox Station.

April 9 —   Lee surrenders the Army of Northern Virginia to Grant in the home of Wilmer McLean at Appomattox Courthouse.

April 12 —   Wilson captures Montgomery, Alabama. Federal troops occupy Mobile.

April 12 —   Grant accords to Gen. Joshua Chamberlain of Maine the honor of accepting the formal surrender of the flags and arms of the Army of Northern Virginia.

April 14 —	John Wilkes Booth mortally wounds President Lincoln at Ford's Theater in Washington.
April 15 —	President Lincoln dies and Andrew Johnson becomes president.
April 21 —	Mosby disbands his rangers.
April 26 —	Gen. Johnston surrenders his nearly 30,000 men to Gen. Sherman.
April 26 —	Booth is trapped by troops and killed.
May 4 —	Gen. Taylor surrenders to Gen. Canby in Alabama.
May 10 —	Confederate guerrilla chief William Quantrill is mortally wounded near Taylorsville, Kentucky.
May 10 —	Union cavalrymen capture Jefferson Davis and his party in Georgia.
May 22 —	Davis is imprisoned at Fort Monroe, Virginia. He will be released in May 1867.
May 23 —	Nearly 200,000 Union soldiers begin a two-day grand review up Pennsylvania Avenue in Washington, D.C.—once more the capital of a united nation.